Marxism and Nationalism

Theoretical Origins of a Political Crisis

Ephraim Nimni

Preface by Ernesto Laclau

PLUTO  **PRESS**

London • Boulder, Colorado

First published 1991 by Pluto Press

Paperback edition first published 1994 by Pluto Press
345 Archway Road, London N6 5AA
and 5500 Central Avenue
Boulder, Colorado 80301, USA

British Library Cataloguing-in-Publication Data
A catalogue record for this book is available from
the British Library

Library of Congress Cataloging-in-Publication Data
Nimni, Ephraim.
    Marxism and nationalism : theoretical origins of a political
crisis / Ephraim Nimni.
        p.   cm.
    Includes bibliographical references (p.   ) and index.
    ISBN 0–7453–0358–7 (hb). – ISBN 0–7453–0730–2 (pb)
    1. Nationalism and communism. 2. Marx, Karl, 1818–1883.
I. Title.
HX550.N3N53   1991
320.5'32–dc20   90–21367
                                                                  CIP

Typeset by Stanford DTP Services, Milton Keynes
Printed in Finland by WSOY

Contents

Acknowledgements

Many people have helped me in the preparation of this book. Special mention must be made of Ivar Oxaal, who warmly supported this project from the beginning, and whose detailed comments to an earlier draft have been very important.

Ernesto Laclau's work had a profound and lasting influence on my intellectual development. He also read an earlier version of the manuscript and made useful suggestions. I am grateful to Talal Asad, too, for his useful suggestions, support and encouragement.

Special thanks to Gerhard Botz from Salzburg University and the people of the Dr Karl Renner Institute in Vienna for their invaluable help with material on Bauer.

I am indebted to a number of colleagues for having taken time to read and comment on various chapters of the book. Particular thanks are due to Bill Brugger, Norman Wintrop, Nira Yuval-Davis, Philip Schlesinger, Alastair Davidson, Bob Jessop and Bryan Turner.

I am grateful to Roderic Pitty for his help with recent Soviet material and to Stephen Fortescue for directing me to the Soviet debate.

Kathleen Weekley read through everything, corrected my faulty grammar, gave me her competent opinion and prevented me from following wrong tracks.

Preface

We are living a period of radical change. The premises and frames of reference of the left, which have dominated its political imaginary since the Russian Revolution, have been shattered by an avalanche of historical changes whose epicentre has been the collapse of the Eastern European regimes in the *annus mirabilis* of 1989. The transformation has been so sudden, it has left so little time to construct new discourses able to give a reading of the changed situation, that a gap has been opened between what most people see and what they are able to account for. Yet the task of theoretical reconsideration has to start, even if belatedly, if we want to make some sense of the world in which we live.

Now, this task can be conceived in two ways. The first is to consider that a certain theoretical approach – Marxism in this case – has failed *in toto* and has to be brushed aside without any further ado. Socialism (at least in its classical formulations) would have not resisted the proof of time, and there would be nothing to learn from going back over its history. Any 'peregrination to the sources' would in this sense be an idle operation. What is needed would be a fresh start, uncontaminated by the sins of the past. This is, I think, a recipe for disaster. Not only because we would be risking throwing the baby out with the bathwater – which is certainly the case – but also because those 'sins of the past' are deeply anchored in our ways of thinking about the world, in our spontaneous reactions to events, in the categories which constitute an only half-conscious horizon which makes sense of our experiences. In politics or in intellectual history there are no Cartesian uncontaminated starting points. If we do not go through the Purgatory of settling accounts with our past, that past will inexorably return in our practices and in our thoughts, as the repressed always does.

One of the two main merits of this remarkable book by Ephraim Nimni is that it helps to start this task of theoretical reconsideration in some fundamental areas of Marxist theorisation. There are no concessions here to the established wisdom, no attempts to disguise the shortcomings of Marxist tradition by presenting them as later distortions of an original, unblemished text. On the contrary, we find in this book a serious deconstructive effort to show the ways in which blindness to the national factor has been recurrent in the history of Marxism right from the beginning. These limitations are to be found even in the highest moments of Marxist theorisation on the national question, the moment in which the specificity and irreducibility of national identities came closest to full recognition – namely Austro-Marxism and Gramsci. The chapter on Austro-Marxism, especially, constitutes, for its scholarship and insightful argumentation, a firstrate contribution to its field. Nimni's book is an example of how a re-examination of the history of Marxism has to proceed by 'reactivating' its 'sedimented' categories; showing the unexpressed assumptions, the non-formulated premises of its main articulations, that led to – now – only-too-visible blind alleys.

The second aspect that contributes to the topicality of this book is its theme: the national question. The book is published at a moment when the disintegration of the Soviet Empire in Eastern Europe has allowed to proliferate the local identities that had been repressed by the previous bureaucratic regimes. Of these identities, the *national* identities within states whose frontiers were largely the result of chess moves by diplomats after the First and Second World Wars are particularly important. On top of that, in the Soviet Union itself the weakening of the bureaucratic role has been accompanied by a violent resurgence of the national identities. The latter are bound to be, whatever form of federalism is implemented in the years to come, a primary factor in any permanent political settlement in the territory of the ex-tsarist/Soviet empire. Nimni's book contributes to the understanding of the historical roots of this process in two ways: both by illuminating the beginning of the intellectual and political discourses which presided over the repression of the national demands during the Soviet period, and by presenting, as a counterpart, the specificity of national identities which made them incompatible with bureaucratic rule.

Nimni has written an excellent book which is a necessary reference point for all those interested in its field.

Ernesto Laclau
November, 1990

Introduction to the 1994 Paperback Edition

When the first edition of this book went to press in 1990, Perestroika was perceived as signalling a more tolerant future for the Soviet Union's nations and nationalities. The perception of Yugoslavia was more mixed. Many Marxists considered that with all its corruption and clientelist practices, the model propounded by the Yugoslavian federal state was at least successful in pacifying the more tempestuous edges of ethnic nationalism. Those Marxists and non-Marxists who thought that 1989 was a year of historical and momentous changes were simply left without superlatives to describe the post 1989 cataclysms, at least in the area of the national question.

The disintegration of the Soviet Union into state-nationalist republics, and the holocaust-like images that global TV stations beam to us from what was once the Yugoslavian Federation, appear, at first sight, to reaffirm the triumphant model of the nation-state. To paraphrase an anti-nationalist Marxist from another period, Rosa Luxemburg, secessionist demands blossom in the post-communist world order like mushrooms after the rain. To the superficial observer, the doctrine of 'one nation one state', is the inescapable legacy of the collapse of communism and the entry requirement for formerly oppressed national communities into our global world.

However, a more balanced analysis shows a different picture. The proliferation of nation-states in the post-communist world is symptomatic of the crisis of the institutional arrangement; in the east as in the west, no ethnic or national group can be surgically isolated in a given territory to form a complete national state without the presence of some ethnic or national minority. In some cases, as in the Baltic Republics of Estonia, the reconstitution of the national state resulted in the removal from the electoral roll of little less than half the population. In a recent article, Yoav Peled called upon Estonia to follow the Israeli case and form an 'ethnic democracy' with full rights for the ethnic majority and partial guaranteed rights for the ethnic minorities.[1]

The development of new ethnic and national states in territories occupied by several national communities is more a reiteration of the symptom of the problem than a solution to the question of self-determination of nations. As Uri Ra'anan argues, it has been a fallacy of contemporary political thought to believe that the international arena is occupied by nation-states or nation-states-to-be.[2]

These arguments are not new and have been well rehearsed by uncompromising Marxist critics of nationalism. But the argument about the impossibility of the nation-state should be carefully separated from the discussion of national communities and national rights. If in our world of migration and globalism the perfect matching of a national community and a state is impossible, this must not be constructed to mean that the nation is fading away.

Here lies the problem of many traditional and contemporary discussions of nationalism, including most Marxist ones. With the collapse of communism and the resurgence of ethnic irredentism, it is more necessary than ever to embark on a process of deconstructing that symbiotic creature called 'the nation-state'. This is not to deny national rights and not because the idea of national identity has lost its validity, but on the contrary, to develop a conceptual framework that encapsulates the reality of national existence in a myriad of forms. These multifarious forms of national existence defy the crude and simplistic conceptual straitjacket epitomised by the slogan 'one nation in one state'. I concur with Fred Halliday in saying that national identities are not axiomatically oriented toward a territory or a state as the myth and ideology of nationalism leads us to believe. They are politicised cultural constructs, not expressing primordial and transcendental links, but the precarious historicity of a changing world. National communities are created, destroyed and re-created by processes that are external to the nationalist discourse. In some case these processes are economic, but more often than not, they relate to extensive political changes in the international order. For example, the creation of a new Israeli nation, as the unintended and unexpected result of Zionist settlement in mandatorial Palestine, was primarily a political act. Zionist ideology aimed at creating a homeland for Jews, but the result was the formation of a new Israeli nation of Hebrew speakers. I hope that this dispels the ambiguity that Fred Halliday detected in a thoughtful and constructive review article of the first edition of this book.[3]

Conceptual liberation from the blinkers of the nation-state can only strengthen our understanding of the national question.

National identities are not destined to be attached to a nation-state. It is possible to argue – as Bauer does – that national identities are enriched and revitalised when they operate in contexts that do not exclude the coexistence of national communities and ethnic groups in the same territorial space.

It is common place in the literature dealing with relations between states to accept that the equivocal concept of 'the right of nations to self-determination' means the right of nations to secede from larger bodies and to create separate national states. As Yael Tamir argues,[4] the popularity of this interpretation rests upon several widely held fallacies, namely that free institutions can only operate within a homogeneous nation-state, that a state can mobilise its citizens only by invoking national ideals and, the most influential and damaging of all, the myth that economic modernisation requires cultural homogeneity.[5] This book tries to show how many Marxist thinkers were seduced by this liberal argument in a way that had disastrous consequences for the development of the Marxist tradition.

In the tight inter-state order that followed the end of the Second World War, irredentism and state secession were curbed by the oppressive logic of superpower competition. Secessionist movements emerged in various regions of the world, but secessionism was always, with one exception, asphyxiated by the cold logic of the inter-state order. If one excludes movements for the independence of colonies, no new national states emerged out of what often were bloody wars of secession, with Bangladesh being the exception that confirms the rule. The end of communism changed this and opened the pandora's box of state secession. Not only did the large communist multinationals disintegrate into ethnically based states with irredentist claims, but the whole process had a knock-on effect on secessionist movements in other parts of the world. In sharp contrast to the experience of only one decade ago, the Organisation of African Unity acquiesced to Eritrea's independence and Quebec may be closer than ever to becoming an independent state. This nationalist explosion motivated an increased concern for a previously neglected subject. As we move toward the end of the century, the study of ethnic nationalism is the fastest growing intellectual industry.[6]

While classical Marxist analyses of the national question remain trapped in the logic of the nation-state, the Austro-Marxist tradition and in particular the work of Otto Bauer present an alternative view which is discussed in detail in this book. It is unfortunate that, to date, there is no full English translation of the work of Bauer. This has resulted in many misinterpretations and misunderstandings of his work. We hope to make available a full translation of Bauer's thought-provoking work very soon, so that the English-reading audience can read the argument at source, without having to rely on interpretations, including of course, my own.

The historical events of the last few years exposed the recurrent malaise of the classical Marxist discussion of the national question, but also made it even more important to deconstruct the institution of the nation-state and to look for novel ways of interpreting the right of nations to self-determination. Within the Marxist tradition, the work of Bauer alone presents itself as a useful, but dated, point of departure for this task.

The first edition of this book had the good fortune of being discussed in a number of thought-provoking reviews and review articles. I am very grateful to Wayne Cristaudo, Brian Jacobs and Louise Hilditch, Claudie Weill and Nora Rtzhel for their constructive criticisms. Fred Halliday took the trouble to write a very useful review article. I am also grateful for Jon Gubbay's kind words, but remain intrigued by his point that Otto Bauer was 'a precocious poststructuralist'.

Sydney, Australia, November 1993

NOTES

1. Yoav Peled, 'Ethnic Democracy and the Legal Construction of Citizenship: Arab Citizens and the Jewish State', *The American Political Science Review*, vol. 86 (June 1992), pp. 432–43.
2. Uri Ra'anan, 'The Nation-State Fallacy' in Joseph Montville (ed.), *Conflict and Peacemaking in Multiethnic Societies* (Lexington Books, Massachusetts, 1990).
3. Fred Halliday, 'Bringing the "Economic" Back in: the Case of Nationalism', *Economy and Society*, vol. 21, no. 4 (November 1992), pp. 483–90. See especially p. 487.
4. Yael Tamir, *Liberal Nationalism* (Princeton University Press, 1993), p. 163.
5. For a forceful anti-Marxist presentation of this argument see E. Gellner, *Nations and Nationalism* (Basil Blackwell, 1983). For a discussion of the logic behind this argument see G. Kitching, 'Nationalism that Instrumental Passion', *Capital and Class*, vol. 29 (1985).
6. Stephen Graubard, preface to the special issue on Nations and States, *Daedalus*, vol. 122, no. 3 (1993), p. 5.

Introduction:
The National Question Revisited

The passionate desire to live in homogeneous national states has incited some of the most important political crusades of the twentieth century. Under diverse historical, geographical and political circumstances, the aspiration for state independence has mobilised ethnic groups through a disparate collection of nationalist ideologies: from Vietnam to Moldavia, from the Reich of the Thousand Years to the resurrection of Zion, from Lithuania to Puerto Rico, from the Vietcong to the National Front, from the Sinn Fein to the Ku Klux Klan. Few, if any, contemporary ethnic groups and national communities have escaped unscathed from this radical transformation of ethnicity. The spectacle of victims of ethnic or national intolerance themselves building national states which then replicate the conditions for such intolerance towards others has been a familiar sight. All this should have indicated that modern civilisation forges a world of nation states, and that freedom (at least for some) and state independence are irrefutably linked. As the world moved towards the cataclysms of World War Two and the subsequent emancipation of colonial peoples, that sardonic paraphrasing of the founding fathers of historical materialism – *A spectre is haunting Europe – the spectre of nationalism* – appeared to be the leitmotiv of modernity.

However, as the twentieth century comes to a close – and despite the current nationalist upheavals in the Soviet Union – the power of the national state appears in the longer run to be in decline. Besieged by economic superpowers and transnational corporations, these states now seek refuge in larger units, thereby jeopardising at least some aspects of the political sovereignty and state independence so passionately fought for only a few decades ago. The image of an informal border crossing between the territories of the Republic of Germany and the French Republic, and the growing political authority of the European parliament which will follow the economic unification of 1992 – bearing in mind that the Thatcherite anachronism is an exception that confirms the rule – would have seemed, only fifty years ago, to be the utopian

1

dream of a drunken visionary; much in the same way as contemporary changes in Eastern Europe would have seemed, in the heyday of Stalinism, the utopian vision of a delirious Gulag inmate.

The prospects of a steady decline of the nation state must not, however, be interpreted as coterminous with the end of the ethnic group or the nation. On the contrary, it signals a rejuvenation of ethnic and national identities. In a 'greener' post-modern world, one intent upon deconstructing universal and all-inclusive identities nurtured by the constraints of industrialisation, the diversities of ethnicity and nationhood have become a powerful rallying point for those who protest against the asphyxiating uniformities of Orwellian bureaucracies. Lithuania, Czechoslovakia and Moldavia are cases in point, but so too are Puerto Rico, Euzkadi, Scotland, Catalonia, the Black and Latino communities in the US and the millions of 'guest workers' in the European community. In the new times, multiculturalism, ethnic diversity and pluralism are the names of the game.

The volatility of the national question disconcerted two of the most formidable ideological protagonists of the twentieth century – liberal democracy and Marxism. Too often, the radical social movements engendered by these ideologies judged nationalism to be a powerful tool for achieving their political projects, only to discover that the nationalism of nation states led to their own undoing.

In the liberal democratic case, faith in human reason and the cast-iron belief that individual freedom must be enshrined in basic rights, went hand in hand with the struggle for national self-emancipation. Such movements invariably led to the establishment of separate national states for aggrieved national and ethnic communities. After World War One, the very liberal democratic 'right of nations to self-determination' – which in practice meant the constitution of separate national states – was one of the most influential political demands of the day. Even the competing Marxist tradition was unable to resist the seductiveness of the slogan; much to the consternation of Rosa Luxemburg it became the cornerstone of the Leninist theory of the national question.

But pivotal liberal democratic principles were soon to be jettisoned in the dynamic interplay between nation states. In a world of competing states, national-state exigencies often clashed with rights of individuals. Much to the consternation of die-hard liberals, reasons of 'national security', 'reasons of state', and, axioms such as 'my country right or wrong', systematically eroded hard earned individual rights in order to guarantee the survival of newly born bureaucratic colossi. From the obscenities of fascism to the absurdities of the Official Secrets Act, the defence of the national state has been portrayed as of paramount importance for the survival of the nation.

Marxism and the National Question

Marxists were more ambivalent towards the rising tide of nationalism, but they, too, were perplexed by it. The Marxist fetish of making sense of every significant social phenomenon by subsuming it within the logic of the universal development of the forces of production, was the blueprint for ingenious but ultimately inapplicable theories of the national question. The heterogeneity of the national phenomenon defies monocausal explanations such as the ones derived from the laws of motion of political economy. It is only fair to point out that this is a problem that transcends Marxism; it is a blind spot that results from a particular aspect of the developmental logic of the Western thought from which the Marxist tradition derives its inspiration. This tradition has always situated reflection on socio-historical patterns within what Castoriadis calls an ontology of determinacy, namely the assumption that 'to be' has only one sense: 'to be determined'[1]. As in many other dimensions of the so-called superstructure, this ontology of determinacy necessitated an explanation of the national question in terms of forces and causal factors exterior to it.

Given that the ontology of determinacy has been a major factor in the development of social and natural sciences, it is no coincidence that the conceptualisation of the national phenomenon presents a series of difficulties and contradictions for all modern social theories. Since the emergence of both Marxism and the social sciences, the concern of theory has been to explain social phenomena by constantly refining a universal logic. Slowly but surely, the apparent mystery of specificities and localisms was to be unravelled by the penetrating force of logically refined, and what were believed to be empirically tested, theories. This task was supposed to enhance human perceptions of social realities – much in the same way as the theory of gravity and the theory of relativity were supposed to enhance the understanding of the way in which the physical universe works. The Tower of Pisa and the Newtonian apple were no longer self-contained phenomena but the result of the laws of gravity – an aprioristic condition that transcended the immediate existence of the tower and the apple. Thus the modern concept of causality emerged in physics as the sometimes empirical, sometimes theoretical, ascertainable combination of conditions that is usually followed by a predictable occurrence that constitutes its effect. [2]

This analytical logic had a profound impact on social theory. Not only the social sciences, but liberal democracy and Marxism were (and are) unmistakably shaped by this epistemological stance, the aim of which is to explain specific and localised problems in terms of an overall developmental logic. Specificities and localisms are both anomalies to be accounted for and stumbling blocks to the efficient performance of those theories. It is, then, no coincidence that both liberal democracy and Marxism have little sympathy for any social phenomenon that resists being subsumed by an all-inclusive logic of analysis.

However, the multifaceted national phenomenon is perhaps one of the most obstinate forms of social contingency: nationalism preaches the importance of the specific over the general; and it provides lengthy justifications for why the national movement is 'unique'. Attempts to explain the nature of this phenomenon in universal terms have clashed with a multifarious reality that resists monocausal explanations. As in the case of early liberal democracy, it is no coincidence that classical Marxism was logically poised to reject the insularity of nationalist movements and the claims to specificity and uniqueness of nationalist ideologies.

But the national question did not disappear because Marxists wished it to do so. A large theoretical gap opened up in the Marxist tradition, a gap that was often concealed by insensitive and stereotypical formulations that had more to do with religious dogma than with a tradition that claims to understand – let alone transform – social reality. Marxist discussions of nationalism were, with few and relatively unknown exceptions, clouded in epiphenomenal terminology. Concrete instances of nationalist agitation were to to be explained in terms of the class struggle or of a pervasive false consciousness that distracted the workers from their real aim: the destruction of the bourgeois order.

The purpose of this book is to try to understand and evaluate the failure of European Marxism to come to grips with the national phenomenon. That the European Marxist tradition flourished and developed outside the area of influence of European culture is evident. As will be shown in subsequent chapters, the generalising and universalising developmental logic that has its historical origins in the European continent is a key factor in the

Marxist failure to conceptualise the diverse forms of the national phenomenon. It is, therefore, essential to understand the European Marxist tradition in detail, not in order to ascertain its general validity, but to discover its historical specificity and thereby avoid the pernicious error of generalising on the basis of European experiences alone.

European Marxism's inadequate understanding and conceptualisation of the national question is acknowledged by most contemporary writers on the subject. The constant repetition of stereotyped formulas, and the failure to provide a sound theoretical analysis of the problem, moved Tom Nairn to open the theoretical section of his seminal book, *The Break Up of Britain*, with a statement of despair:

> The theory of Nationalism represents Marxism's great historical failure. It may have others as well, and some of these have been more debated: Marxism's shortcomings over imperialism, the state, the falling rate of profit and the immiseration of the masses are certainly old battlefields. Yet none of these is as important, as fundamental, as the problem of nationalism, either in theory or in political practice. [3]

Nairn goes on to argue that this failure was inevitable but we are now in a position to understand it. Here, however, it will be argued that there is nothing inevitable about it – unless the paradigms of eurocentric evolutionism and economic reductionism remain uncontested features of the Marxist discourse on the national question.

Another widespread and no less influential Marxist argument attempts to show the logical impossibility of a general analysis of this issue.[4] According to this position, every national formation will have its own internal logic which is not translatable to other situations. The essence of this argument is that there is not a National Question but national questions. The apparent plural relativism of this interpretation is paradoxically the result of the deterministic unity of the main theme of classical Marxism. This is the dispiriting argument that '*social classes are the sole and unique agents of social transformation*'. Consequently, the diversity of national questions is the expression of the impact of this unique and privileged agency in a plurality of situations. Thus the impossibility of theorising about the national question stems from the assertion that, ultimately, the national phenomenon has no logic of its own, but its transformations are only the reflection of the laws of motion of political economy. The 'plurality' and 'flexibility' of this analysis are a convenient way to hide and excuse the dogmatic unity of the theoretical stance which sustains it.

One aim of this book is to establish that this interpretation was both intellectually abortive and politically disastrous. It caused a theoretical blindness within the mainstream Marxist tradition that was responsible for many important defeats of Marxism in the West and the East. The importance of the national question for both the Marxist tradition and the socialist movement is currently highlighted by the menace that national separatism poses to the unity of the Soviet Union. More significantly, its importance is also indicated by the fact that Marxist movements in the non-European world – and outside the area of influence of the Red Army – have been successful only when they have also expressed powerful national sentiments.

Marxist Parameters for Analysis of the National Question

The most influential European Marxist discussions on the national question are characterised by a recurrent thematic unity and a relatively cohesive line of argument despite important political and intellectual differences. The theoretical and epistemological base of this thematic unity will be called the Marxist parameters for the analysis of the national question. These parameters are: a) the theory of the universal evolution of the forces of production, b) the conceptualisation of the economic identity and the determining role of forces of production, and c) the eurocentric bias in concrete discussions of the universal process of change. These parameters refer to three areas of analysis widely considered crucial in defining the characteristic identity of historical materialism. They have shaped a theoretical framework that has severely limited the capacity of a number of influential Marxist traditions to understand the theoretical and political importance of the national question.

The theory of evolution refers to an understanding of social transformation as a process which can be grasped in universal laws of historical development. History is understood as a progressive series of transformations through universal and hierarchically defined stages; in Marx's words, 'The country that is more developed industrially only shows, to the less developed, the image of its own future.'[5] Local variations and historical zigzags do not affect the overall pattern.[6] These stages of transformation inevitably lead to a classless society.

The concept of evolution is one of those rarities in the history of ideas which have had a lasting impact in the different branches of the social sciences and which have provided an equally influential paradigm in the natural sciences. At first sight it seems that the discursive logic that lies behind this concept realised the long-cherished dream of many philosophers to find the organising principle that rules both the natural and social worlds.

Karl Marx was determined to establish that scientific and objective laws of motion were equally applicable to the social and natural worlds. He found in the success of the theory of evolution in the natural sciences a valuable source of encouragement for his belief that an objective and scientific analysis of the process of social transformation was possible and desirable.[7] The Marxist fascination with theories of evolution results from the generalising properties of these theories. The crucial factor in explaining social change is not a heuristic self-explanation of social developments, but the overall universal mechanism that makes possible the process of social transformation. For Marx, as for various subsequent generations of Marxists, the relationship humanity–nature is simultaneously the 'natural' history of humanity and the very place where the 'species being' is constituted through the process of labour and production. Consequently there is only one universal history, that of human beings in relation to nature. This relation constitutes the locus of the history of production, of industry and of science.[8] The notion of development as an evolutionary sequence from a lower to a higher stage is found not only in the abstract prose of Marx's *Preface to the Contribution to the Critique of Political Economy*, but finds concrete expression in his works on the European and the non-European world. It is present in the works of Engels and, as shown in the following chapters, is the basis for Kautsky's, Lenin's, Luxemburg's and Bernstein's more specific discussions of the national question. In the preface to the first German edition of his magnum opus, Marx enunciates this position with pristine clarity:

One nation can and should learn from others. And even when a society has got upon the right track for the discovery of the natural laws of its movement – *and it is the ultimate aim of this work, to lay bare the economic law of motion of modern society* – it can neither clear by bold leaps nor remove by legal enactments, the obstacles offered by successive phases of its normal development. But it can shorten and lessen the birth-pangs. (emphasis added) [9]

Classical Marxism regarded the equating of its principles of social evolution with those of natural evolution as a sound criterion of scientificity. Marx saw in the impressive advances of the natural sciences a further justification for the evolutionary logic of historical materialism. He borrowed from the natural sciences what he considered to be scientific criteria of objectivity and, in this way, was insensitive to the specificity and non-reducibility of the realm of the social. Only those Marxist schools that seriously engaged in a debate with the neo-Kantian tradition, or with this tradition's heirs in the social sciences, developed some awareness of the problem of the specificity of the forms of the social. It will be shown that the Gramscian and Austro-Marxist traditions were able to see the heterogeneity of the national question because they were prepared to question the uncritical Marxist appropriation of the methodological principles of late nineteenth century natural sciences.

The second parameter configuring the Marxist theory of the national question is the theory of the economic determination of the forces of production. This theory is a form of *economic reductionism*, because it declares that all meaningful changes within the social arena take place in the sphere of economic (class) relations. Marx himself expressed this theory in terms of his well-known metaphoric distinction between base and superstructure. The superstructure is shaped and determined, after various stages of more or less complex mediations, by the activities and processes of change that occur at the level of the base. This conceptualisation of relations of causality has been expressed in a variety of ways by different Marxist traditions and its most influential version is the so-called theory of determination in the last instance.

The classical Marxist axiom that productive forces determine, directly or indirectly, the behaviour of the superstructural phenomena created insurmountable problems for the analysis of the national question. As many Marxist revolutionaries learned at their peril, national identities cut across class positions, and national communities did not always respond to class interests. In view of the difficulties in explaining the existence and political activity of nationalist movements using the rationale of the evolving forces of production, classical Marxists were forced to utilise a battery of concepts and ideas that were, at best, perceptive insights ingeniously contorted to comply with the dogma of the economistic model.

In criticising the teleological speculations of German idealism, Marx and Engels did not build adequate safeguards into their theory to prevent their disciples falling into the mirror-image stance: a mechanistic-materialist interpretation of the process of social change. In the period following the deaths of the founding fathers of historical materialism, mainstream Marxism tended towards rigid and mechanistic methods of analysis which reached their peak around the turn of the century. This was the period in which the national question was of paramount importance for the young European socialist movement. While the Bolshevik tradition offered a partial renovation by criticising the excesses of the mechanistic Marxism of the Second International, the economic reductionist perspective remained alive in the works of Lenin, Trotsky and Stalin. This time it was elevated to a category of dogma by a political movement which regarded itself as the avant-garde of the proletariat, and which dismissed criticisms with a manichean sense of self-righteousness. But if the end of Stalinism and the subsequent disenchantment with the Soviet system, coupled with the identity crisis of the European socialist movement, brought about more innovative and daring approaches during the 1970s and 1980s, very little of this innovation was directed towards resuscitating the ailing fortunes of the Marxist theory of the national question.[10]

The notion of economic determination has another dimension that completes the privileged position of the forces of production, namely the equation of material existence and the economy via the concept of production. The Marxist notion of production encapsulates the axiom of human existence: the need to obtain food and shelter to secure basic needs of life. In this way, material existence (being) and production are logically unified in an indivisible field. If material existence compels production, this compulsion must be located outside the area of voluntary action, otherwise the 'compulsion' fails to compel. The economy emerges as the realm in which Marx's 'dull compulsion of material life' produces the laws of motion of material production independently of human will. Classical Marxism thus justifies the primacy (in terms of existential causality) and the objectivity (in terms of its independence from human will) of the economic realm.[11]

This abstract discourse permits a number of logical permutations, some of which are connected with bitter methodological disputes that haunt the Marxist tradition. For our discussion of the national question, one of the most relevant disputes is what Chantal Mouffe defined in a seminal article as the difference between what she called 'epiphenomenality' and class 'reduction-ism',[12] two positions that identify different attitudes towards the so-called superstructural realm.

Epiphenomenality refers to a situation where every aspect of the superstructural phenomena is a mere reflection of the economic base. In this sense, a correct understanding of the dynamic of this base is a necessary and sufficient condition for a complete explana-tion of what occurs at the level of the superstructure. Every move-ment of the superstructure is accounted for as a reaction to changes taking place at the level of the base; thus economic rela-tions of production are the unique source of causality.

A class reductionist approach represents an important shift of emphasis within the same conceptual framework. Social classes are considered the only possible historical subjects so that ideologies and other superstructural phenomena (such as nationalism and the national arena in general) 'belong' to the paradigmatic area of influence of a class position. This does not prevent the superstruc-tural phenomena from having a certain relative autonomy from the economy as a whole. While all types of contradictions are ulti-mately determined by economic (class) positions, they may not transparently and immediately reflect the positions of those classes. Political and other activities may advance or delay (accord-ing to the circumstances) the outcome of the relations between classes (class struggle).

The first form of economic reductionism, epiphenomenality, is best represented in the mechanistic understanding of the works of Marx and Engels held mainly by the leading schools of the Second International (with the exception of Austro-Marxism). The second position, class reductionism, allows for a limited flexibility in the evaluation of the role of the superstructural phenomena. It influ-enced the positions of the Bolsheviks and the Third International.

The epiphenomenalist interpretation has deservedly lost most of its credibility today, given that the complexity and intricacies of contemporary societies defy the validity of analytical patterns based on relations of causality determined by immutable iron laws.

The class reductionist paradigm has proven to be more resilient; it continues to inform influential contemporary Marxist discussion of the national question.[13] The most challenging feature of this concept has been the notion of determination in the last instance. The national phenomenon cannot, according to this ingenious argument, simply be reduced to the effects of economic forces. A more or less complex system of mediating stages defines the influence of the economic base over cultural and political levels, creating a delaying effect, which gives to the superstructure a relatively autonomous existence. According to this formulation, national communities are not directly subsumed into class ideologies, and may even pre-exist a given class configuration. But the social and behavioural functions must satisfy the conditions of existence of the dominant mode of production and their concomitant ruling classes. Nationalist movements may only act as catalysts for changes that are about to take place, or are taking place at the level of the forces of production.

The perspective of economic reductionism has vexed the Marxist tradition for generations, seriously undermining its ability to understand the nature of what it called superstructural phenomena. Subsequent chapters examine how economic reductionism restricts Marxist discussions of the national question.

In order to overcome the damage inflicted by the recurrent use of these paradigms, a dramatic intellectual transformation is required to regenerate the vitality of the socialist tradition. If a more sensitive discussion of the national question is to emerge, it must start by demolishing completely the crumbling edifice of economic reductionism – from its basic foundation to its superstructure.

The third parameter, the eurocentric bias in concrete case studies, is strictly speaking derived from the two categories previously discussed. It is not a separate analytical tier and cannot be understood without reference to economic reductionism or the theory of evolution. It warrants separate consideration, however, because of its important methodological consequences when the Marxist analysis of the national question is applied to the non-European world.

The Marxist tradition is trapped in the paradoxical situation of claiming to be a universal theory of social emancipation, while it uses an ethnocentric methodology to conceptualise social formations located outside the area of Western culture. Eurocentrism, then, refers here to the construction of a model of development which universalises empirically observed European categories of development: the process of social transformation in different societies is understood and conceptualised in terms of the Western developmental rationale; the more 'advanced' industrial (European) society shows to the less developed 'the image of its own future'.[14]

With the possible exception of the revisionist tradition, no school of Marxism argued for the explicit superiority and hegemony of the European culture over the rest of the world. Indeed, the notion of the cultural superiority of one society over another is clearly an anathema to the universalistic values of the Marxist tradition. Yet, in spite of its genuine universalistic aspirations, the conceptualisation of human development and the rationale for the emancipation of the human species as a whole was constructed as a form of discursive rationality and as a political project directly derived from the main experiences of the European Enlightenment. This created an intriguing paradox: classical Marxism derived its universal evolutionary paradigm from its parochial reflections on European history. But classical Marxists were not aware of these inconsistencies. Marxist claims to scientificity portrayed their theories as being immune from any suspicion of cultural relativism.

A tradition that claimed to have discovered the laws of motion of human history and to understand the evolution of the forces of production with the precision of the natural sciences cannot have been aware of its cultural biases. But the concepts of classical Marxism, the notions of class, capitalism, feudalism and mode of production, emerged as forms of analytical reflection on the history of European societies. More importantly, they resulted from a discursive practice that to all intents and purposes is distinctly European:

> Marxism is an intrinsically European current of thought, which unites several of the most characteristic traits of European civilisation as a whole: the sense of history inherent in the Judeo-Christian tradition, and the Promethean urge to transform nature that has manifested itself since the Renaissance and specially since the industrial revolution. Transplanted to Asia, to societies most of which did not have this sense of history, and none of which traditionally had such a vision of man as *maître et possesseur de la nature* (in Descartes's well-known phrase), it caused a profound shock. Nor did Marxism escape unchanged from the encounter.[15]

Classical Marxism could either have maintained its claim to universality by putting its sense of European history in perspective and catering for a plural world or, alternatively, sustained a sense of European history and culture and abandoned its claim to universality. Neither path was chosen: classical Marxian notions of evolution invariably located the European West at the highest stages of historical development, thus subsuming the major stages

of universal development into a European sense of historical continuity. The revisionist and centrist factions of the Second
International supported, at times, the 'civilisatory mission' of
some forms of 'progressive colonialism'. Before this, Engels considered that the colonies best suited for independence were those
populated by Europeans:

> In my opinion the colonies proper, i.e., the countries occupied
> by a European population – Canada, the Cape, Australia – will
> become independent: on the other hand, the countries inhab-
> ited by a native population, which are simply subjugated –
> India, Algeria, the Dutch, Portuguese and Spanish possessions –
> must be taken over for the time being [following the Revolution]
> by the proletariat and led as rapidly as possible towards
> independence.[16]

Even Lenin, while providing a novel articulation between class
and colonial struggles, maintained that the more 'advanced' social
formations were located in industrial and capitalist Western and
Central Europe.

The notion that the ruling ideas of every society are the ideas of
the ruling class is at the heart of Marxist theory. Classical Marxists
were acutely aware of the relativity of the claims to universalism of
the dominant ideas in different historical periods. Even in the case
of the national question, the classical Marxist perception was a
form of relativised historicism: the nation was conceived as a
social formation that originated in the process of transition from
feudalism to capitalism.

It seems remarkable today that classical Marxists were unaware
of the relative historical location of their own works, never developing Marxist analyses of the origins of their own ideology. For it
is clear that the main corpus of Marxist literature emerged at a definite historical period and could not, therefore, escape the influence of the hegemonic ideas of its time. Not only did the
Industrial Revolution and the rationale of the Enlightenment
provide the historical context for the emergence of Marxism, but
also this theory and practice emerged at a time when European
colonialism was about to reach its peak. Had the criteria used to
evaluate other ideological practices been used for the evaluation of
Marxism, the latter's eurocentric bias would most certainly have
been detected. The opposite occurred, as Anouar Abdel Malek
explains:

The nation is conceived as the socio-economic formation with the state emerging from the disintegration of the feudal system in Western Europe; and it is seen as concomitant with the emergence of the capitalist system. This definition, which belongs to classical historical sociology, was taken up again and refined by the Marxist theoreticians, notably Stalin. This tacit consensus expresses, of course, the unity of the socio-historical framework which gave rise to the notion. Thus the right to national existence of other social formations prior to the capitalist system will be challenged, even though they present the same features which were said to be constitutive of the modern nation: geographical unity, historical continuity, a single language, a single unified economic market and a unified cultural consciousness ... the real problem is the extrapolation of European Experience– designated as *normal*, and thus given objective priority – to the experiences of other peoples. The European origins of the social sciences lead to Eurocentrism – the world is conceived in Europe's image, invited to conform to it, and rejected, if it creates an exception.[17]

From this emerged comparative criteria by which to evaluate the non-European nations and assign a place on a continuum between 'progressive' and 'reactionary' nations. The further a social formation departed from Western European models, the more reactionary it was. This form of ideological and political mapping resulted from the epistemology that configures classical Marxist discourse and which renders its own discursive practice immune from critical evaluation.[18]

The eurocentrism of classical Marxism arises from the overdetermination of the two parameters discussed above: the mechanistic perception of historical evolution and the ontological privilege of the process of production. This is the point at which many attempts to overcome the eurocentric bias of classical Marxism fail. For there cannot be a criticism of this bias if at the same time there is no attempt to criticise Marxist ontology and epistemology.

Overview of the Book

An attempt has been made to delineate the specific theoretical constraints which prevented classical Marxism from developing a understanding of the different dimensions of the national question. In the following chapters it will be shown how the analytical paradigms discussed above configured the most important aspects of concrete European Marxist discussions of the national question.

In the first chapter, the work of Marx and Engels will be analysed. Contrary to the general opinion that their positions on the national question were informed by circumstantial events, it will be argued that they exhibit a good deal of coherence and unity, despite the fact that their positions were never comprehensively stated in any single work or sustained argument.

The work on the national question by the most influential figures of the Second International will be evaluated in the second chapter. Against the assertion that at the time of the Second International Marxist theory was not codified as a rigid orthodoxy, it will be argued that the main works of the different and conflicting traditions were influenced by a doctrinaire and mechanistic stance. In all cases excepting the Austro-Marxist school they failed adequately to conceptualise the national phenomenon. Leninism had to break with the rigidities of the Second International in order to make sense of the diverse Russian reality. The third chapter argues that this partial break sensitised the tradition to the political dimension of the national question, while it nevertheless retained a doctrinaire class reductionist perspective which severely limited its ability to come to grips with other substantive aspects of the national question.

The work of Antonio Gramsci provided a partial, but significant, break with class reductionism. In Chapter 4 it will be argued that his conceptualisation of important aspects of the political arena outside the paradigmatic field of class determination constitutes a qualitative change in the ability of Marxism's capacity to conceptualise the national question. However, Gramsci remained insensitive to the plurality of the national phenomenon, and particularly to the existence and development of different ethno-national communities within the framework of the same state. Gramsci took for granted that states are 'national', avoiding a discussion of the problematic relation between nations and states.

The last three chapters will discuss the writings of Otto Bauer and suggest that his work on the national question is one the lost gems of European Marxism. Notions such as the community of fate and the national character appear to be useful categories of analysis when stripped of the essentialism of nationalist discourses. However, some important aspects of Bauer's work remain trapped in the strait-jacket of economic reductionism. The class reductionism of his historical case studies seems to contradict the richness and multidimensionality of his theoretical analysis. In this sense, two different Bauers appear to be writing *Die Nationalitätenfrage und die Sozialdemokratie*.[19] The first, the Austro-Marxist intellectual, fresh out of the environment of *fin-de-siècle* Vienna, expresses brilliant and innovative ideas, matured through his debate with Max Adler against the neo-Kantians and classical Marxism. The second, the party man, is loyal to the dogmas of economistic Marxism and is severely restrained by the need to demonstrate allegiance to the doctrinal teachings of Marx and Engels.

The terminology used in the Marxist tradition to refer to the national arena belongs to a highly contested field. It is, therefore, important to clarify the meaning of certain key terms used in this work. *Classical Marxism* is used to define a tradition which sees social classes as protagonists of the process of social transformation. It also refers to original theoretical statements of historical materialism. Classical Marxists referred to the *national question* as the totality of political, cultural, ideological, economic and legal relations within and between national communities. I see no reason not to continue using this term, which is interchangeable with *national phenomenon*. *Nations* are for classical Marxists fully formed national communities, usually in possession of a national state. *Nationalities* are national communities not fully developed as nations. The distinction between these two concepts is unclear, so the term *national communities* will be used instead to cover both cases. This also highlights the cultural and communitarian aspects of the national phenomenon. A national state is the ideal and usually unobtainable synthesis between a complete national community and a state. Whenever the word nation appears it denotes a closer connection with the *national state* rather than with the national community. *Nationalism* is a political and ideological movement whose main concern is the well-being of the national community – be it real or fictitious. Sometimes, nationalisms 'make' national communities. Nationalism was unanimously defined by classical Marxists as a bourgeois phenomenon alien to Marxism.

1

The Perplexing Legacy of Marx and Engels

The historical and theoretical essays of Marx and Engels on the national question reveal superficial discussions, apparent conceptual gaps and great differences in interpretation from one historical context to another. It is no coincidence, then, that a significant group of scholars and historical analysts maintain, in a variety of influential works, that the founding fathers of historical materialism had no theoretically coherent approach to this issue. Some also argue that Marx and Engels treated each national movement on an ad hoc basis and that their attitude was often dictated by fleeting political events.[1]

Insofar as lack of theoretical coherence is considered the main characteristic of Marx and Engels' approach to the national question, this argument is incorrect. It will be argued here that they did in fact have a coherent view of this question, even if there is no single corpus of literature that presents their theories in an unequivocal manner. The social-evolutionary and economic reductionist parameters of analysis provide a coherent basis for the formulation of a theory of the national question which is compatible with the apparently contradictory positions that Marx and Engels held in relation to various movements of national emancipation. This largely unwritten, but nonetheless real and influential perception provided the intellectual basis for the way in which subsequent generations of Marxists comprehended the problem of nationalism.

Two considerations were decisive in the formulation of Marx and Engels' understanding of the national question. The first was their adherence to a universal but, at the same time, historically located model for national development. This is the model state–language–nation. The second concerned the capacity of national communities to evolve from lower to higher stages of development of productive forces. This is the theory of historical versus non-historical nations.

State–Language–Nation

For Marx and Engels, the modern nation was the direct result of a process whereby the capitalist mode of production superseded feudalism, causing concomitant dramatic changes in the process of social organisation. The transition to a capitalist economy impelled a number of Western European social formations to evolve into more linguistically cohesive and politically centralised units. Feudal society was slowly united under the structure of the nascent modern state.[2] The destruction of local differences followed, initiating the process whereby each population became uniform, which was considered an important condition for the formation of a market economy.[3]

In Marx's view, one of the strongest indicators of this process of uniformisation was the emergence and development of Western European languages. A crucial characteristic of the capitalist mode of production is the intensification of the division of labour, coupled with a growing interdependence among the different units of production, holding together a mass of dispossessed labourers free to sell their labour power in the market. Capitalism breaks the isolation of feudal units, increasing the interaction of the various participants in the newly formed market. This in turn necessitates a medium for efficient communication. According to Marx and Engels, Western European languages emerged to fulfil this role and to consolidate distinct and recognisable linguistic units based on the embryonic absolutist state.[4] From this account, it is possible to derive two important observations which help to define the meaning of the notion of a modern nation. It must fulfil the following criteria:

a) Hold a population large enough to allow for an internal division of labour which characterises a capitalist system with its competing classes; and
b) occupy a cohesive and sufficiently large territorial space to provide for the existence of a viable state.[5]

This understanding of the process of formation of modern nations is easily derived from Marx and Engels' observation of the process of formation of national states in Western Europe, particularly France and, to a limited extent, England. Above all, it adheres to the view that the French Revolution provided the model for national development. The founders of historical materialism regarded the process of national consolidation which took place after that revolution as a model for national formation in other 'less developed' parts of the world. Given the importance of the French model of national formation in Marx and Engels' thought, it is useful briefly to discuss the process of national formation in that country, particularly during the period of the Revolution.

The Jacobins and other French revolutionaries believed that the best way to establish a democratic state was to follow a path of tight centralisation and linguistic standardisation. Pursuing this political project, the Jacobins perceived the existence of non-Parisian French-speaking peoples within the boundaries of the French state as a considerable menace to this process of uniformisation. However, the geographical area occupied by the French absolutist state was inhabited during the best part of the pre-revolutionary period by a conglomerate of linguistic communities, some of which spoke Romance languages (Langue d'Oc, Langue d'Oil, Catalan), other Celtic languages (Breton), and other ancient pre-Latin languages (Euzkera). The language of the court of Versailles, which subsequently became 'French', was spoken only by a minority of the state's population. As Pierre Giraud demonstrates,[6] during the Middle Ages there was not one French language but several. Each province spoke its own dialect.

During the period preceding the Revolution, the language of Paris began to exercise its definitive supremacy, becoming the official language of the state. After 1789, this process was greatly encouraged by the revolutionary government, anxious to create a national state with a uniform language for all its citizens. It was not an easy task. According to Brunnot,[7] of a total population of about 25 million inhabitants, between six and seven million did not understand Parisian French, a similar number were capable only of holding a very basic conversation in this language; ten million were bilingual, using their respective dialects as their mother tongue and Parisian French as the lingua franca. Only three million inhabitants of Paris and surrounding areas spoke 'French' as their mother tongue and an even smaller number were capable of reading and writing in this language.

When this situation was reported to the 1791 constitutional convention, the revolutionary government intensified its efforts to spread the use of the French language as quickly as possible. Two closely connected reasons account for this: the wish to create a democratic and tightly centralised state and the need to ensure the hegemony of the Parisian bourgeoisie against pockets of feudal and aristocratic resistance in remote locations. Given the close association between Parisian French and revolutionary aims, it is hardly surprising that the counter-revolution was stronger in those areas where French was hardly spoken – Brittany for example. A tightly centralised state was bound to destroy the administrative and cultural autonomy of the non-French national communities.

The combination of cultural imperialism and tight administrative centralisation led to an almost complete destruction of the cultures and languages of the non-Parisian French national communities. As their animosity towards the Parisian bourgeoisie grew, these communities became sites of counter-revolutionary activities. Responding to a reaction generated largely by their own insensitivity, the Jacobins equated the national identity of these unfortunate peoples with counter-revolution. The Jacobin deputies Barère and Grégoire presented a submission to the constitutional assembly of 1794 with a telling title: *Report on the need and means to destroy rural dialects (patois) and universalise the use of the French language*. This work eloquently illustrates the ideas and generalised positions of the Jacobins on what we may call today national minorities.[8] One year later the same deputies advanced the following revolutionary slogan: 'In the one and undivided Republic, the one and undivided use of the language of freedom', a slogan which, as Rosdolsky argues, conveniently forgot that French was also the language of the court of Versailles and of pre-revolutionary absolutism in general.

This tendency to use the French language as the cultural medium for the advancement of revolutionary goals was noted by Marx in his famous refutation of Lafargue's attempt to abolish all national differences.

> the English laughed very much when I began my speech by saying that our friend Lafargue and others had spoken '*en français*' to us, i.e. a language that nine tenths of the audience did not understand. I also suggested that by the negation of nationalities, he appeared quite unconsciously to understand their absorption by the *model French nation*.[9]

Marx, however, did not draw any theoretical conclusions from this incident and continued all his life to believe that the French model was the universal path for national development. He and Engels believed that state centralisation and national unification, with the consequent assimilation of small national communities, was the only viable path to social progress. Their preference for large centralised states was not only a strategic consideration, but also formed the basis for their unwritten conceptualisation of the national question, inspired by the parameters of analysis discussed above. This can be seen in their discussion of the civil society, the national state and what they called the historical nations.

Marx took the concept of civil society from Hegelian political philosophy. For Hegel this is the place where individual self-interest receives its legitimation and becomes emancipated from religious and other considerations, which until the formation of the civil society limited the free play of individual interests.[10] This definition of the civil society should be not confused with Hegel's definition of the state. Civil society is based on the needs of a 'lower kind', which are best defined in the concept of 'Verstand' (knowledge, understanding in the concrete mechanical sense). The state is the expression of a higher level of reason which Hegel calls Vernunft (an ethical principle that permits essential understanding or consciousness). For Hegel, the state is the consciousness of freedom, but in a way that allows the enjoyment of that freedom in conjunction with others, while in the civil society people realised their freedom without regard to the freedom of others.[11]

Marx was certainly influenced by the Hegelian conceptualisation of the civil society and its relation to the state, but he located that relationship in a different perspective, by attempting to conceptualise the developmental historicity of both concepts within the context of the process of production. Civil society emerges, for Marx, at a specific stage of development of the productive forces. Here he inherited the evolutionist-universal perspective developed by Hegel, but he explicitly rejected its idealistic base. This becomes clear when Marx argues in the *German Ideology* that the modern state, in its very constitution, is unable to overcome the egoism of civil society, because 'mere political emancipation' (the bourgeois state) leaves intact the world of private interest (civil society). He concludes that:

> Civil society embraces the whole material intercourse of individuals within a definite stage of development of productive forces. It embraces the whole commercial and industrial life of a given stage, and, insofar, transcends the state and the nation, though, on the other hand again, it must assert itself in its foreign relations as *nationality* and inwardly must organise itself as state. (emphasis added)[12]

This is an important consideration. The general form of the civil society is present in the more specific forms of state and nationality. Given that the civil society is only the reflection of the dominant forces within it, it follows that in the capitalist mode of production the dominant class (the bourgeoisie) determines the form and content of the civil society, while the civil society itself, in the format described by Marx, cannot exist outside capitalist relations of production.

The implications of Marx's discussion of the theoretical status of the civil society are important for the discussion of the national question. In Marx and Engels' terms, the modern nation is a historical phenomenon that must to be located at a precise historical period: the era of the ascendance of the bourgeoisie as a hegemonic class, the time of consolidation of the capitalist mode of production. In this context, the different treatment given by Marx and Engels to different national communities acquires meaning and coherence. The modern nation is an epiphenomenal result of the development of the bourgeoisie as the hegemonic class, and the former must be evaluated on the merits of the latter. If it represents a higher stage of development of the productive forces in relation to a predetermined process of historical change, if it abolishes the feudal system by building a national state, then the nationalist movement deserves support because it becomes a tool for progressive social change. If, however, the nationalist movement emerges among linguistic or cultural communities incapable of surviving the upheavals of capitalist transformation (because they are too small or they have a weak or non-existent bourgeoisie) then the nationalist movement becomes a regressive force because it is incapable of overcoming the stage of peasant-feudal social organisation. As will be shown, Marx and Engels repeatedly argued that national communities incapable of constituting proper national states should vanish by being assimilated into more progressive and vital nations.

This social evolutionist and epiphenomenalist understanding appears in every analysis by Marx and Engels of the concrete features of national movements. It constitutes their theory of national development, though the general theoretical question is not addressed specifically in any single work. However, in order fully to understand the implications of Marx and Engels' position on the national question, the problem of their recurrent terminological ambiguity must be clarified.

The Terminological Ambiguity

In various European languages the concepts of people, nation and nationality can have different and confusing meanings. The difficulty is compounded by the no less perplexing and indiscriminate use of this terminology in specialist literature. These terms can either be taken as synonyms or as meaning different things in different situations, creating a terminological confusion that is seldom clarified with clearcut definitions.[13] Marx and Engels are no exceptions to this: in their work the meaning of nations, nationalities and modern nations is not always clear.[14]

In English and French the word nation usually refers to the population of a sovereign state, but is sometimes taken to mean clearly identifiable national communities which lack a national state (for example, the Welsh nation or the Catalan nation). Nationality has two different and confusing denotations:

a) A synonym of citizenship, juridical definition of membership of a state usually defined by entitlement to a passport (British nationality, French nationality).

b) A community of culture and/or descent, which also incorporates some of the meanings of the more contemporary term ethnicity. (English nationality, Welsh nationality).[15]

Marx and Engels generally used the term nation in its English and French meaning to designate the permanent population of a nation state. The word nationality, however, was used in its Central and Eastern European denotation, to designate an ethnocultural community that had not achieved full national status because it lacked a state of its own.[16] In Marx and Engels' works, nationalities will either become nations by acquiring a state of their own (Poland, Ireland), or alternatively they are said to be historyless peoples ('Geschichtslosen Völker'), national communities which lack historical vitality because of their inability to consolidate a national state. These non-historical nationalities are intrinsically reactionary because of their inability to adapt to the capitalist mode of production. Their survival is only guaranteed in the old order, so by necessity they must be regressive, in order to avoid extinction.

Consequently, modern nations are for Marx and Engels what we may call today nation states; ethno-cultural and linguistic communities with their own states. Nationalities are ethno-cultural and linguistic groups not developed into full nations because they lack their own states. This model of national formation is greatly inspired by the historical development of the French and, to a lesser extent, the British case, which as 'the most advanced nations' must serve as models for 'less developed' national communities.

There is another dimension to Marx and Engels' discussion of national communities. Nations, as noted earlier, were for Marx one of the concrete forms of the general form of civil society. This only comes into existence as a result of a specific configuration of certain classes, which in general respond to the characteristics of the capitalist mode of production. Since the bourgeoisie is the universally dominant class in this mode, civil society gives legitimacy to bourgeois class domination by creating the impression that the class requirements of the bourgeoisie to reproduce its conditions of existence are the general requirements of society as a whole. Moreover the state in its national form is responsible for regulating the best possible conditions for the fulfilment of these general requirements. Following this logic, which is at the centre of Marx and Engels' evolutionary discussion of the development of capitalism, it is possible to envisage a chain of events that will destroy the foundation of every form of class society via the emancipation of the proletariat. Thus the achievement of this final goal of abolishing capitalist relations of production has far-reaching consequences for the nation. It could be schematised in the following way: the abolition of the capitalist mode of production will bring about the end of:

a) civil society as an entity reproducing the conditions of existence of class societies;
b) the bourgeoisie as the hegemonic class of the civil society and the proletariat as the subordinated oppressed class;
c) the state as the instrument through which the bourgeoisie controls the civil society, and
d) the nation as the framework for the existence of the bourgeois state.

As the framework for the existence of the capitalist (national) state, the nation creates a linguistic unit essential to the consolidation of capitalism's conditions of existence, by generating a medium of communication (language) and a focus of identity which gives a general appearance to the sectarian interests of the bourgeoisie (nationalism). Thus, in terms of this unilinear and eurocentric process of development, the nation is crucially linked with the fate of the capitalist state, because both are concrete epiphenomenal expressions of the civil society – the mechanism which created them in the first place. Once the state is abolished (or withers away), a similar fate awaits the nation. Consider the statement in *The Communist Manifesto*: '... the proletariat must first of all acquire political supremacy, must rise to be the leading class of the nation, it is, so far, itself national, though not in the bourgeois sense of the word.' One is presented with a tactical ploy to gain power from the bourgeoisie in its own terrain, since the nation will be abolished by the advancing tide of history:

> National differences and antagonisms between peoples are daily more and more vanishing owing to the development of the bourgeoisie, to freedom of commerce, to the world market, to uniformity in the mode of production and in the conditions of life corresponding thereto. The supremacy of the proletariat will cause them to vanish still faster.

Marx and Engels expected the proletariat to become the national class for a short period, believing this to be a transitional but historically necessary step in order to advance to a higher developmental stage, the abolition of the national state. In this sense Marx's ironic remarks on Lafargue's speech do not indicate that he rejected the abolition of nations as such, merely that he refuted the idea that such a stage of development had come to pass at the time of the meetings of the First International.

The parameters of analysis briefly discussed here help to give coherence to the apparently contradictory formulations of Marx and Engels on the national question. Their support for the right to self-determination in the Irish and Polish cases, as well as their opposition to any self-determination for the so-called Southern Slavs, can be thus explained in terms of the rigid evolutionary model, epiphenomenal economism, and the eurocentric approach which permeated their interpretations of the processes of social change. These parameters, concerned as they are with the universal impact of the process of transformation of the productive forces, are insensitive to the specific circumstances which bring about the emergence of actual national movements. Marxist epistemology is concerned only with the impact of universal processes of social transformation and is therefore blind to those aspects which cannot be directly derived from the laws of motion of political economy. The nation is understood to be a by-product of productive forces. It comes into existence to secure the domination of the bourgeoisie during the transition to, and consolidation of, the capitalist mode of production. A clear effect of this model is best illustrated by one of the most unfortunate aspects of Marx and Engels' conceptualisation of the national question, the theory of the historyless peoples.

The Theory of the Nations Without History

Bozě! ... Ach nikdo není na zemi Kdoby Slavům [sic] spavedli-vost činil?[17]

The way in which Marx and Engels related to a number of stateless or numerically small national communities has been a subject of embarrassment and amazement for a considerable number of commentators within the Marxist tradition, from the Second International right up to recent works on the subject.[18] However, the most detailed and illuminating discussion of this unfortunate use of Hegelian terminology can be found in Rosdolsky's seminal work. With the exception of his thorough research, there have been few attempts to understand Marx and Engels' position on the subject, and no attempt to locate their bizarre analysis in the context of their overall theoretical positions. It is therefore necessary to try to provide a link between the theory of non-historical nations and the general Marxist discussion of the national question.

As has been noted, the idea of progressive centralisation as the economy develops from a lower to a higher stage is at the heart of Marx and Engels' analysis of the national question. This premise, as Ian Cummings asserts,[19] 'runs like a red thread through Marx's writings'. Since this is an axiomatic point of departure for many discussions of national movements, it is hardly surprising to find that Marx and Engels regarded every form of nationalist ideology and activity as aimed towards the formation and consolidation of national states. Nationalist ideology is for Marx a mere epiphenomenon of the growth of the nation.[20] One of the main problems with this is that it leads to both a gross overestimation of the structural need of the bourgeoisie to build a national state, and also to a parallel underestimation of cultural and ethnic factors (insofar as they are not explained as an epiphenomenon of the economy) in the process of the formation of national communities. The problem here is not only the use of Western European models of development, but also a capital-centred emphasis in the discussion of all aspects of the national phenomenon. Nationalist movements and communities are always defined in terms of their position or functionality within the capitalist system.[21] Once the goal of national communities is defined as the formation of national states, the difficulty is how to explain the existence and behaviour of nationalist movements that are neither capable of nor willing to form such a state.

If, according to the Marxian interpretation, the growth of the nation only heralds the formation of national states (so that the bourgeoisie can secure its hegemonic position) the inescapable logic of this analysis, as has been noted, dictates that national communities incapable of constituting national states are acting against the tide of history. Such communities perform a reactionary function since they cannot develop a healthy and hegemonic bourgeoisie, a condition *sine qua non* for the subsequent proletarian revolution. An even more serious and disturbing conclusion, however, is that these usually small national communities are not only functionally but intrinsically reactionary relics of the past, which must disappear to pave the way for social progress. Since for Marx and Engels the only purpose of national agitation is the drive to build a national state, those national communities whose size precludes their becoming viable independent economic units have no *raison d'être*. If they wish to follow a path of national revival, they will become socially regressive because they cannot adapt to the capitalist mode of production and therefore must remain feudal enclaves in order to subsist as independent entities. Furthermore, according to Marx and Engels, such enclaves have no choice but to associate closely with those reactionary forces which oppose the progressive unifying role of the bourgeoisie. These unfortunate national communities ('ethnographic monuments' in Engels' words) must perish culturally and politically in order to make way for the unifying role of the bourgeoisie. Closely following some of the worst excesses of Hegelian political philosophy, Marx and Engels called these national communities historyless peoples ('geschichtslosen Völker').

The central idea behind this dubious concept of non-historical nations is that peoples ('Völker') who have proven incapable of building a state over a period of time will never be able to do so.[22] Hegel makes a sharp distinction between nations and states. For him, a group of people may exist as a nation, but in such a condition the nation is unable to contribute to the unfolding of world history. A nation, according to Hegel, will only fulfil its historical mission if it is capable of building a stable state. Therefore it is no accident that those whom Hegel calls 'uncivilised peoples' have no history, because they have been proven incapable of having a state. From this theory Marx and Engels drew the logic of their evolutionary paradigm. Hegel argued, perhaps for the first time, that history cannot be conceived as a mere recording of change, but must primarily be considered in terms of the development of human agency. His teleological notion of history indicates not only the direction but also the stages of evolution towards a higher stage of freedom embodied in a superior state. Thus earlier or 'less developed' civilisations must give way to more advanced forms of social organisation which will inevitably result in a superior state. However, what fate awaits those national communities unable to achieve a higher degree of statehood, or those nations which lost their national state, or even those which never had a national state? On this issue, Hegel's position in *Philosophy of History* is clear: peoples ('Völker') who had been proven incapable of building a state will never be able to do so and are damned culturally to vanish in the stream of history.

Hegel distinguishes between state and nation while arguing that the supportive base for the former is the latter. A nation, in Hegelian terms, is held together by natural and emotional ties: kinship, language and other means of union. Translating this argument into more contemporary terminology, nations are first and foremost ethno-cultural communities. The state preserves the ethnic link, but its specificity is derived from something different – the ethical ideal derived from the genius of the national spirit ('Volksgeist'). The particular national spirit of each nation develops as a consequence of the harmonic interaction of the particular elements which constitute the whole: the people, the civil society, ethnic links, the rulers, and so on. Since the national spirit is the result of this harmonic interaction, it becomes a discrete unit independent of its constitutive elements. In this way it takes an objective form by generating the state and its institutions, but this only occurs if the national spirit is capable of a significant contribution to the development of freedom. If this condition is fulfilled, then this spirit has a place in history. National communities which have such a spirit then become 'historical nations, bearers of the world spirit' ('welthistorische Volksgeister').[23]

This is well explained by Hegel in the *Encyklopädie der philosophischen Wissenschaften im Grundrisse*:

In the existence of a Volk, there is a substantial purpose to become a state, and to maintain themselves as such; a Volk without a state formation (a nation as such) had actually no history, as the people before their state formation existed and others yet exist, as wild nations.[24]

The national communities incapable of creating a national state are not the bearers of the world spirit. Because they do not contribute to the unfolding of civilisation, they are peoples without rights ('rechtlos') and, as Hegel states, they 'count no longer in history'.[25] Also, for Hegel, not all nations have the same rights; the rights of 'barbarian nations' are certainly not equal to those of 'more civilised nations', the true bearers of the spirit of freedom. 'The civilised nation is conscious that the rights of barbarians are unequal to its own and treats their autonomy as only a formality.'[26]

These speculations are perhaps one of the weakest features of Hegel's political philosophy and are certainly in direct opposition to a historical materialist conception of history. It is indeed strange to find this conceptualisation echoed in the works of the founding fathers of historical materialism. The revival of Hegelian terminology, particularly in the context of the 1848 revolutions, was coupled with an increasing usage of abusive language vis a vis communities that did not conform to the path to national development discussed above. The intense hostility to these national communities can be ascertained from the following quotations.

Spaniards and Mexicans:

> The Spaniards are indeed degenerate. But a degenerate Spaniard, a Mexican, that is the ideal. All vices of the Spaniards – Boastfulness, Grandiloquence, and Quixoticism – are found in the Mexicans raised to the third power.[27]

Scandinavians:

> Scandinavism is enthusiasm for the brutal, sordid, piratical old norse national traits, for the deep inner life which is unable to express its exuberant ideas and sentiments in words, but can express them in deeds, namely in rudeness towards women, perpetual drunkenness and wild berserk frenzy alternating with tearful sentimentality ... Obviously, the more primitive a nation is, the more closely its customs and way of life resemble those of the old norse people, the more 'scandinavian' it must be.[28]

Chinese:

> It is almost needless to observe that, in the same measure in
> which opium has obtained the sovereignty over the Chinese,
> the Emperor and his staff of pedantic mandarins have become
> dispossessed of their own sovereignty. It would seem as though
> history had first to make this whole people drunk before it could
> raise them out of their hereditary stupidity.[29]

North African Bedouins:

> The struggle of the Bedouins was a hopeless one, and though
> the manner in which brutal soldiers like Bugeaud have carried
> on the war is highly blameworthy, the conquest of Algeria is an
> important and fortunate fact for the progress of civilisation ...
> and even if we may regret that the liberty of the Bedouins of the
> desert has been destroyed, we must not forget that these same
> Bedouins were a nation of robbers, whose principal means of
> living consisted in making excursions upon each other, or upon
> settled villages.[30]

This is only a sample. Marx and Engels were, to put it mildly,
impatient with and intolerant of ethnic minorities. This is clear
from their private correspondence, the most infamous example of
which is the characterisation of Lasalle as a 'Jewish Nigger'.[31] But
the dichotomy historical-non-historical nations was revived by
Marx and Engels in the context of the 1848 revolutions while discussing the revival to national life of the Czechs, Slovaks,
Ukrainians (Ruthenians) and Serbs, all of which were Eastern
European national communities which spoke Slavonic-related languages. These diverse national communities were constituted into
a fictitious unit called the Southern Slavs. The reasons for this can
be understood in the context of Marx and Engels' model of
national formation, discussed above. If the conditions of a
national community do not allow for the formation of a viable
state, the national community has to be assimilated into a larger
state and a more viable national community, with 'democracy as
compensation'.[32]

In Marx and Engels' view this process of national assimilation is
not only highly desirable, but it cannot be opposed. Nations
which are incapable of forming national states and still persist in
their claim to nationhood oppose the inexorable process of development of the capitalist mode of production, by virtue of their

claim to national existence in a capitalist world which they cannot possibly survive. The conclusion that Marx and Engels drew from this was that, if national survival is to occur, then the national community in question must seek to return to the state of affairs that preceded capitalist transformation, a retrograde step in the evolution of humanity.

As Rosdolsky rightly argues, the old Hegelian terminology served a useful purpose in the Marxian analysis of the Slavonic national communities. These unfortunate peoples were defined as non-historical in much the same way as Hegel used the term for the same peoples a century before. The Hegelian 'Volksgeist' was replaced by the notion of the capacity to enter the capitalist mode of production, but much of the metaphysical social evolutionist logic survived to demand the disappearance of the Southern Slavs. These national communities were understood by Marx and Engels to be incapable of having national states of their own because they were either too small or they lived in areas of mixed population in the midst of a 'more energetic race' (usually German but also Magyar), where the other national community was considered more advanced and better equipped in terms of its class composition to constitute a national state:

> Bohemia and Croatia (another disjected member of the Slavonic family, acted upon by the Hungarian, as Bohemia by the German) were the homes of what it is called on the European continent 'Panslavism'. Neither Bohemia nor Croatia was strong enough to exist as a nation by herself. Their respective nationalities, gradually undermined by the action of historical causes that inevitably absorbs into a more energetic stock, could only hope to be restored to anything like independence by an alliance with other Slavonic nations.[33]

Thus, if the Slavonic East European nationalities cannot constitute national states, their only hope for survival is to constitute a federation of Slavonic nations under the leadership of the Czar of all Russia, the 'bulwark of European reaction'. The democratic movement in the Austro-Hungarian monarchy will, according to Marx and Engels, assimilate these 'relics of peoples', transforming their culture and national identity into the 'superior' German and Magyar culture, granting to them a democratic way of life as a compensation. But given that national communities persist in preserving their 'backward' national identities and culture, they can only subsist on condition that they locate themselves within the sphere of influence of the equally backward Russian absolutism. So these national communities can survive only in semi-feudal conditions and their survival can only be guaranteed by the backward Russian empire.

Engels provided the theoretical justification for this analytical logic in the following way:

> There is no country in Europe which does not have in some corner or other one or several fragments of peoples, the remnant of a former population that was suppressed and held in bondage by the nation which later became the main vehicle for historical development. These relics of a nation, mercilessly trampled under the course of history, as Hegel says *These residual fragments of peoples (Völkerabfalle)* always become fanatical standard bearers of counter revolution and remain so until their *complete extirpation* or loss of their national character, just as their whole existence in general is itself a protest against a great historical revolution.
>
> Such in Scotland are the Gaels, the supporters of the Stuarts from 1640 to 1745.
>
> Such in France are the Bretons, the supporters of the Bourbons from 1742 to 1800.
>
> Such in Spain are the Basques, the supporters of Don Carlos.
>
> Such in Austria are the panslavist Southern Slavs, who are nothing but *residual fragments of peoples*, resulting from an extremely confused thousand years development. This residual fragment, which is likewise extremely confused sees its salvation only in the reversal of the whole European movement, which in its view ought to go not from west to east, but from east to west.[34]

Here we find with remarkable clarity, as Rosdolsky points out, the repetition of the eurocentric pattern which first emerged with the French Revolution and which constitutes the theoretical basis for Marx and Engels' analysis of the national question. The revolution will destroy the particularism of small nationalities, incorporating them into the higher and developed nations, becoming in this way the vehicle for emancipation from feudalism and superstition. German is the 'language of liberty' for the Czechs in Bohemia, in the same way as French is for the Occitans and Bretons in the French state. As the Jacobins perceived the non-French nationalities as intrinsically reactionary, so Marx and Engels regarded the Southern Slavs in the Austro-Hungarian empire in the same light.[35]

The argument that so strongly denies the non-historical nations the right to self-determination and historical continuity also sustains a strong justification for the emancipation and state independence of the so-called historical nations. These are national communities capable of being agents of historical transformation which will further the formation of a strong capitalist economy. Marx and Engels strongly supported the right to state independence of the Irish and Poles, as both were considered historical nations that did not have a national state. In this sense the right to self-determination (meaning state independence) is not an absolute right, but is the right of some nations, those which can become agents or vehicles of social transformation – for themselves and for the nations that oppress them. The most important example was Poland.[36]

Similar observations were made by Marx and Engels on the Irish question. They reasoned that England could not embark on a true revolutionary path until the Irish problem had gone. Marx conclusively shows how the occupation of Ireland underdeveloped the country by making it an appendix to the British economy.[37] The separation and independence of Ireland from England was not only a vital step for Irish development but was also essential for the British people since 'A nation that oppresses another forges its own chains [because] the average English worker hates the Irish worker as a competitor who lowers wages and standard of life' and this proletarian antagonism is nourished by the bourgeoise in its goal to divide the workers.[38]

This does not, however, apply to the non-historical nations. In terms of Marx and Engels' analytical logic there is no *contradiction* or *incoherence* in this. The Irish and Polish national movements are perceived as advancing the course of progress by constituting national states capable of developing a healthy contradiction between the proletariat and the bourgeoisie. Furthermore, their state independence will be a considerable help for the proletarian struggles within the nations that subjugate them. The non-historical nations, by contrast, either cannot develop a bourgeoisie, because they are peasant nations, or they cannot develop a state of their own, because they either live in a mixed area of residence or they are too small to create an internal market. Thus these nations must seek alliances with the defenders of the old order: the irresistible flow of progress requires either the voluntary assimilation or the annihilation of these national communities. If they persist in maintaining their national identity in alliance with reactionary forces in a revolutionary situation, they will simply be trampled over by the forces of progress.

The contrast between Marx and Engels' perceptive discussion of the Irish question and their ethnocentric attitude towards the Southern Slavs has puzzled and surprised many observers and commentators. The differential treatment received by different national communities in the struggle for self-determination requires an explanation. The most common one is that Marx and Engels had no theory on the national question and so were inconsistent in their discussion of it. Their analyses of concrete national situations are considered to be connected to circumstantial political events and devoid of any theoretical significance. This is the view of Löwy and Davis, among others.[39]

However, even a superficial evaluation of the works of Marx and Engels shows that this is not the case. The presence of important traces of Hegelian historicism in their universal evolutionary theory, and the related understanding of the national state as a historical construct to secure the conditions of existence of the bourgeoisie, make it inconceivable that their discussion of the national question is simply an ad hoc construct. If all historical devices have a functional purpose in terms of the overall movement of history, why should the national phenomenon be an exception? On the contrary, the systemic view of the process of evolution of humanity through different modes of production and their concomitant forms of social organisation must provide the analytical tools to conceptualise the nation within definite historical boundaries. The emergence of every national state is for Marx and Engels indissolubly linked with the universalisation of the capitalist mode of production and the hegemony of the bourgeoisie. The viability or otherwise of every national state is tested against this fundamental theoretical assumption. Each of their concrete analyses of specific national communities, from the firm advocacy of the right to self-determination of the Irish and Poles, to the harsh treatment of the Southern Slavs, is guided by this principle.

A second influential explanation of the embarrassing statements about the Southern Slavs is put forward by Bloom.[40] Referring to Engels' scornful attacks on these peoples, he argues that most of them 'must not be taken into account', because Engels was more prone to 'political generalisations' and he was 'rather more severe' than Marx with small nations. The implication of this argument is that Marx should be disassociated from this analysis because it was Engels who promoted the use of Hegelian terminology as well as being guilty of a certain 'German jingoism' in his youth. Such an explanation is partly accepted by Davis, and Rosdolsky [41] appears also to suggest the same argument.

This conclusion is unjustified for two main reasons. First, as noted above, Marx also indulged in a derogatory denunciation of small and non-Western European national communities. Second, and more important, it is unthinkable that Marx and Engels, in a relationship of close collaboration and joint revolutionary work, would disagree over such a fundamental question. As David Fernbach suggests in his introduction to the 1848 writings, the reason for Engels' recurrent use of Hegelian terminology was mainly a consequence of the division of labour between the two partners. Engels was responsible for work on the national question. If the senior partner was in disagreement with the views of the junior partner, he never made this difference explicit. Had such a difference existed, it would have been extraordinary, given the importance of the issue during the period 1848–52.

Mehring too, in a comprehensive study of the writings of Marx and Engels in the *Neue Rheinische Zeitung*, argues that there is no clear way to determine the origin of the majority of the articles of this newspaper (most of the attacks on the Southern Slavs appeared here). As a rule, the writers worked in close collaboration on these pieces. Consequently it is hard to escape the conclusion that the articles containing the Hegelian derogatory terminology were also written in close collaboration and agreement, and were not the result of Engels' idiosyncratic approach to the problem.[42]

Another, perhaps more sophisticated, interpretation of the embarrassing use of the ethnocentric Hegelian terminology is discussed in Haupt and Weill's well-documented article on the Marxian heritage on the national question.[43] According to this thesis, the persistent use of such descriptions should be understood in the same context and domain in which they were used, namely the arena of political action. Haupt and Weill reason that this language is neither the result of any aprioristic elaboration, nor does it arise from a careful and systematic thinking of the problems involved. It arises from the heat of the fervour inspired by the 1848 revolutions. In this context Marx and Engels perceived the twin tasks of the democratic and revolutionary forces to be the destruction of the political system established by the congress of Vienna of 1815, and the independence of 'big' historical nations oppressed by multinational empires.

But, Haupt and Weill argue, this strategy did not take into account the interests of the small national communities (which

Marx and Engels considered to be 'backward peasant nations'), which needed the equilibrium of the multinational empire to counteract the assimilationist pressures of their larger neighbours in order to maintain their national individuality. The movements for national revival among the small Slavic national communities were pushed, by the incapacity of the revolutionary movement to provide a solution to their national aspirations, into the arms of the counter-revolutionaries, because by preserving the status quo they were not forcing assimilation upon themselves.[44] Thus, according to this argument, Marx and Engels drew theoretical conclusions from the transitory and conjunctural circumstances of the 1848 revolutions, by defining these unfortunate peoples as intrinsically reactionary.

While Haupt and Weill's hypothesis has the important merit of providing a plausible historical context for Marx and Engels' bizarre analysis, it is not entirely satisfactory for two main reasons. Firstly, Marx and Engels maintained their strong animosity towards the small Central European national communities throughout most of their political careers. In 1855, in an article in the *New York Daily Tribune*, Marx argued that 'one part of the Austrian Slavs consists of tribes whose history belongs to the past' and Engels repeated this same argument in an article about Russia.[45] In 1882, one year before the death of Marx, Engels declared in response to a criticism by Kautsky that he had no sympathy for the 'small slavonic groups' and 'ruins of nations', who looked to the Czar for salvation. Moreover in 1885 Engels, in a letter to August Bebel, argued that:

> The European War is beginning seriously to threaten us. These miserable remnants of former nations – Serbs, Bulgarians, Greeks and other dishonest rabble [*Raübergesindel*] – over which philistine liberals gush in the interests of Russia, are unwilling to grant each other the very air they breathe and seem to be compelled to cut each others' greedy throats. That each of these tiny tribes can determine whether Europe is to be at war or peace serves these nationalistic philistines right. The first shot has been fired at the Dragoman, where and when the last shot will be fired, no-one knows.[46]

The second weakness of Haupt and Weill's argument is that, as is shown above, Marx and Engels used their offensive terminology, and the Hegelian concepts, not only in writing about the Southern Slavs, but also with respect (or rather disrespect) to other national communities. In using this language they created a system of equivalences which clearly implied the creation of a dichotomous analysis of national communities. On the one hand were the historical great European nations: generally speaking, the standard-bearers of the process of 'civilisation and progress'. On the other hand were the small, non-Western and Central European nations: usually 'barbaric and reactionary'. This division implies that the pattern of national development in Western and Central Europe should be considered normal and universal, and lack of compliance with it implies reaction and retrogression. In conceptualising the national phenomenon in this way, the emerging theoretical categories of analysis go beyond the specific case of the 1848 revolutions.

Bauer, in his important work on the national question,[47] provides an ingenious way out of this embarrassing analysis by arguing that the concept of non-historical nations is not an absolute criterion but the result of a set of historical circumstances occurring at a particular period in the process of development of the forces of production. Under different circumstances connected with the development of a more advanced stage of capitalist development, these non-historical nations will 'awake to national life'. Bauer felt uneasy about the categorical and deterministic use of the concepts of historical versus non-historical nations, but nevertheless accepted them as the theoretical point of departure, if only to change their meaning radically.

Rosdolsky's Critique of the Concept of 'Non-historical Nations'

Roman Rosdolsky, the distinguished Ukrainian Marxist scholar, provides the most comprehensive, detailed and scholarly written work on the subject of the non-historical nations. Fortunately, this important work has been recently translated into English.[48] Though some of his conclusions appear to lack sufficient critical discussion, his work should be praised for its detailed evaluation and systematic use of primary sources.

The first part of Rosdolsky's work is devoted to a comprehensive presentation of the attitudes of the *Neue Rheinische Zeitung* and of Marx and Engels towards each of the Eastern European national communities under discussion, presenting an initial tentative explanation of the reasons for their attitude towards these communities. According to Rosdolsky, one factor that must be taken into account is the complexity of the national problem in Austria, and the difficulties faced by anyone attempting to provide a solution to the conflicting claims of the national movements under consideration:

> On one side were plebeian peoples, only just awakened to a new historical life, without their own national bourgeoisie and working class, as yet scarcely capable of building their own states. On the other side, however, was the German bourgeosie, which felt as much at home in the Slavic lands of the monarchy as it did in Germany itself, since it inhabited the cities of these lands and commanded their trade and industry. Because of its whole class situation, the German bourgeosie was as little capable of renouncing its privileged position as the Hungarian or Polish nobility was of renouncing the exploitation and domination of its subjects (Hintersassen)[49] who spoke a foreign tongue.[50]

The clear cultural and political domination of the German bourgeoisie over territories inhabited by national communities of Slavic descent and culture, made the acceptance of any form of national emancipation of the latter (meaning national-territorial state sovereignty) by the German bourgeoisie an impossibility. Rosdolsky argues that to ask the German bourgeoisie voluntarily to give up their hegemonic position in these Slavonic countries was tantamount to questioning the ability of the German bourgeoisie to participate in the revolution. So, he continues, Marx and Engels found themselves in an acute dilemma: support for the emerging national communities would alienate the German bourgeoisie, the 'most advanced class at the time', the very basis of the 1848 revolutionary fervour. Rosdolsky reasons that Marx and Engels had 'no other choice' but to support the 'progressive bourgeoisie', even if this meant encouraging harsh national repression of the non-viable national communities. The Czech provinces were, according to Rosdolsky who quotes Marx in 'Herr Vogt',[51] 'in the middle of Germany' and, in language that is more in tune with a reactionary and nostalgic 'völkisch' nationalist rhetoric than the analytical wit of a distinguished Marxist scholar, he argues that if the Slavic national communities were to constitute national states, they would have represented 'Einen Dorn im Fleische des künftigen grossdeutschen Reiches ...'.[52] If this were not enough, Rosdolsky identifies a second major problem: the underdevelopment of the Czechs and other Southern Slav national communities vis a vis the German bourgeoisie. The Czechs and South Slavs were 'neither mature, nor strong enough' to establish independent states; had they been formed they could all too easily have become 'bounty of Czarism' ('Beute des Zarismus') and 'vanguard positions' ('Vorposten') of the latter in Central Europe.

By posing the problem in these terms, Rosdolsky is falling into the same paradigmatic trap that made Marxian analysis so insensitive to the plight and national awakening of those communities which did not conform with the pattern of development of Western European national communities. Rosdolsky is repeating Marx's epiphenomenal analysis by arguing that every national movement exists to build a national state, and that national awakening is only progressive where there is a strong bourgeoisie. He qualifies his analysis, however, by arguing that the danger of counter-revolution could have been kept under control had these national communities achieved autonomy and equality of rights at the cultural, linguistic and political levels. But Rosdolsky also asks the rhetorical question, 'What could have moved the German bourgeoisie to unilaterally resign their privileges?' Here he believes that to propose a programme of national cultural autonomy, as was suggested fifty years later in the Brno (Brünn) congress of the All Austrian (Gesamtpartei) Socialist Party, was a utopian solution.

Rosdolsky concludes his analysis by arguing that, given the conjunctural relations of forces, the German revolution could only give power to the German bourgeoisie and to the Hungarian and Polish aristocracy, the junior partners of the former. This thesis leads him to the conclusion that the victory of the revolutionary forces would have had to coincide with an even greater oppression of the so-called non-historical nations. Rosdolsky[53] attempts a critical defence of the German left and of Marx and Engels when he argues that it was impossible for them 'to identify objectives that went beyond this objective "barrier" (Schranke) of the revolution'.

Consequently, the left was unable to reconcile the antagonisms which, according to Rosdolsky, were irreconcilable at that particular historical period. The left had no other option but to adopt a position in favour of the progressive bourgeoisie and to declare as their natural enemies the populations that resisted the political hegemony of the German bourgeoisie and the Polish and Hungarian nobility. In other words, the German left had to declare entire national communities counter-revolutionary. This posed a theoretical problem for the left as well as for Marx and Engels:

This unusual distinction between nations and not between social classes had to be explained, this is to say, deduced, from the history or from the *nature* of these nations. In this situation it seemed 'natural' for the revolutionary 'left' to recur to the traditional Hegelian doctrine of 'historical' and 'non historical' peoples (Völkern) as a mechanism for self deceit, escaping to the terrain of historical mythology to cover for the fatal objective difficulties of the revolution. The Hegelian reminiscences of the Neue Rheinische Zeitung were very useful for this purpose. (emphasis added)[54]

Rosdolsky's arguments could be summarised in the following way: firstly, the objective conditions did not allow for the emancipation of the Southern Slavs; even if it had been possible for them to gain some form of national emancipation they were too backward to constitute modern nations. Secondly, the revolutionary left had no alternative but to oppose the demands of these unfortunate national communities, even if they were struggling against a vicious form of oppression. The victory of the bourgeoisie was supposed to pave the way for the eventual emancipation of humanity as a whole in the form of the impending proletarian revolution. If in order to achieve this goal whole national communities were culturally and politically obliterated, the left had to shrug its shoulders and wonder about the heavy price paid for the development of progress. So, according to Rosdolsky, the mistakes of the revolutionary left were conditioned by historical circumstances and were, in this sense, unavoidable.

Thus Rosdolsky argues that one must judge the left not in terms of our 'contemporary perceptions of the national question', but in the context of the historical circumstances of the period in question.[55] His conclusions are problematic in a number of ways. Firstly, the theory of nations without history, as Rosdolsky is well aware, does not only embrace the small Slavonic national communities. It was also applied to a variety of nations, both large and small, which in Marx and Engels' judgement were not capable of a revolutionary transformation of their societies (the Welsh, the Scots, the Quebecois and the Mexicans are but a few examples). The widespread use of the theory denotes a more systematic conceptualisation than the conjunctural explanation proposed by Rosdolsky appears to indicate.

Secondly, it seems that Rosdolsky falls into the paradigmatic theoretical trap which logically leads to the formulation of the theory of non-historical nations. By sustaining the argument that historical circumstances were not yet ripe for the emancipation of the Southern Slav national communities, he is implicitly accepting the teleological model of social evolution behind the Hegelian theory of non-historical peoples. This influence was also noted earlier, when evaluating the social evolutionary parameter inherited by the Marxian tradition from the works of the founding fathers. The epiphenomenalist equation:

modern nation = national state = hegemony of the bourgeoisie

is accepted by Rosdolsky, considerably weakening his case against Marx' and Engels' abusive attitude towards the Southern Slavs.

Thirdly, Rosdolsky fails to see the link between his well-documented section on Marx and Engels' evaluation of the national question and their overall theory of evolution. He argues that the revolutionary left could not overcome the objective circumstances in which the struggle for the emancipation of the Southern Slav national communities was taking place, and therefore it had to oppose their struggle for national emancipation to prevent further delays to the development of a revolutionary class (the bourgeoisie). The problem in this argument is not the objective conditions, but the use of epistemological constructs which lead to a conceptualisation of the lack of maturity of these conditions. Rather than the objective circumstances, it was the numbing effect of the epiphenomenalist epistemology that prevented the German left from conceptualising the national problem in such a way as to take into account the national development of the Southern Slavs. Marxist epistemology required the definition of a developmental continuum in which the national state must be historically located to function as a vehicle for the crystallisation of bourgeois power. National communities which do not follow this developmental path cannot fit the theoretical model, and are declared deviant exceptions to be rectified at the best possible opportunity. This is perhaps the single most important explanation for the lack of a sensitive analysis of the national phenomenon in the works of Marx and Engels, as well as in subsequent generations of Marxists discussing the national question.

Conclusion

Contrary to the assertions of Davis, Löwy and other analysts and commentators, it has been argued that the work of Marx and

Engels on the national question can be understood as a coherent corpus of literature, even if the theoretical arguments which sustain their analysis have not been explicitly conceptualised. The modern nation is a clearly defined and historically located political phenomenon. It represents a mechanism for consolidating and securing the conditions of existence of the bourgeoisie. The theory of the non-historical nations is not a curiosity, a slip of the tongue, an ad hoc argument or a regrettable mishap. It is rather the result of the formulation of the rigid universal laws of social evolution which define the precise historical location of the modern nation and by default render obsolete national communities that cannot fulfil this eurocentric political criterion.

The analytical parameters outlined in the introduction to this book inform the conceptual requirement that every modern nation must form a national state to further the development of the bourgeoisie. Furthermore, the formation of a national state is a sine qua non functional requirement for the survival of a national community in a capitalist mode of production. National communities incapable of forming national states are hindering the development of the progressive centralisation and uniformisation of humanity, and must therefore be assimilated into more vital and 'energetic' nations capable of forming national states with democracy 'as compensation'. The national state is the condition for a mature bourgeoisie and the prerequisite for the final contradiction that will render both the nation and the state historically obsolete. The 'model' for national development is that of the 'large' Western European nations, particularly France, but also British England, which is considered a 'successful' case of assimilation of the celtic fringe, with the important exception of Ireland – a 'historical' nation.

The perception of the national community outlined above is the nucleus of the *misleading heritage of European Marxism*. It informed the positions of the main debates within the Second and Third Internationals, and it configurated the framework in which subsequent generations of Marxists thought about the national question. The epistemological requirement which demands the historical location of the national phenomenon within a hierarchical, universal and developmental continuum must be seriously challenged if the Marxist tradition is to provide a more sensitive discussion of the multidimensionality of the national arena. Only those Marxist theories capable of breaking with the abortive rigidities of the above mentioned parameters have managed to provide a more sensitive analysis of the national phenomenon.

The work of Otto Bauer and the Austro–Marxists would be the single most important exception to this misleading analytical stance of classical Marxism, the impact of which on the most influential traditions of the Second International we must now examine.

2

The Second International and the National Question

Leszek Kolakowski in his influential book on the history and development of the Marxist theory argues that the Second International 'may be called without exaggeration the Golden Age of Marxism' because:

> Marxist doctrine had been clearly enough defined to constitute a recognisable school of thought but it was not so rigidly codified or subjected to dogmatic orthodoxy as to rule out discussion or the advocacy of rival solutions to theoretical and tactical problems.[1]

While this may be superficially the case, particularly when the proliferation of debates and thinkers is taken into account, the apparent plurality of approaches hides a more dogmatic and deterministic approach to the fundamental features of historical materialism. The Second International's left, right, and centre wings became leading exponents of the parameters of analysis discussed in the introduction above, which choked the analytical creativity and imagination of the movement in more ways than one. The conceptualisation of the national question is one of the many examples of this dogmatism. A significant exception in this analytical outlook was the emergence and development of the *Wiener Marxsche Schule* (Viennese Marxist school) which was later to take the name of Austro-Marxism. This will be discussed in Chapter 6.

As Kolakowski argues, the Second International was characterised by a prolific discussion of a number of controversial issues, of which the national question was one of the most hotly debated. Though there was a genuine attempt to come to grips with an important problem perceived to have been insufficiently discussed by Marx and Engels, the possibilities of conceptualising the issue in a novel and imaginative way were denied from the start by the orthodox framework of analysis.

This chapter will examine the most influential arguments on the national question debated during this historical period, taking the view that the factional split that resulted from the revisionist debate in many ways determined both the configuration of ideas in the Second International, and the intellectual legacy of the period as a whole. Because of their intellectual originality and influence in the debate on the national question, the Marxist-Leninist and Austro-Marxist traditions will be considered in separate chapters.

Kautsky and Luxemburg on the National Question

Rosa Luxemburg and Karl Kautsky represent two different and often contradictory approaches and political strategies in the years preceding World War One. Luxemburg was the outstanding figure of the radical left of the Second International and Kautsky was the most influential intellectual figure of the so-called centrist or orthodox faction. Many contentious issues separated them, but in spite of their differences it is possible to detect a common departure in their conceptualisation of theory and discussions about strategy. This is the direct equation of political and social institutions with the most meaningful features of the economic order. Every social institution represents an agent in the class struggle and socialism will evolve out of the capitalist mode of production in a mechanistic way, in much the same way as capitalism was perceived to have evolved out of the feudal mode of production.

Heavily influenced by earlier forms of a social darwinian logic, Kautsky[2] developed his analysis of the process of social transformation in terms of what he called 'The natural necessities of the capitalist mode of production'.[3] He understood history as a series of interrelated stages of linear development, the iron laws of evolution, which will lead history to its inexorable end: the abolition of capitalism and the socialist transformation of society. Communities, like all other superstructural social institutions, are mere tools or instruments in this process: 'All communities have economic functions to fulfill! This must, self evidently have been the case with the original communist societies which we encounter at the threshold of history.'[4]

Rosa Luxemburg's major theoretical work, *The Accumulation of Capital*, is also committed to the same analytical logic:

[Imperialism is] ... The political expression of the accumulation of capital in its competitive struggle for what remains still open to the non-capitalist environment ... Though imperialism is the historical method for prolonging the career of Capitalism, it is also a sure means of bringing it to a swift conclusion ... But the more violently, ruthlessly and thoroughly imperialism brings about the decline of non-capitalist civilisation, the more rapidly it cuts the very ground from under the feet of capitalist accumulation.[5]

The prophetic nature of this prediction is deeply rooted in the nature of what was earlier termed the epiphenomenalist analysis. The perception that the process of social transformation will eventually and necessarily result in the collapse of the capitalist mode of production arises from a view of the base-superstructure relationship as transparent which, in turn, is determined by a mechanistic interpretation of the function of the laws of motion of political economy. This logic deeply influenced Kautsky's and Luxemburg's analyses and prevented a multidimensional and imaginative understanding of the national question, which during this period was of enormous importance for the theory and strategy of the workers' movement. The legacy of Karl Kautsky on the national question will be discussed first.

THE NATIONAL QUESTION IN KAUTSKY'S WORK

In an influential work on the national question, Kautsky argued that the classical form of the modern state is the national state. But these classical forms only exist as tendencies; they seldom develop in a perfect form.[6] For Kautsky, as for Marx, the origin of the modern nation was unequivocally located in the period that led to the consolidation and development of the capitalist mode of production. Kautsky further argued that the basic requirement for the development of a modern nation is a common language. National languages, he says, had most probably developed from idioms used by traders. With the creation of internal markets and the development of free wage labour, the nation emerges embracing all classes in society.

Thus, for him, nationalism is the expression of the interests of commercial capitalism and the cover for 'the most sordid profiteering'.[7] The central factor in the formation of nations has been language: with modern economic development, the need for all those who speak the same language to be united in a common state became a priority in the process of social organisation. This point is crucial in the development of Kautsky's argument; not only is the linguistic unification of the modern state a causal explanation for the formation of modern nations, but also the existence of a common language becomes a 'methodological yardstick' for the process of national development. Languages play the role of barometers of the stage of development of the productive forces.[8] The level of national development is measured by the degree of linguistic unification of the state under consideration, which in turn denotes the level of hegemony achieved by the bourgeoisie of that particular nation. For Kautsky, languages are the basic medium of social intercourse, and the full development of capitalism out of the feudal mode of production requires as a condition sine qua non the formation of a market, which in the first instance is where this extended intercourse takes place. For market forces to be able to interact without hindrance, a medium of communication must be defined and institutionalised. A common language becomes a functional necessity of the new state, delimiting the administrative and territorial boundaries of the linguistic unit in the process of becoming a nation.

For Kautsky, then, language constitutes the system of communication through which the interaction required for the formation of markets takes place. However, the process of linguistic consolidation is not an abrupt transition. It is a gradual process of evolution in which different dialects and languages merge to form the common base for the interaction process. The constituent parts of the emerging economic system face a darwinian dilemma: either they adapt to the new socioeconomic condition or perish in the process, trampled over by the irresistible forces of 'progress'. According to Kautsky, this process is at times painful,[9] but the laws of capitalist development are inexorable. The fate of modern nations is linked to the fate of capitalism, and all this is expressed in the evolution of modern languages: 'To the extent that international communications expand, the need is felt for a medium of international communication, for a universal language'.[10] Yet this cannot and will not be a constructed language like Esperanto. Neither will it be one of the civilised contemporary languages such as French, English or German. The universal language will result from the mutual assimilation of the most important contemporary languages as the process of economic development brings into a single system the different national economies.[11] However, according to Kautsky, this process cannot be achieved as a result of political or extra-economic coercion, as was taking place in Czarist Russia at the time that he wrote his essay on modern nations.

National assimilation is the essential and necessary outcome of the amalgamation of market forces, so it cannot be imposed by political decree. Linguistic difference is merely a symptom, not the problem; the real locus of the problem has always to be at the level of the economy. To clarify this point, Kautsky refers to the Irish question:

> The Irish case is a clear proof that the solution to the 'linguistic question' would not be enough to suppress a national antagonism, while the economic conditions that created this antagonism in the first place still persist.[12]

He argues that after centuries of British colonisation in Ireland, and the subsequent loss of Gaelic as the national language, Ireland did not became part of Britain through the loss of its national language.[13] This was because the country was exploited and colonised rather than integrated into the British economy. In the same way, Kautsky argues that the national communities in Czarist Russia and the Austro-Hungarian empire will not assimilate out of forcible compulsion. But neither the languages of the small Slav national communities nor the Irish Gaelic have any future. The relentless process of assimilation of all nations into an international community will simply mean that the languages of the small national communities will vanish first. At most, Kautsky states, these national languages will remain for 'domestic use' in the same way as 'old family furniture' is conserved for 'family veneration' but has little practical use.[14]

The languages spoken in the international trade and communication centres will slowly take the place of the more peripheral ones, until one of them assimilates the others. But only 'economic considerations' will decide the victor, not considerations of 'grammar or musicality':

> The need for a universal language is nothing else but a symptom of the need for the union of all nations that constitute modern civilisation into a single economic territory, which will undo national barriers.[15]

In concrete terms, only the more advanced and developed nations will survive the initial process of assimilation; small communities like the Czechs are bound to disappear in 'the near future'.[16] To the extent that capitalism develops in Bohemia, the importance of the Czech language decreases and the importance of German increases. However, Kautsky advises the Czechs to find solace and consolation in the fact that the same fate awaits larger and more advanced national communities.

Kautsky's position on the national question remained unchanged through his long and active political life. Twenty years after *Die Moderne Nationalität*, he wrote a polemical article attempting to refute Otto Bauer's contention that national communities will survive capitalism. In this article, Kautsky restates his orthodox position:

> Once we have reached the state in which the bulk of the population of our advanced nations speak one or more world languages besides their own national language, there will be a basis for a gradual reduction leading to the total disappearance of languages of minor nations, and finally, to the uniting of all civilised humanity into one language and one nationality.[17]

Kautsky's discussion further solidifies the epistemological premises of classical Marxism. Each national community or nationalist movement must fit into the process of social transformation determined by universal and inflexible laws. Interpretations of the general behavioural patterns and the historical meaning of concrete national communities are informed a priori by concepts derived from these epistemological premises. Under these conditions, the national phenomenon can only be rendered intelligible within a framework compatible with the teleology of a universal and linear process of social evolution which leads to the eventual dissolution of the nation.

So, for example, if the working class is granted the privilege of being the social stratum which will preside over the dissolution of national ties, it becomes impossible for it to claim any kind of connection with the national phenomenon other than to assist in the process of bourgeois consolidation, which in itself contains the seeds of destruction of the nation. Working class attachment to the nation is thus rendered impossible. Equally important, any conflictive relation between nations is not analysed on its own terms, but in terms of a possible general progressive outcome of the process of change. Since Kautsky ascribes no importance or meaning to cultural diversity, the shattering of the cultural existence and values of more backward national communities in the quest for universal human progress is always an acceptable and very often a desirable outcome. Indeed, cultural diversity has no place within the rigidity of his categories of social evolution and is therefore a utopian principle.

In a similar way, Rosa Luxemburg argues that it is always necessary to sustain a healthy and objective perspective in the analysis
of the national question. Anything which does not fit the general
logic of epiphenomenal Marxism is thereby viewed as an illegitimate concern. In her work these analytical tools are taken to the
inescapable conclusion that nations are only temporary
phenomena.

THE REJECTION OF THE NATION: THE WORK OF ROSA LUXEMBURG

Rosa Luxemburg was probably the most uncompromising Marxist
commentator on the national question. She became involved in
countless debates on the topic, particularly in relation to Poland,
her native country. Her constant involvement in discussions on
the national question led one of her most important biographers
to comment that she had an 'insatiable appetite for public polemics on the subject'.[18] Her unrelenting opposition to any concession to nationalism or to the widely accepted right of nations to
self-determination must be understood not only as the result of
the logic of epiphenomenalism, but also in the context of her
analysis of the contemporary situation in her native land. She was
in principle opposed to the creation of an independent Polish
state.

Around the turn of the century, the demand for the liberation of
Poland became one of the key political demands of the young
European social democracy. This followed a long tradition dating
from the works of Marx and Engels in which Polish independence
was considered to be of paramount importance for the development of the revolutionary forces in Europe. Luxemburg challenged
this view, arguing that the Polish working class in the areas of
occupation should join forces with their fellow workers in their
respective multinational states, rather than join the Polish petty
bourgeoisie for what she regarded to be the utopian liberation of
Poland, only to create a bourgeois Polish state. She acknowledged
that Marx was justified in campaigning for the emancipation of
Poland in 1848, but towards the end of the century conditions had
changed dramatically; Czarist Russia showed clear signs of developing a capitalist economy, and this should change the Marxist
perception of Russia and Poland.

If the independence of Poland in 1848 was supported because it
helped the development of the capitalist forces of production, it
must, given the dramatic change in the socioeconomic

circumstances, be opposed at the end of the century for the same reasons. Czarist Russia was no longer a semi-feudal economy, but an embryonic capitalist state. In a polemical article published in the theoretical journal of the German socialist party, *Die Neue Zeit*,[19] in response to a previous article by a group of socialist activists from the city of Cracow,[20] Luxemburg argued that since the removal of the tariff boundary between Russia proper and Congress Poland, the area of Poland under the occupation of Czarist Russia, industry had mushroomed in Congress Poland. The effect was to tie this part of Poland to Czarist Russia, on which it depended for the maintenance of its markets. She concluded that the Polish bourgeoisie was economically linked to Czarist Russia and was therefore not interested in an independent Polish state. A Polish state would create customs barriers that would jeopardise the expansion of markets of the bourgeoisie in Congress Poland. The same criterion applied to the Polish textile industry since it depended for its markets on Czarist Russia. Consequently Luxemburg argued that there were 'sound and objective economic reasons' for the bourgeoisie of Congress Poland not to support the movement for Polish unification.

However, the petty bourgeoisie was another matter. While acknowledging that this group was by no means united, and that certain sections had done well under the annexation to Czarist Russia, Luxemburg argued that the backward nature of the cottage industry generated very good reasons for petty bourgeois support for the unification of Poland, since the small industry had been obliterated by the Russian-connected big industry. These petty bourgeois, she reasons, with their 'very backward' productive methods, with no capital and in a state of near bankruptcy, had good reasons to be dissatisfied with the partition of Poland. She believed that the emergence of large-scale industry was the direct result of Russian annexation, and that the petty bourgeoisie was 'trampled over' by big industry. That was how it became

> the adoptive parent of that orphan national aspiration ... the bourgeois intelligentsia is initiated into the national sentiment by the brutal system of Russification ... and only those [intellectuals] who had not been absorbed into industry protest against their exclusion from the civil service and are at the forefront of nationalist agitation.[21]

Rosa Luxemburg concluded that only two class factions had a tendency towards nationalism: the declining petty bourgeoisie and the intelligentsia that could not find its place in the more advanced capitalist structure resulting from Poland's incorporation into the Czarist economy.[22] Given this configuration of forces, she argued, in principle the unification of Poland would be a retrograde step, since it would impede the development of capitalism and consequently would only benefit those reactionary forces which wanted to return Poland to a previous stage in its developmental process. The proletariat cannot take sides with backward forces in the process of development:

> If the proletariat would consider Polish independence as its own political program, this will be against the process of economic development. This will not only be of no help in the fulfilment of its task as a class, but, on the contrary, it will produce an ever widening gap between itself and its goals and aspirations.[23]

In her doctoral thesis submitted to the University of Zurich,[24] Luxemburg expanded this argument, providing an impressive economic substantiation of the structural link between the Polish and Russian economies. The central argument of the work is that the emergence of Polish industry took place between 1850 and 1870. The introduction of a railway system accelerated the process of capitalist development even further. After 1877 Polish industry was stimulated by the introduction of protectionist policies by the Czarist government and, like St Petersburg and Moscow, the kingdom of Poland became one of the most developed regions of the Czarist empire. In 1886, according to Luxemburg, the 141 largest factories in Poland sold 53 per cent of their production to Russian markets, and in 1898 the whole of the Polish textile industry sold more than 50 per cent of its production to Czarist Russia. On the basis of an impressive array of statistical data, Luxemburg concluded that the Polish bourgeoisie had benefited from, and been strengthened economically by, its close connection with the Russian market. The industrialisation of Poland would go ahead accompanied by a growing Polish proletariat, which would eventually transform Poland into a socialist society. In view of this, the separation of Poland from its Russian markets would bring the process to an end without any gain for the socialist cause. In the same way as the economic activity between Polish and Russian business interests tended to have the effect of destroying national separatism, a strong community of interests would emerge between the nascent Polish and Russian proletariats. The political consequence of this analysis of the economic tendencies of the kingdom of Poland was that self-determination, meaning a separate national state, was a retrograde step. By cutting Polish industry from Russian markets the class struggle could only be slowed.[25]

Rosa Luxemburg's analysis of the Polish case aroused bitter controversies not only among Polish socialists but in the whole socialist international. The tactical and political implications of her thesis fuelled discussion as to whether the working class and its political organisations should support national liberation movements or whether social emancipation should take priority. In terms of Luxemburg's analysis, the priorities are clear. National oppression is only one aspect of the process of oppression in general, which is the direct result of the division of societies into classes. The main task of the working class is to abolish the very root of the system of oppression, the class society. Since all forms of oppression are derived from the need to sustain class divisions, the emancipation from class societies will necessarily bring about the end of the oppression of nations. This analysis generated vigorous discussion within the Second International, motivating Lenin to write a series of influential articles on the national question.[26]

The intransigent position of Rosa Luxemburg and her supporters finally split the Polish socialist camp. The Polish Socialist Party (PPS) favoured the reconstitution of Poland, and its branches in the parts of Poland under foreign occupation campaigned for a reconstitution of a Polish state. In 1893 Luxemburg and her supporters founded the Social Democratic Party of the Kingdom of Poland and Lithuania (SKDKPiL) which campaigned against the creation of a separate Polish state.[27] Luxemburg consistently argued against the PPS, accusing its members of being 'social patriots' (a term which she herself coined and used for the first time in the socialist movement). The theoretical and political conflict between the PPS and the SKDKPiL grew in intensity and in the course of the debate Luxemburg developed a strong theoretical and political animosity towards the national liberation movements of small national communities.

In the heat of the argument, Luxemburg adopted uncompromising positions that puzzled many commentators.[28] In her analysis of the Russian situation, she discussed the position of the small national communities of the Czarist empire with the same lack of sympathy and understanding which characterised Marx and Engels' discussion of the situation of the Southern Slavs. She was a strong supporter of the principle of state centralisation to achieve larger markets that will permit capitalism to arrive at its maturity. Small states only delay the process of socialist transformation.

In an article published in *Die Neue Zeit*,[29] Luxemburg argued that the Russian middle class was immature since it sat and watched the freedom of Russia being destroyed because of the conflicts between the various national groups:

> the many Kirgiz, Baschirs, Lapps and others, the remainders and ruins of former nations had no more to say in the social and political life of Russia than the Basques in France and the Wends in Germany.[30]

She then asked rhetorically how these numerous nationalities could constitute a parliament and concluded that in two days 'they will tear each other's hair out'.[31]

Clearly the model which emerged from her doctoral thesis, on the lack of economic viability of Poland as an independent state, informs much of Luxemburg's strategical and theoretical analysis on the national question. The only 'healthy objective criterion' on which to judge a nation's performance was its capacity to develop productive forces that would help it to evolve towards socialism. However, Nettl argued that the denial of the Polish right to self-determination (the creation of a separate Polish state), was not the same thing as the denial of a separate Polish nationality. Luxemburg always recognised, Nettl claimed, the distinctive national identity of the Poles.[32] Without denying that it is possible to sustain the principle of national identity while arguing against the creation of national states, this seems an incorrect characterisation of Rosa Luxemburg's position, since for her the unity of the nation was unacceptable under capitalism, because it cut across classes. Her analysis did not permit the conceptualisation of any unitarian, autonomous social phenomenon that had this effect. For Luxemburg social classes are not only the causal explanation of superstructural phenomena, they are also constituted into clear and distinguishable units with no genuine common interests. If Nettl is right in arguing that Luxemburg recognised the distinct national identity of the Poles, this was presumably of bourgeois and proletarian Poles alike, a position totally incompatible with her basic premises. At best, it is possible perhaps to argue that Luxemburg was prepared to recognise the principle of nationality in a future classless world, or to accept the national identity of a uniform proletarian national community, but neither of these possibilities applied to the Polish nation of her time, or indeed to any other national community.

It was only in 1908, when Luxemburg wrote her major series of articles entitled 'The Question of Nationality and Autonomy[33] that her main ideas were presented in a theoretical and systematic way. In this series of articles she argued that the very concept of nation is temporary, not an absolute standard of measurement. It is no more than the particular way in which the bourgeois society encapsulates its structural arrangement. To talk about a theoretical 'right of nations' valid for all nations at all times is for Rosa Luxemburg a metaphysical cliché such as the rights of man and the rights of citizens. The scientific nature of historical materialism demonstrates that rights are not 'universal and absolute', but are determined by the 'material conditions of production' of the period.[34] It is not possible to conceptualise any so-called super-structural phenomena outside a strict determination by the forces of production. It is unthinkable to conceptualise superstructural phenomena that transcend the immediate economic conditions of causality. For this type of Marxist interpretation, to refer to general principles outside the immediate sphere of production is illegitimate, because it means locating these principles outside the parameters of the epiphenomenal relations of causality.

On the basis of this argument, Luxemburg reasoned that the position of socialists on questions of nationality is not guided by some universal abstract principle, but depends primarily on the concrete circumstances of each case, which differ in each country and change with time.[35] To support the right of nations to self-determination is to be in favour of an abstract and metaphysical right, and Marxists cannot sustain such universal rights on the national question. To talk about the right of nations to self-determination is for Luxemburg like positing the 'right' of workers to eat from 'gold plates' or to sustain the right to work in a world in which unemployment is a structural feature of social organisation.[36] On the national question, she concludes that:

> In a society based on classes, the nation as a uniform social and political whole simply does not exist. Instead there exist within each nation classes with antagonistic interests and 'rights'. There is literally no social arena, from the strongest material relationship to the most subtle moral one, in which the possessing classes and the self-conscious proletariat could take one and the same position as one undifferentiated national whole.[37]

Since, in the capitalist world at least, the nation as a uniform entity does not exist, support for the right of nations to self-determination implies at best support for a non-existent entity and at worst support for the bourgeoisie which uses the nation as a smokescreen to present its sectarian interests as the general aspirations of the community. Also, following her Polish discussion, there is another important impediment to the formulation of a general theory of national self determination: to support the right of self-determination for small national communities 'incapable of constituting a proper state', is a retrograde step which impedes the development of the bourgeoisie and the emergence of a victorious proletariat.

From this review of the main ideas of Kautsky and Luxemburg on the national question, it is possible to recognise the nature of the paradigmatic trap which severely curtailed the ability of both Marxist thinkers to conceptualise the national phenomenon: the logic of epiphenomenalism. Both writers, in spite of profound and lasting disagreements over conceptual and strategical issues, were bound to a limited analysis of the national phenomenon by an epistemological stance which could only recognise the position of a so-called superstructural phenomenon in terms of a chain of causality directly derived from the conjunctural relations of classes in a limited historical setting. An observed change in this relation between the most important classes represented, for Kautsky and Luxemburg, an unmistakable sign that a similar change is taking place at the level of the superstructure. This renders an autonomous theoretical analysis of the national question a conceptual impossibility.

If the national issue has no logic of its own but is determined by events outside its topographical location, it is impossible to deduce its nature even from a generalised observation. Transformations in the function of the national phenomena are always exogenous to the events under consideration and cannot be examined in an isolated analysis. Similarly, it is impossible to ascertain causal connections with events located outside the relations between the fundamental classes. Only transparent relations of causality are recognised. The epiphenomenalism of the Second International was not restricted to the so-called left or centre, but became a central paradigmatic feature of turn-of-the-century Marxism.

National communities were to be understood only in terms of the universal development of the forces of production and even under these circumstances they remained closely linked to the fate of the bourgeoisie. In the same way as the bourgeoisie was considered a transitory class – destined to be abolished in the course of the transformation of capitalism into socialism – the nation was also a transitory category, resulting from the bourgeois bid for hegemonic power and destined to collapse with it. This shortsighted conceptualisation of the national question was an important factor in the resounding Marxist defeat in its struggle against nationalism on the eve of World War One. The narrowly focused chain of causality which was the cornerstone of epiphenomenalism was only to be partially corrected by the Leninist critique of Kautsky and Luxemburg, and by the more flexible interpretation of the national question advocated by Lenin and Stalin.

Revisionism and the National Question

Superficially the word revisionism appears easy to define: it means Bernstein's (and his supporters') evaluation of classical Marxism and their attempt to revise some aspects not considered relevant to their period. However, the task is not that easy. As Kolakowski argues, the term revisionism has never been precisely defined and in present day Marxist discourse it is little more than an arbitrary label affixed to any group or individual who in any way criticises Marxist orthodoxy.[38] Labedz goes as far as to say that 'revisionism' implies a certain institutionalisation of a form of Marxist orthodoxy to the point where the use of the word becomes to classical Marxism what heresy is to religious thought.[39] Fortunately, for the purposes of our discussion it is not necessary to engage in such hair-splitting debate on orthodoxy and heterodoxy. The term revisionism will be confined to its original meaning, namely the critique of classical Marxism emanating from the works of Eduard Bernstein and his followers. The alleged parallels between their work and the variety of Marxist and post-Marxist discussions lumped together in what R. Miliband called the new revisionist spectrum[40] are of no theoretical importance. In the work of Miliband revisionism is merely a descriptive oppositional category.

However, even within the debates in the Second International revisionism was only a cohesive and homogeneous position in the writings of many of its critics. Its relative unity consisted in its critique of classical Marxism by way of placing greater emphasis on the paradigms of social evolution and rejecting the notion of the revolutionary collapse of the capitalist mode of production. Revisionism not only doubted the classical Marxist notion of the inevitable collapse of capitalism, but it was also sceptical of the notion of the immiseration of the proletariat and the idea that society is polarised into two antagonistic fundamental classes. The consequence of this criticism of classical Marxist notions of economic determination was the development of a vision of the political arena as a more autonomous dimension. This does not mean that revisionism was free from the parameters of analysis that imprisoned classical Marxist conceptions of the so-called superstructural arena. Instead, this relative liberation from the straitjacket of economism was replaced by an even stronger dependence on notions of universal social evolution. Revisionism merely displaced the traditional Marxist privileged agent of social change (the working class) in favour of another privileged agency (the ethical-progressive human being emerging out of modernity). If revisionism 'revised' Marxist epistemology, it was only to change its format and relation of priorities, maintaining its developmental logic intact. History maintained its *telos*, but the ethical progressive being replaced class as the agency of social transformation. In this sense it is difficult to understand why Miliband sees any continuity between Bernstein and the recent post-Marxist debates, for what characterises the latter is precisely the rejection of any ontologically privileged historical agency capable of being the universal agent of change.

BERNSTEIN'S CRITIQUE OF CLASSICAL MARXISM

Two elements precipitated the crisis of orthodox Marxism in the context of the German socialist party. The first was the vision of bourgeois democracy sustained by the majority of the socialist parties before World War One. As Joll argues, no socialist party could escape the difficulties presented by its own existence as a mass party, forced to operate in a political system to which it denied legitimacy and which it consciously sought to destroy.[41] When the socialist parties were marginal to the process of policy making it was possible to maintain a principled position by rejecting the system in toto. But when, as in the case of France and Germany, the socialist parties became leading political actors, with a possibility of at least sharing parliamentary power, this dilemma was a continuous source of internal debate.

The second element that precipitated the ideological crisis of the Western European socialist parties was the perceived failure of the theory of the immiseration of the masses and subsequent class polarisation. With the consolidation of the bourgeois democratic state, a multiplicity of social strata emerged, blurring the traditional distinction between the bourgeoisie and the proletariat. Not only was the working class just a segment of the population of the main industrialised states, but it also became difficult to determine with any degree of certainty the class location of a substantial section of the population. This problem was continuously to shadow Marxist discussions.[42] The emergence of the revisionist critique of orthodox Marxism has to be understood as a response to the disjunction between classical Marxist theories and the observable tendencies of capitalism.[43]

In his major work *Die Voraussetzungen des Sozialismus*,[44] Bernstein begins his criticism of orthodox Marxism by examining the distribution of wealth in a number of West European countries and then asserting that the theory of the immiseration of the masses is not sustained by facts.[45] Is then socialism an unattainable utopia? Not for Bernstein. The shortcoming of classical Marxism is the misunderstanding that socialism and the abolition of capitalism are dependent on the pauperisation of the proletariat. Socialism will be the result of what he calls the irreversible advances of democracy in industrial societies. Socialism is not only the collectivisation of the means of production, but the fulfilment of the theory and practice of democracy in the widest possible array of social relations. From this Bernstein concludes that socialism is not the result of the fulfilment of the corporate aims of the working class, nor does it represent any objective need of the latter. For him socialism results from the universal embodiment of human interest, the interests of all human beings qua humans.

Bernstein was critical of those cadres in the socialist movement who were contemptuous of what he called contemporary societies and were prepared to demand sacrifices from contemporary generations for the achievement of a socialist goal in a distant future. This is the context in which he formulated his famous slogan: 'What is generally called the ultimate goal of socialism is nothing to me, the movement is everything'. This statement was of course ambiguous and was distorted by his orthodox critics. Bernstein did not mean that socialists should limit their horizons and work only towards the achievement of limited immediate goals, but simply that immediate sacrifices for the sake of a distant socialist future are out of the question.[46]

This statement also constituted the focus of the classical Marxist backlash against Bernstein's ideas, and should not be confused with the prevailing reformism of the trade union movement in Britain, France and Germany. While trade union reformism and Bernstein's revisionism may coincide at certain points of immediate policy, there are a number of fundamental differences between them. Reformism referred to the gradual consolidation of the achievements of the trade union movement and the working class. Such an approach was corporatist in nature; political activity was subordinated to the daily needs of the trade union movement. In the German socialist party, many reformist leaders voted with classical Marxists on issues of principle that had little relevance to their day-to-day political activity. This position becomes clear in a letter from I. Auer, a trade union leader, to Bernstein:

> Do you think that it is really possible for a party that has a litera-ture going back fifty years, an organisation going back forty years, and a still older tradition, to change direction like this in the twinkling of a eye? ... My dear Ede, one doesn't formally decide to do what you ask, one doesn't say it, *one does it*! ... our whole activity is the activity of a Social democratic reforming party. A party that reckons with the masses simply cannot be anything else.[47]

Defence of what the reformist leadership considered to be the immediate interests of the working class required both a defensive political stance and a demarcation of the working class as a corpo-rate entity with clearly defined boundaries.[48] But Bernstein was arguing precisely the opposite: socialism was considered to be part and parcel of the democratic tradition and as such was not in the corporate individual interests of any one section of society, but in the interests of the community as a whole. While reformism was closing boundaries for the working class, revisionism represented an effort to break with the corporatist isolation of that class.[49]

But, as Laclau and Mouffe ask, if class unity can only be recon-stituted at the political level, in what sense is this a class unity? At this point Bernstein introduced an element that became crucial for the revisionist discussion of the national question: the notion of the evolutionary and progressive nature of human history. He accepted without reservation the evolutionary parameters of classi-cal Marxism, making it an important milestone of his discussion of the development of industrial societies.

> Now, to whatever degree other forces besides the purely eco-nomic, influence the life of society, just so much more also does the sway of what, in an objective sense we call historic necessity change. In modern society we have to distinguish in this respect two great streams. On the one side appears an increasing insight into the laws of evolution and notably economic evolution.

With this knowledge goes hand in hand, partly as its cause, partly again as its effect, an increasing capability of directing economic evolution.[50]

Thus the more advanced a society is, the less dependent it becomes on economic forces, and the greater the possibility of a conscious human agency that directs the process of social transformation. Bernstein appears to be arguing that, with technological development, the iron laws of history tend to play a less determinant role. If this is the case, the process of technological development introduces an element of growing indeterminacy in the process of historical development. However, this apparent indeterminacy is controlled by another element which gives intention and coherence to the process of social evolution: the ethical dimension of human behaviour and the notion that socialism is an ethical principle which emerges out of the rational development of modernity.

For the Marxism of Kautsky and Luxemburg, socialism was the embodiment of the objective interests of the working class and only as such did it become an ethical principle. In opposition to this idea, Bernstein argued that socialism appeals to humanity as a whole; technology liberates humanity from determination by the laws of motion of political economy, and the more civilised a society becomes the greater the need for co-operation between different social forces. The result of this is a historically constructed ethical subject, increasingly liberated from the tyranny of political economy and concerned with the need to cooperate with other human beings. Thus a new ethical subject emerges out of the civilisatory process of modernity, replacing the working class as an agent of social transformation because of its capacity to master the environment through an ever more sophisticated technology. The higher the level of 'civilisation', the less the dependency on economic forces and the greater the possibilities for realising the great ethical ideas of socialism.

Bernstein's linear and one-dimensional perception of human progress owes more to classical Marxism than many of his Marxist critics care to admit. Peter Gay argues that Bernstein distorted the classical Marxist concept of evolution because it eliminated its dialectical dimension.[51] Even if one admits that Bernstein was hostile to the use of Hegelian dialectics and saw its influence on Marxism as pernicious, the consequences of his evolutionary vision were not that different from those of classical Marxism. Humanity was seen in terms of a hierarchical and universal process of social transformation of social structures. It matters little whether this evolution was the result of a dialectical process or the product of cooperation between different social subjects.

> What is the crucial distinction between Marxist theory and socialist doctrines preceding Marx? It is the emphatic and profound achievement of a form of developmental thought [Entwicklungsgedanken] and the conceptualisation of evolution [Evolutionsbegriff], that was taken to its most significant consequences, in a way in which it was not done by any other socialist thinker, before Marx or during his lifetime.[52]

The methodological result of this analysis is a model of social transformation which locates concrete societies in terms of a heuristically constructed social continuum. This is precisely the essence of the evolutionist parameter discussed earlier.

BERNSTEIN AND THE NATIONAL QUESTION

Bernstein's faith in the progressive nature of the process of social evolution had a profound effect on the way in which revisionism conceptualised the national question. The idea that the Western state moves to higher levels of democratic achievement as the process of historical development unfolds led Bernstein to the following reflection:

> if one starts from the sentence in the Communist Manifesto 'The proletariat has no fatherland'. This sentence might, in a degree, perhaps, apply to the worker in the forties without political rights, shut out of public life. To-day in spite of the enormous increase in the intercourse between nations *it has already forfeited a great part of its truth and will always forfeit more, the more the worker by the influence of socialism moves from being a proletarian to a citizen.* The workman who has equal rights as a voter for state and local councils, and who thereby is a fellow owner in the common property of the nation, whose children the community educates, whose health it protects, whom it secures against injury, *has a fatherland* without ceasing on that account to be a citizen of the world. [53] (emphasis added)

This shows the extent of Bernstein's positive assessment of what the Victorians called the irreversible advances of progress and civilisation. For Bernstein, the question of the national identity of the working class was directly linked to their participation in the affairs of the state through the electoral system. Nationhood was essentially a political issue, related to the nature of the state apparatus; cultural and ethnic considerations are absent from his analysis. In fact, he opposed nearly every type of nationalism which represented in his view 'an atavistic regression to a pre-democratic epoch'.

Bernstein believed that the state had a crucial role to play in the process of nation-building. As the bearers of social and scientific progress, 'the great historically developed nations' were essential to the development of humanity. A future socialist society would not 'dissolve the unity of the developed nations' but set them on a new basis.[54] His model for national development was based on the example of the parliamentary nation states of Western Europe. The pre-eminence of the state on the process of national development was clear in his writings.

> The state is historically the creator of nationality. Race and linguistic community have provided the [basic] material, but this would never have been formed into a nation without the state.[55]

Following his optimistic evaluation of the positive role of 'civilisation and progress' in human development, Bernstein considered that he was witnessing a gradual change taking place in the relationship between nation states. A new internationalism was beginning to provide the concepts and rules for a more equitable international code of rights. He distinguished between what he called ethnological nationalism – the tendency to establish new nation states on the basis of language and ethnic origin – which he condemned as reactionary and regressive, and what he termed sociological nationalism – the social restructuring of population groups into larger units – which he praised as progressive and forward-reaching.[56]

While opposing nationalist arguments within the German socialist party, Bernstein was not prepared to support a generic condemnation of nationalism. He rejected Kautsky's and Luxemburg's class reductionism by opposing the view that the historical process will lead to the destruction of national differences. Modernity, he reasoned, changes the character of nationalism and makes it acceptable to the aims of the workers.[57] He also opposed the anti-national rhetoric of the radical left, arguing that the break-up of the nation was 'no beautiful dream' and German social democracy should not be indifferent to the German nation carrying out what Bernstein believed to be 'its honourable share in civilising the world'.[58]

This phrase implied a positive attitude towards European colonial ventures. Paradoxically, Bernstein rejected ethnic and cultural nationalism while expressing faith in the superiority of European values. On the issue of colonialism, he sharply disagreed with Kautsky and Luxemburg:

> The assumption that the extension of colonies will restrict the realisation of socialism rests at the bottom of the altogether outworn idea that the realisation of socialism depends on an increasing narrowing of the circle of the well to do and an increasing misery of the poor.[59]

Clearly he misunderstood the critique of colonialism that came from the left and centre of the German socialist party. For him, colonies were one aspect of progress and civilisation and, as such, were an important part of the development of industrial societies. In this sense he believed that the socialist party should be a strong advocate of colonialism:

> if we take into account the fact that Germany now imports yearly a considerable amount of colonial produce, we must say to ourselves that the time may come when it will be desirable to draw part of this products from our own colonies.[60]

Reasons of capitalist expediency dictate that the socialist party should become a fully fledged partner in the colonial enterprise, but would this situation contradict the ethical postulates of socialism which Bernstein asserted so vehemently? Not at all,

> but if it is not reprehensible to enjoy the produce of tropical plantations, it cannot be so to cultivate such plantations ourselves ... It is neither necessary that the occupation of tropical lands by Europeans should injure the natives in their enjoyment of life nor has it hitherto usually been the case.[61]

Bernstein's advocacy of a form of humane colonialism is consistent with the revisionist analysis of the role of civilisation and progress. If some societies (i.e. Europe) achieve a 'higher level of civilisation and development' then their occupation of 'less developed' societies will be for the benefit of those less developed peoples. Not only will humane colonialism benefit colonials and natives alike but, as a matter of principle, natives have no exclusive rights to their own lands:

> Moreover, only a conditional right of savages to the land occupied by them can be recognised. The higher civilisation can ultimately claim a higher right. Not the conquest, but the cultivation of the land gives the historical legal title to its use.[62]

The evolutionary analysis constructs a new subject, the industrial and civilised democratic being who takes over as the agent of social transformation. An ethical notion of socialism becomes intelligible from the superior morality of this modern democratic subject. Many of Bernstein's socialist critics rushed to denounce the non-Marxist nature of this analysis, and the introduction of neo-Kantian categories of analysis was blamed for this idealist deviation.

It would be illegitimate, however, to disassociate this analysis completely from classical Marxism, even if Kautsky, Lenin and the radical left relentlessly criticised and denounced Bernstein's views. The link expressed in the works of Marx and Engels between bourgeois nation state formation in historical European nations and the progress towards the socialist transformation of society had a clear impact in the work of Bernstein. Furthermore, Marx was not exactly tolerant towards the 'peculiarities' of many non-European national communities, and Kautsky and Luxemburg themselves argued that 'less developed' nations should relinquish their right to self-determination and be assimilated into more 'civilised' nations so that the cause of progress could be advanced. In fact, Bernstein's analysis should not be considered an aberration of classical Marxism, but a controversial albeit possible development of the unilateral evolutionism that coloured classical Marxist interpretations of the national question. If the emergence and legitimate existence of national communities are to be located in a universal-historical continuum, then there is no escape from a hierarchical interpretation of national development, or from the argument that, given the uneven nature of the process of development, some nations are 'more civilised' than others. As we shall see, Leninism provided the first partial critique to this eurocentric discourse.

Bernstein was even more explicit in his humane colonialist position in a number of articles published in the *Neue Zeit* and *Sozialistische Monatshefte*.[63] In an essay published in the *Neue Zeit* devoted to the British colonisation of India, Bernstein argued that it was 'not fair' to blame the British empire for the famine in that country. On the contrary, the British reforms of the Indian political system would help to alleviate such crisis. If the Indian population still fell victim to famines it was 'their own fault' since, given the 'backwardness' of the population, 'it is not easy to help Indian peasants'. The 'well intended' reforms of the British clashed with 'religious and other prejudices' of the Indian population.[64]

In a famous article discussing the Armenian genocide in Turkey at the beginning of the century, Bernstein wrote a passionate plea supporting the situation of the unfortunate Armenians. However, the theoretical part of this article gives a unique insight into Bernstein's eurocentric and dogmatically evolutionist position with regard to national and colonial questions. According to Bernstein, in Africa there are 'tribes that give themselves the right to slave trafficking' and they can only be dissuaded from such purposes by more 'civilised nations'. From this he concludes that 'Peoples that are enemies of civilisation and incapable of achieving higher level of culture have no right to request our sympathy when they rise against civilisation'.[65]

Bernstein agrees with critics of colonialism that certain methods used to subdue 'savages' are cruel and unethical, but he makes clear that this does not mean that such 'savages' should not be subdued, since 'the right of civilisation should prevail':

> For a struggle for emancipation to awake our interest ... it must have a civilising character: this may either be peoples or nations that develop a cultural life of their own and rebel against a foreign domination that hinders their development, or the uprising of progressive classes against the subjugation they suffer from more backward ones. To every people [volk] that gives evidence of its capacity to develop a national cultural life we should recognise the right to nationality ... If some time ago, the proposition to support savages and aborigines in their struggle against capitalism was made from a socialist point of view, this was only the result of a romanticism whose inconsistency could be easily demonstrated by simply observing the consequences of such a proposition.[66]

He goes on to argue that support for the struggle of aborigines against capitalism cannot be sustained by any serious socialist argument, and this proposition only makes sense if the eurocentric bias of the debates of that period is taken into account.

The epiphenomenalism of the various sections of the Second International prevented any serious intellectual or political challenge to this proposition. The works of Kautsky and Luxemburg on the national question show a similar eurocentric bias. In the first footnote to this revealing article, Bernstein is full of praise for Rosa Luxemburg's article on the national struggles in Turkey:

> This essay was almost finished when I received the relevant copies of the *Sachsisten Arbeitzeitung* [the Workers Newspaper of Saxony] with the articles of Miss Luxemburg on social democracy and the national struggles in Turkey. From the contents of this article the reader will be able to judge how much I agree with the arguments and conclusion of that excellent work.[67]

While Luxemburg opposed all forms of colonialism, Kautsky was ambivalent about its progressive role, supporting settler colonialism but opposing other forms of imperial colonisation.[68]

> consequently, with reference to settler colonialism, even if in many occasions we are obliged to criticise the treatment given to the natives, we cannot reject the act of colonisation. On the contrary, we must see it a a powerful lever for the development of humanity, and for this reason the latter has a debt of gratitude to this policy.[69]

Bernstein's support for colonialism is derived from the unilinear and Eurocentric understanding of social evolution. But even the possession of a 'civilised culture' is not yet enough to attract socialist support for national liberation: 'The liberty of some insignificant nationality outside Europe, or in Central Europe cannot be compared with the development of the large and highly civilised peoples of Europe'.[70]

After clarifying the theoretical standpoint of revisionism vis a vis national and colonial questions, Bernstein proceeds to tackle the main theme of his article, the massacres of Armenians in Turkey. Turkish society is presented as a prime example of 'oriental decadence' and the Turkish state as incapable of overcoming its internal disintegration. The main religion of the Ottoman empire (Islam) constituted, according to Bernstein, an important factor in the 'Ottoman backwardness'. Even if the Muslims 'propagated culture' through southern Europe, they 'did not know how to preserve it' or 'continue with its development':

the religion they professed – Islam – did not stop them from becoming barbarians; quite to the contrary, under the influence of the conditions of *the orient*, this religion encouraged them. In accordance with its fundamental conceptions and its precepts [Islam] results in reality as a religion of barbarians, that is to say, nomads, traders of the old style and peasants who still live in local communities. (emphasis added)[71]

The racialist[72] tone of this argument is clear, but even Bernstein must concede that religion on its own cannot hinder historical development, so after this observation on Islam, he went on to argue that what prevented Turkey from becoming a modern state was its inability to assimilate the ethnic communities under its rule. And what, according to Bernstein, is the reason for this state of affairs? 'Simply, they are a barbarian people, violence is mixed with indolence.'[73]

Edward Said would have been hard put to find a better example of the nature and aims of orientalism, the Western image of the East, which he so vividly describes in his remarkable book.[74] In orientalism in particular, and European knowledge of non-European societies in general, historicist evolutionism (of which Bernstein was just one exponent) asserted one universal human history which either culminated in the West or was observed from the vantage point of Europe.[75]

Bernstein's optimism in 'progress and civilisation' fuelled a complacent and profoundly ethnocentric perception of the national phenomenon. While the revisionist enthusiasm for colonial ventures was unique in the context of the Second International it would be wrong to regard it as an aberration. The unilinear notions of social evolution – with and without dialectics – which permeated most of the classical Marxist works on the national question are not unconnected with these ideas.

This chapter began with Kolakowski's evaluation of the Second International. In the light of the preceding discussion, how can we accept Kolakowski's assertion that the Second International was the golden age of Marxism because Marxist theory was not so rigidly codified or subjected to a dogmatic orthodoxy? The previous discussion has confirmed that at least on the analysis of the national question there was a certain rigidity and eurocentrism. Kolakowski himself appears to recognise this when he describes what were the central beliefs of the different Marxist formations. According to him, in the period of the Second International a Marxist was a person who accepted, among others, the following propositions:

The interests of the proletariat are identical on the world scale, and the socialist revolution will come as an international event, at all events in the advanced industrial societies.

In human history, technical progress is the deciding factor in bringing about changes in the class structure, and these changes determine the basic features of political institutions and the remaining ideology.[76]

These notions of universal evolution did in fact represent the basis for a 'rigid codification of a dogmatic orthodoxy' – in spite of Kolakowski's assertion to the contrary – preventing an imaginative understanding of the multifarious forms of the national question.

3

Marxism–Leninism and the National Question

The Specificity of Marxism–Leninism

In terms of the simplified evolutionary notions which prevailed in the thought and actions of the leaders of the Second International, the October Revolution was an inconceivable event. But to regard Lenin's break with this evolutionism as an attempt to justify that revolution is an equally misleading over-simplification. In his early works[1] he criticised Western forms of epiphenomenalism relentlessly, while paradoxically claiming total adherence to the principles of classical Marxism. In this chapter it will be argued that the incompatibility of these claims was reflected in Lenin's ambiguous discussion on the national question.

A great deal has been written about Lenin's and the Bolsheviks' contributions to Marxism but, as Marcel Liebman argues, a great part of it is sterile historiography. This results from the extraordinary paradox that one of this century's most subversive political theories was converted into a theoretical system that justifies an authoritarian political order.[2] While not denying that certain features of Marxism–Leninism lend themselves to a sectarian, dogmatic and manichean perception of the political arena, it is important to understand the reasons for the emergence of Marxism–Leninism in terms of its factual (but not theoretical) break with classical Marxism, and not as an a priori justification of the nature of the Soviet state. If this rather more productive line of enquiry is taken, one dominant factor prevails: the specificity of the Great Russian situation. The causes of the Bolsheviks' break from epiphenomenalism must be found in the social and political structures of Czarist Russia which defied attempts to extrapolate rigid Western models of development. Located at the periphery of Europe and inhabited by more than one hundred national communities, Czarist Russia's social and political order was different from that of Central and Western Europe.

During the nineteenth century generations of democratic thinkers (including Marx himself), regarded Czarist Russia as a backward

European state. But the concept of backwardness is always an oppositional category; it must be defined in terms of its opposite, the idea of progress. Given the all-inclusive contextual nature of the universal process of development espoused by classical Marxists, the comparative criterion that gave meaning to Russian backwardness was the notion of a more advanced Western European situation. This prevented any constructive understanding not only of the specificity of Czarist Russia, but also of the non-European world in general. If Lenin and the Bolsheviks were to provide an understanding and a guide to action for the non-Western European world, they had first to break with the logic of epiphenomenalism.

The Leninist strategic break with epiphenomenalism had a profound impact on the way in which the Marxist-Leninist tradition conceptualised the national question. Above all, three aspects of Lenin's arguments influenced the new approach to the national question: the emphasis on the political dimension; the theory of the revolution, and the theory of imperialism and combined and uneven development.

For Lenin – following the Russian experience – the relentless process of the historical development of the productive forces is not enough to guarantee the required conditions for the construction of a socialist order. The socialist project also requires an efficient and organised party of the proletariat, armed with the correct theoretical and methodological tools. Only in this way can a guide to action in complex conjunctural situations be provided. The party can only be effective if it becomes a disciplined organisation of professional revolutionaries.[3] The apocalyptic vision of the collapse of capitalism is then replaced by a more voluntaristic understanding of political struggle.

But Lenin's argument opens the Pandora's box of classical Marxism. The conditions and relations of production no longer determine the spatial location of the political forces. Political actors, in the form of the disciplined revolutionary party, intervene in the political arena without any obvious economic reason. What impels them to act is their understanding of their objective conditions of existence and their subjective commitment to the revolutionary cause. In spite of this, Marxism–Leninism follows the analytical logic of classical Marxism: reality must be understood as the result of objective conditions of existence which are determined by the logic of the process of production. But these conditions have no meaning for the project of social transformation. It is only through the voluntary intervention of the enlightened avant-garde that they have any significance for the project of the revolutionary transformation of society. Marxism–Leninism then opens a dimension of indeterminacy at the level of the economy, since the arena of political struggles can no longer be deduced from the transparency of the process of production.

The gap opened at this level is immediately closed at the political level by the presence and wilful action of the enlightened revolutionaries, who give meaning to the process of change by understanding and acting upon the objective conditions. The attempt to close at the political level the indeterminacy identified at the level of the economy, while at the same time maintaining the privileged position of the economic (class) dimension, is a source of permanent theoretical tension, a tension which Marxism–Leninism never managed to fully resolve.

The expansion of the political field permitted Marxism–Leninism to discuss the political dimension of the national question, free from the limits of the transparent relations of causality which characterised the epiphenomenalist discussion. The relative autonomy of the national phenomenon allowed Marxist–Leninists the strategic use of national demands to advance the cause of the revolution.

Lenin also transformed the classical Marxist theory of the revolution by arguing that the bourgeois democratic revolution must be transformed into a socialist revolution by the proletariat, enabling the latter to take over political power at the end of the process. According to this view, the specific circumstances of Russia enabled the bourgeois democratic and the socialist revolutions to take place almost simultaneously while at the same time maintaining a separate identity. This conceptualisation of the Russian situation allowed the Bolsheviks to sustain the general argument of classical Marxism in terms of the universal class determination of a revolutionary situation and, at the same time, to justify the developmental multilinearity of that situation. Bourgeois and socialist revolutions were determined by different classes in every case, but in Russia proletarian power in the form of the Soviets was constituted before the crystallisation of the bourgeois democratic state.

Two aspects of the Leninist conceptualisation of the revolution are crucial for the understanding of the Bolshevik position on the national question. Firstly, bourgeois democratic and socialist revolutions may occur simultaneously, or the latter may closely follow the former. However, both revolutions have distinct and contradictory identities because they respond to hegemonic projects of different classes.[4] The transition from one revolution to the other is essentially a political act, the result of the actions of the avantgarde revolutionaries. Consequently the transition from one revolutionary situation to the next is the result of activity which takes place outside the process of production. Yet the identity of the revolutionary process is determined by forces endogenous to the process of production, since they respond to the hegemonic project of fundamental classes. The paradoxical nature of this argument requires a rigorous separation of identities at every moment of the revolutionary process, a condition that is logically incompatible with the transitional nature of the revolutionary situation.[5] This confusing distinction subsequently becomes the cornerstone of the Marxist-Leninist analysis of the national question. As will be shown, national self-determination is a bourgeois democratic demand which must be supported in backward circumstances, but opposed when the bourgeois democratic revolution reaches its maturity.

The concept of uneven development appears at first glance to be simple. Capitalism develops in different ways in different countries and as a result of this certain states are ahead of others on that great universal freeway of capitalist development. Not only are certain nation states ahead of others, but they use their commanding position to ensure that that their leadership remains unchallenged. Competition between the leading nation states increases and consequently, more 'less developed' regions of the world fall into the hands of, and are exploited by, these competing powers. Increasingly, capitalism becomes a single universal system, eventually engulfing the whole world with its developmental logic. But this imperialist subjugation of the 'backward' world does not necessarily result in a stable and comfortable situation for the leading national states. The very backwardness of the East is converted into an asset by its ability to imitate modern forms of economic, social, and political organisation. This has the net effect of paving the way for the possibility of a challenge to the hegemony of the very nation states which introduced the more advanced methods into those 'backward' societies.

This process of change and transformation is a far cry from the regular and predictable process envisaged by Marx in his preface to *Capital*.[6] 'Backward' societies do not resemble the 'advanced' capitalist states at a previous stage of development, partly because their process of change is faster, but also because their development is combined with the elements of backwardness, creating a condition of transition that is both novel and unique.[7]

Although it rejects the prescription of a developmental linearity, the idea of uneven development follows the logic of the evolutionary paradigm of classical Marxism. The use of notions of backwardness and progress are defined in accordance with the Western European experience, and the constant identification of stages in a developmental process denote a tendential movement defined by an a priori epistemological stance. This concept did, however, break the sterile linearity of epiphenomenalism, allowing a more flexible understanding of the political dimension of movements for national emancipation, by way of a conceptual framework that permits the analytical evaluation of specific circumstances.

The hierarchical element of the notion of uneven development locked Marxism–Leninism into an exclusively political analysis of the national arena, inhibiting the understanding of those aspects of the national phenomenon which transcended the immediate conjunctural political stage, such as culture and ethnicity. Similarly, the class reductionist dimension of this approach required every nationalist movement to respond to the political project of a fundamental class. In this way it prevented an understanding of those aspects of the national phenomenon which transcend a class location.

At the same time, the novel political understanding of the imperialist stage of capitalist development required a revised conceptualisation of the national question. Revolutionary conditions were no longer internal to the state or region under consideration; they were also the results of the contradictions of imperialism as a world system.

The Marxist-Leninist Theory of the National Question

> Regarding national problems, the [Marxist] social sciences have still done practically nothing.[8]

Around the turn of the century, the major point of reference on the national question for the majority of socialist parties was the resolution of the congress of the Second International held in London in 1897. Lenin considered this resolution of great importance for the nationalities policy of the Bolshevik party, to the extent that he quotes it in full in his article on 'The Right of Nations to Self Determination':

This Congress declares that it stands for the full right of all nations to self determination (*Selbstbestimmungsrecht*) and expresses sympathy for the workers of every country now suffering under the yoke of military, national or other absolutism. This congress calls upon the workers of every country to join the ranks of the class conscious (*Klassenbewusste*) workers of the whole world in order jointly to fight for the defeat of international capitalism.[9]

The only clear aspect of this resolution is its vagueness, which is the main cause of the difficulty in ascertaining the real meaning of the slogan 'the right of nations to self determination'. This ill-defined formulation was the end result of the controversial debate which took place, particularly within the Polish delegation, over the issue of Polish self-determination.[10] As H. B. Davis argues, the call for self-determination is hopelessly vague on the crucial issue of whether it means state independence or some other status for the national community in question.[11] In the Austro–Hungarian empire, the principle of national-cultural autonomy was the socialist party's interpretation of the concept of self-determination. Kautsky did not express a clear opinion on the subject, the radical left rejected the principle completely and the revisionists made the principle conditional on the achievement of a 'higher degree of civilisation'.

Lenin and the majority of the Bolshevik party (with the possible exception of Bukharin), took a clear and uncompromising position on the issue:

if we want to grasp the meaning of self determination of nations, not by juggling with legal definitions, or 'inventing' abstract definitions, but by examining the historico-economic conditions of the national movements, *we must inevitably reach the conclusion that self determination of nations means the political separation of these nations from alien national bodies, and the formation of an independent national state.*

Later we shall see still other reasons why it would be wrong to interpret the right of self determination as meaning anything but the right to existence of a separate state.[12] (emphasis added)

For Lenin, self-determination meant only the secession of national communities from multinational states to form their own separate national states. That is to say, it meant the exclusive right to separation in the political sense, and not the right either to federation or to autonomy. In 'The Right of Nations to Self Determination', Lenin states that 'it is not difficult' to see from a social democratic point of view that this right means neither federation nor autonomy, although he concedes that, when speaking in abstract terms, these two concepts do come under the general category of self-determination.

> The right to federation is simply meaningless, since federation implies a bilateral contract ... Marxists cannot include the defense of Federalism in general in their program. As far as autonomy is concerned, Marxists defend not the 'right' to autonomy, but autonomy *itself*, as the general democratic principle of a democratic state with mixed national composition ... Consequently, the recognition of 'the right of nations to autonomy', is as absurd as the the 'right of nations to federation'.[13]

This position was by no means universally accepted in the Bolshevik party. A minority of Russian Bolsheviks rejected the notion altogether, employing arguments similar to those sustained by Rosa Luxemburg. Another small group of Bolsheviks, particularly members of non-Russian national communities, demanded a broader definition. The Armenian Bolshevik Stephen Georgievich Shahumyan argued, contrary to Lenin's ideas, that the right to self-determination could mean not only secession but also other forms of devolution, including autonomy or federation. In a letter to Shahumyan, Lenin restated his opposition to this interpretation, arguing that federation is an agreement between equals and cannot be implemented if only one party agrees to it. Lenin also insisted that federations weaken economic links and that, all circumstances being equal, he preferred a centralised state. With the characteristic forthrightness of his polemical writings he argued:

> The right to self-determination does not imply only the right to secede. It also implies the right to federal association, the right to autonomy, you write. I disagree entirely. It does not imply the right to *federation*. Federation means the association of equals, an association that demands *common* agreement. How can *one* side have a right to demand that the other side should *agree* with it? That is absurd. *We are opposed to federation in principle* [emphasis added], it loosens economic ties and is unsuitable for a single state. You want to secede? All right, go to the devil if you can break economic bonds, or rather, if the oppression and friction of 'coexistence' *disrupt* and ruin economic bonds.

You don't want to secede? In that case, excuse me, but don't decide for me; don't think that you have a *'right'* to federation.[14]

Given the nature of Lenin's interpretation, it would have been more precise to call this principle the right of nations to an independent state, or the right to statism.

In order to be properly understood, Lenin's advocacy of the right to state separatism must be viewed both in relation to his definition of the role of the party and the notion of 'democratic centralism', and also in the context of the previously discussed taxonomical and hierarchical conceptualisation of social development. The role of the party and democratic centralism will be discussed later in conjunction with Lenin's evaluation of national culture and his polemical stance in relation to the project of national cultural autonomy.

To justify his position on self-determination, Lenin follows a conceptualisation of national communities that is initially based on Kautsky's analysis. In 'The Right of Nations to Self Determination' he argues that, throughout the world, the period of the final victory of capitalism over feudalism is 'linked' to the emergence and development of national movements. The economic rationale which lies behind this linkage between class determination and the emergence of national movements is expressed thus:

> for the complete victory of commodity production the bourgeoisie must capture the home market, and there must be politically united territories whose population speak a single language, with all obstacles to the development of that language and its consolidation in literature eliminated. *Therein is the economic foundation of national movements* ... unity and unimpeded development of language are the most important conditions for genuinely free and extensive commerce on a scale commensurate with modern capitalism.[15] (emphasis added)

Lenin argues that unity of language is one of the most important conditions for an unrestrained exchange of goods between different peoples, and it is therefore a requirement for the initial development of capitalism. When market forms establish their preponderance over other forms of social distribution, a common language becomes a crucial requirement for the consolidation of the capitalist mode of production. Following this analytical logic, he concludes that the tendency of every national movement is towards the formation of national states, where such organisational requirements of modern capitalism can best be satisfied.[16] In other words, the economic logic and organisational tendencies of the capitalist mode of production define the functionality of the formation and consolidation of national states, and the subsequent emergence of national movements is the superstructural response to this organisational tendency. Given that the hegemonic class in the process of development and consolidation of capitalism is the bourgeoisie, the presence of national movements is the superstructural response to the needs and requirements of the bourgeois class.

Thus far, Lenin's theoretical analysis appears to be almost identical to the one put forward by Kautsky. Both refer to the nation as the outcome of the emerging capitalist system and see in the preponderance of national movements an expression of bourgeois hegemony. Both give crucial importance to language as the nucleus of the national community, and both conspicuously fail to distinguish between the specific configuration of the emerging capitalist state and the characteristics of national communities. In summary, both exhibit the main features of the class reductionist analysis. The bourgeoisie and the nation are connected in a relation of causality from the former to the latter.[17]

From the Kautsky-Lenin assertion that the national state is the typical form of state organisation under capitalism, Lenin derives his original contribution to the debate on the national question: the theory of the right of nations to self-determination. While he appears to accept the basic premises of the Kautskian position, he differs from Kautsky on a fundamental point: the principled application of the right to self determination (meaning of course state independence) to every national community. But as will become clear shortly, this does not mean the principled acceptance of the right of secession in every case.

Lenin justifies the advocacy of the right to state secession by referring to the periodisation of the capitalist mode of production discussed earlier. Given that the typical state under capitalism is the national state, the advocacy of the right of nations to constitute separate national states will assist in ensuring the optimal development of the productive forces under capitalism, particularly in those areas of the world in which the bourgeois democratic revolution is not yet in full swing. In this sense, for Lenin, the national question must be looked upon within 'definitive' historical limits,[18] meaning the taxonomy of stages that give shape to the process of uneven development. In discussing the role of the national state in the development of the capitalist mode of

production, Lenin makes a clear distinction between two historically different periods.

The first is that of the collapse of feudalism and absolutism. This
is the time when the bourgeois democratic state is formed and the
national movement becomes a mass movement under the hegemony of the bourgeoisie. In this case the national struggle
deserves the support of the incipient proletariat, because it is a
struggle against feudalism and absolutism, for civil and political
liberties and for democracy, the main characteristics of a democratic republic, which is 'the best possible political shell for
capitalism'.[19]

The second period is that of fully formed capitalist states, with
long established constitutional regimes and, above all, a highly
developed antagonism between the proletariat and the bourgeoisie. Here the bourgeoisie has consolidated power and developed
the capitalist mode of production to its creative limits. At this
stage of capitalist development, support for nationalist movements
is tantamount to supporting the bourgeoisie at the expense of the
proletariat.

From this Lenin infers that national movements should be supported if their aim is to overthrow absolutism and to build a bourgeois-democratic state. But it would be an 'immense error from the
point of view of the proletariat' to support the nation when the
bourgeois-democratic movement achieves its maturity and the
antagonism between the bourgeoisie and the proletariat is highly
developed.[20] It is interesting to note the rigidity with which Lenin
applied these criteria to a number of European states, notwith-
standing his argument that the two periods are not 'walled off'
from each other but are connected by 'numerous transitional
links'. In spite of this, Lenin stated that, 'there can be no question
of the Marxists of any country drawing up their national program
without taking into account all these general historical and concrete state situations'.[21] He argued that bourgeois democratic revolutions in Eastern Europe did not begin until 1905, while in
Western and Central Europe they took place during the period
1789 to 1871.[22] His formalistic presentation of the stages of development of the bourgeois democratic revolution results from the
epistemological requirement to identify every moment of the
developmental process within the field of determination of class
positions, which leads him to the absurd claim that in Western
Europe nationally uniform states became the general rule at the
close of the period of consolidation of bourgeois democratic
revolutions.[23] Consequently, he argues, to seek the right of self-

determination in the programmes of the Western European socialist parties is 'to betray one's ignorance on the ABC of Marxism'.[24]

Lenin was ambivalent towards the actual pursuit of state
separatism:

> It is not difficult to understand that the recognition by Marxists
> of the *whole of Russia*, and first and foremost by the great
> Russians of the right of nations to secede in no way precludes
> *agitation* against secession by Marxists of a particular *oppressed*
> nation, just as the recognition of the right to divorce does not
> preclude agitation against divorce in any particular case.[25]

Given that the bourgeois democratic revolution only began in
Czarist Russia in 1905, and taking into account that the process of
uneven development experienced by that diverse multinational
state created developmental peculiarities, the concrete features of
the national question in Russia were diverse and different from
those experienced in Western Europe at the same early stage of the
bourgeois democratic period.[26] This argument permitted Lenin to
maintain the developmental taxonomy of classical Marxism, while
sustaining an analysis which took into account the specific conjunctural situation of Czarist Russia. According to Lenin, 57 per
cent of the population of Czarist Russia was not of ethnic[27]
Russian extraction, and national oppression there was harsher
than in other multinational states. As a result of the peculiarities
of the process of uneven development, capitalism was more
advanced in some of the peripheral national communities than in
the ethnic Russian centre, while at the same time some of the
Asian national communities were only on the 'eve' of the 'bourgeois democratic stage'. The combination of harsh national
oppression with a wide range of developmental diversity resulted
in the 'urgent' political need to resolve the question by the principled application of the right of nations to self-determination.[28]

Rosa Luxemburg vehemently opposed the notion of a right of
nations to self-determination[29] and consequently disputed Lenin's
arguments. The polemic between Lenin and Luxemburg is a good
illustration of the differences between the class reductionist and
epiphenomenalist position on the national question. Luxemburg
denied that nations had rights while Lenin was prepared to grant
them certain qualified rights. While maintaining a strict class
reductionist position, Lenin understood that a relative autonomy
of national movements will advance certain strategic objectives of
fundamental importance for the party of the proletariat.

Luxemburg rejected the notion of national rights because there was no direct connecting relation of causality between national existence and the aims of the working class. If she was prepared to talk about rights at all, it was exclusively in terms of the rights of the working class.[30] She failed to see the bourgeois democratic revolutions in the same perspective as that of the Bolsheviks because she was not interested in any political movements that did not directly advance the objectives of the working class.

Lenin, however, appreciated the strategic importance of operating in the political arena and forging tactical alliances with political groupings not directly connected with the working class. As H. B. Davis argues, Lenin opposed the complete rejection of nationalist demands, even if he did not agree with them,[31] because he saw that the strategical importance of the national question – an essentially political issue – transcended the immediate position of nationalist movements. Consequently he realised the fundamental importance of not allowing nationalist movements to monopolise national demands. Luxemburg was blinded to this dimension because of her exclusive concentration on working-class politics and therefore she was not interested in political demands that were not directly connected with the root cause of all forms of oppression, the oppression of the working class. Lenin understood that the national question posed a specifically political problem that had to be resolved at the political level.

Agreeing with Otto Bauer that a socialist commonwealth cannot include national communities by the use of force,[32] Lenin saw that the specificity of national oppression required a specific political solution to the national problem. However, this solution could only be achieved following the socialist transformation of the capitalist mode of production:

> ... while being based on economics, socialism cannot be reduced to economics *alone*. A foundation – socialist production – is essential for the abolition of national oppression, but this foundation must also carry a democratically organised state, a democratic army, etc. By transforming capitalism into socialism the proletariat creates the *possibility* of abolishing national oppression; the possibility becomes *reality* 'only' – 'only'! – with the establishment of full democracy in all spheres, including the delimitation of state frontiers in accordance with the 'sympathies' of the population, including complete freedom to secede.[33]

In this remarkable statement, Lenin is not only radically breaking from epiphenomenality, but is also pushing the class reductionist position to its very limits. The socialist transformation of society is essential but not sufficient to overcome national oppression. In addition to the socialist transformation of the process of production, a full democratisation of the apparatus of government is required to resolve basic democratic demands such as the rights of national communities.

This argument begs an important and unresolved question: is it possible to have a form of social organisation based on socialist production that does not democratise the political arena? The question is strictly unthinkable for epiphenomenalism given the transparency of relations of causality, but it represents an unresolvable dilemma for class reductionists, for if the answer is affirmative, as Lenin appears to imply, then in what way is socialist production (the hegemony of the proletariat) essential in the determination of the nature of the political arena? If there is a clear difference between these two dimensions, the democratically organised state appears not to be the outcome of proletarian hegemony – the economic cannot explain the political. On the other hand, if the answer is negative, there is no justification for any form of political activity that transcends the strictly corporatist demands of the working class, for the organisation of socialist production will resolve all forms of political oppression – the position of Luxemburg and a return to epiphenomenalism.

A solution to this dilemma is to conceptualise the political and economic dimensions as separate fields in the pursuit of the goals of socialism. But such a separation is an unthinkable position for class reductionism, because it implies an autonomous dimension of the political arena. This dilemma exemplifies the achievements and failures of the Leninist theory of the national question. Lenin was able to see the formidable strategic importance of the national question in the political domain, and the requirement for a specific form of democratic politics to solve issues of national oppression. However, by trying to recognise the class identity of every national movement, Lenin severely limited the possibility of achieving his first goal, to develop the specific forms of national politics required for the consideration of issues of national oppression.

But his most complete and definitive break from epiphenomenalism in the arena of the national question relates to his appreciation of the revolutionary potential of the countries dominated by imperialism. One of the most important aspects of Lenin's theory of imperialism is that it transformed the capitalist arena into a world system in which a small group of central national states oppresses a large group of peripheral social formations. The antagonistic nature of the relationship between dominant national states and the peripheral oppressed peoples constitutes the main contradiction of the imperialist system. National liberation movements of national communities under the oppression of imperialism are, for Lenin, progressive because they break the imperialist chain at the weakest link.

Lenin's theory of the right of nations to self-determination, coupled with his appraisal of the role of imperialism, results in the articulation of the inherent class conflict of the capitalist system with the inherent national conflict of the imperialist stage. The process of national liberation added a radical new dimension to the Marxist conceptualisation of revolution, which in turn required a reappraisal of the revolutionary imagery.

> To imagine that social revolution is *conceivable* without revolts by small nations in the colonies and in Europe, without revolutionary outbursts by a section of the petty bourgeoisie *with all its prejudices*, without a movement of the politically conscious proletarian and semi-proletarian masses against oppression by the landowners, the church, and the monarchy, against national oppression, etc. – to imagine all this is to *repudiate social revolution*. So one army lines up in one place and says 'We are for socialism', and another somewhere else and says, 'We are for imperialism', and that will be a social revolution! Only those who hold such a ridiculously pedantic view could vilify the Irish rebellion by calling it a 'pustch'.
>
> Whoever expects a 'pure' social revolution will *never* live to see it. Such a person pays a lip-service to revolution without understanding what revolution is.[34]

According to Lenin, liberation from national oppression is one of the most important demands in the colonial world in the era of imperialism. The slogan of national self-determination will allow the working class to put forward a concrete programme against national oppression, creating the conditions for the workers to assume the leadership of the national movement.

A second important consequence of Lenin's theory is that it allows the development of a conceptual framework which explains why revolutions are unlikely to occur in advanced capitalist states, but are more likely to occur in peripheral societies and in places where the development of the productive forces will not assure the supremacy of the proletariat. Again, Lenin draws the class reductionist approach to its conceptual limits. He clearly understands the revolutionary potential of nationalist movements, and the specificities of the revolutionary struggle outside the European world, but the strait-jacket of class reductionism prevents him from conceptualising these – by his own account – non-class antagonisms, outside the paradigmatic field of class determination.

If national liberation movements are to move towards socialism, this will take place only under the leadership of the working class (and, of course, its avant-garde party), even in places where an industrial proletariat hardly exists. The paradox of this analysis could have been avoided by rejecting – as Mao eventually did – the ontological privilege of the proletariat in the process of socialist development, but such a proposition was precluded by the limitations of class reductionism.

Lenin's contribution to the Marxist debate on the national question was summarised by Stalin in the following way:

> Formerly the national question was usually confined to a narrow circle of questions concerning primarily civilised 'nationalities'. The Irish, the Hungarians, the Poles, the Finns, the Serbs, and several other European nationalities. This was the circle of unequal peoples in whose destinies the leaders of the Second International were interested. The scores and hundreds of millions of Asiatic and African peoples who are suffering national oppression in the most savage and cruel form, usually remained outside their field of vision'.[35]

Lenin's break from epiphenomenalism enlarged the concept of self-determination to the point where it became a tool in the anti-imperialist struggle of the non-European world. This resulted in an intense politicisation of the national question. 'Putting Politics "in Command", meaning his obstinate, inflexible, constant and unflinching tendency to ... highlight the *political* aspect of every problem'[36] was the main advantage and the main weakness of Lenin's theory, as we shall see. But before evaluating the work of Stalin, it is necessary to discuss Lenin's interpretation of national culture.

In the article 'Critical Remarks on the National Question'[37] Lenin addresses the question of national culture, which he considers to be of 'enormous importance' to Marxists (meaning, of course, those who subscribe to the Bolshevik interpretation of Marxism). Here Lenin argues for a specifically Bolshevik position on the subject, distinct from what he calls 'bourgeois propaganda' and from the programme of 'national cultural autonomy'[38] (the latter was a programme for national decentralisation which Lenin and Stalin wrongly believed was adopted by the Austrian Socialist Party in the Brno [Brünn] conference, and was supported by the majority of socialist parties of the non-Russian national communities in Czarist Russia). Lenin believed that it was important to discuss the issue of national culture for two related reasons.

Firstly, he regarded what he believed to be the Austrian position on national cultural autonomy as dangerous for the fundamental organisational principles of the Bolsheviks, because it implied the decentralisation of the party and state, which contradicted the fundamental Marxist-Leninist notion of democratic centralism.

The congress of Vienna-Wimberg decided in 1897 to divide the Austrian Socialist Gesamtpartei into a federal organisation of six ethno-national parties, and the congress of Brno (Brünn) resolved in 1899 to call for the organisation of the Austrian state on a federal and multinational basis, with central power devolved into six autonomous national regions, and no linguistic privilege to be granted to any of the participant national communities.[39] If the principle of national cultural autonomy (the Austrian 'personality principle')[40] was to be translated to the Russian situation – as the Bund and other socialist parties of national minorities demanded – it would have implied the decentralisation of party and state, a clear anathema to the organisational principle of democratic centralism as first sketched by Lenin in 'What is to be done?'

Secondly, the programme of national cultural autonomy was supported by many influential socialist organisations among the non-Russian national communities and the Jewish Bund was actively campaigning for its implementation in Russia. Lenin and the Bolsheviks clearly understood that the support of the non-Russian national communities was essential for the success of the Bolshevik position. They saw the need to forestall the danger of a possible alliance between the Mensheviks and the non-Russian socialist parties on the basis of the programme for national cultural autonomy.

Faced with this challenge, Lenin sketched an original programmatic position for the Bolsheviks, whose positive dimension was the right of nations to self-determination, and whose negative side was a ferocious attack on the concept of national cultural autonomy and a denial of the unity of national cultures. This situation also constitutes the background for Stalin's famous book, *Marxism and the National Question*, which will be discussed below.

The Leninist conceptualisation of national culture, is perhaps one of the best examples of the limitations of class reductionism for the analysis of the multifarious nature of the national phenomenon. Lenin argued repeatedly that in every nation there are two cultures: that of the bourgeoisie and reactionary forces, and that of the proletariat. The cultural unity of national communities is nothing but the hegemonic ideology of the bourgeoisie in disguise:

> Politically conscious workers have understood that the slogan of 'national culture' is a clerical or bourgeois deception – no matter whether it concerns Great Russian, Ukrainian, Jewish, Polish, Georgian or any other culture. A hundred and twenty five years ago, when the nation had not been split into bourgeoisie and proletariat, the slogan of national culture could have been a single and integral call to struggle against feudalism and clericalism. Since that time, however, the class struggle between the bourgeoisie and the proletariat has gained momentum everywhere. The division of the 'single' nation into exploiters and exploited has become an accomplished fact.[41]

For Lenin, then, the conflict between the bourgeoisie and the proletariat does not allow for the existence of a single national culture. The cultural domain is an area of the so-called superstructure and must therefore be explained in terms of the field of class determination. He conceded that, on the eve of the bourgeois revolution, it was possible to speak of a 'single' national culture, because it had a certain 'progressive' role in relation to the hegemonic struggle of the bourgeoisie. However, in attaching a strictly political meaning to the notion of national culture, Lenin ignores any possible ethno-historical or contemporary-relational dimension, that is a dimension which transcends the field of class determination.

In his 'Critical Remarks on the National Question', Lenin strongly attacked arguments in favour of a proletarian participation in the national culture. He argued that this discussion was required because of 'the increase of national vacillations among the different national [non-Russian] Social Democrats',[42] as well as other 'pro-nationalist tendencies' in Russian society. In rejecting the argument in favour of the unity of the national culture sustained by the Bundist P. Liebman, Lenin argued that in every national community there are 'toiling and exploited masses whose conditions of life inevitably give rise to the ideology of democracy and socialism', but every capitalist nation possesses a 'bourgeois dominant culture' which makes the slogan of national culture the slogan of the bourgeoisie.[43] To conceptualise the national culture as an undivided unit is unthinkable in terms of his class reductionist position, and consequently he advances the idea of the existence of two nations in every modern nation.[44] The significance of the concept of national culture is determined by the objective alignment of classes in a given country, which implies that in capitalist societies the national culture is the culture of the bourgeoisie.

> Developing capitalism knows two historical tendencies in the national question. The first is the awakening of national life and national movements, the struggle against national oppression, the creation of national states. The second is the development and growing frequency of international intercourse in every form, the breakdown of national barriers, the creation of the international unity of capital, of economic life in general, of politics, science, etc.[45]

Lenin then goes on to argue that both tendencies are the 'universal law' of capitalism, which will eventually result in a process of 'assimilation', a tendency which manifests itself 'more and more powerfully with every passing decade'. Here again he is reverting to the analysis of classical Marxism, which regards the national community as a passing phase in the development of capitalism.

The principle of nationality 'is historically inevitable' in bourgeois societies. Lenin therefore recognises the 'historical legitimacy' of those movements in the process of consolidation of the capitalist mode of production. But this recognition must be prevented from 'becoming an apologia' for nationalism, it must be strictly confined to the period in which the nationalist movement is a 'progressive force' so that 'bourgeois ideology' does not obscure 'proletarian consciousness':

> Marxism cannot be reconciled with nationalism, be it even of the 'most just', 'purest', most refined and civilised brand. In place of all forms of nationalism, Marxism advances internationalism, *the amalgamation of all nations in the higher unity*, a unity that grows before our eyes with every mile of railway line that is built, with every international trust, and every workers association that is formed.[46] (emphasis added)

The proletariat supports 'everything that makes the ties between nationalities closer' or 'tends to merge nations'.[47] The Austrian programme of national cultural autonomy was a 'refined dimension' of nationalism, and could not therefore be supported by the Bolsheviks. On the organisational aspect of the state, Lenin argues that:

> Marxists are, of course, opposed to federation and decentralisation, for the simple reason that capitalism requires for its development the largest and most centralised possible states. *Other conditions being equal*, the class conscious proletariat will always stand for the larger state.[48]

Lenin accepts the transitional nature of national communities, implying that the process of development of the productive forces will lead to the international unity of all working peoples, meaning by this the eventual disappearance of national boundaries. This process of international assimilation must take place as a result of the developmental logic of capitalism and, subsequently, socialism, but should take place free of coercion. Any form of coercion or compulsion to assimilate will have the reverse effect. This argument becomes clear in Lenin's position on the debate over whether it should be compulsory to learn Russian:

> The Russian language has undoubtedly been of progressive importance for the numerous small and backward nations. But surely you must realise that *it would have been* of much greater progressive importance had there been no compulsion. Is not an 'official language' the stick that *drives people away* from the Russian Language?[49]

From Lenin's opposition to the compulsory use of any language, it appears that he maintained a pluralist position on the linguistic question.

> Why will you not understand the *psychology* that is so important in the national question and which, if the slightest coercion is applied, besmirches, soils, nullifies the undoubtedly progressive importance of centralisation, large states and a uniform language? But the economy is still more important than psychology: in Russia we *already* have a *capitalist* economy, which makes the *Russian language essential*.[50]

On the one hand, Lenin believed that ethnic minorities held to national and linguistic identities as a psychological reaction against coercion and forced assimilation. On the other hand, he believed that state centralisation and national uniformity were essential for the achievement of the Marxist-Leninist goals but to achieve them, he was not prepared to risk alienating the non-Russian ethno-national communities.

The solution to this dilemma, paradoxically, was to invoke the iron laws of capitalist development, the very laws which were rejected in his discussions on the role of the party, the revolution, imperialism and uneven development. He asserted that economic forces in every case worked against a split-up of large states, and therefore the actual implementation of the right of nations to self-determination was, in most cases, against the logic of the process of economic development. The existing centrifugal forces were mainly psychological in their origin:

> The mass of the population knows perfectly well from daily experience the value of geographical and economic ties and the advantages of a big market and of a big state. They will therefore resort to secession only when national oppression and national friction make joint life absolutely intolerable and hinder all and any economic intercourse ... as long as national oppression is permitted, the victim minority was receptive to nationalist agitation; once this oppression ceased, the *psychological basis for nationalism and separatism will vanish*. And what better way could there be of striking at the very root of national antagonism than to guarantee to every nation the right to complete political freedom?[51]

Obviously Lenin was wrong on three counts. First, he was wrong to view the awakening of national identity as mere reaction to national oppression. He failed to see the cultural content of national existence and the desire of members of national communities to preserve their cultural heritage, even if that went against what he believed to be objective economic interests.

Second, he was wrong to believe that all problems of separate national identity will be solved by the constitution of separate national states. By overemphasising the political dimension he overlooked the cultural and ethnic dimensions of the national question. Lenin shows a remarkable insensitivity to the ethnic culture of the Soviet nationalities when he argues that the Russian language plays a 'progressive' role. As the Lithuanian academic A. A. Prazauskas argues, the compulsion to learn the Russian language, the supercentralisation of the administration, and the under-representation of non-Russians in the central apparatus of the party greatly contributed to the alienation of non-Russians from the Soviet system.[52] The constitution of separate national states does little to resolve this problem. Most territorial states are not ethnically homogeneous and national separatism often emancipates one ethnic or national community by compounding the oppression of others. Prazauskas argues that:

> the resolution of the national question depends directly and in the closest way upon the degree of democratisation and the development of democracy in a given society. In the limits of a bureaucratic model of socialism in general there were no mechanisms which could have expressed national interests and secured the timely resolution of problems.[53]

Third, Lenin was wrong to perceive national culture as divided by class loyalties. National communities often have a sense of collective identity that transcends class divisions. As Gramsci was later to argue, the working class also had a stake in the cultural national identity. The Marxist-Leninist concept of the two nations ascribes a fixed class to every national identity and consequently precludes an understanding of the transformative potentiality of national identities. Successful Marxist movements outside the area of influence of the Red Army were always supported by strong nationalist sentiments.

Lenin's errors of judgement in relation to the national question are all connected to the debilitating impact of class reductionism. The requirement to locate national movements and national identities within the field of class determination inhibits the understanding of the role of national culture, sees national identity only as a political force, and over-emphasises the role of economic forces in the determination of national identities.

Stalin and the National Question

Sympathetic discussions of Marxist Leninist theories,[54] tend to diminish the importance of Stalin's contribution. If Stalin is the *enfant terrible* of the Bolsheviks, then he should be detached as much as possible from Lenin. However, it is important not to obscure the fact that he was regarded in the early years of the Bolshevik movement as the highest party authority on the national question. In 1913 he left for Vienna, possibly sent by Lenin,[55] to study the theories of the Austro-Marxists on this issue and to produce a monograph on the Bolshevik theoretical position on the subject. The importance of the national question for the Bolshevik party has already been discussed and Stalin, being a token member of a non-Russian nationality, was in an ideal position to foster the much needed sympathy of the ethnic minorities towards the Bolshevik project.

The 'marvellous Georgian who sat down to produce an article',[56] as Lenin wrote to Gorki, in fact produced a mediocre monograph when compared with the calibre of the works of Lenin and other Bolsheviks. Stalin engaged in a discussion of Otto Bauer's theories without seeming to understand them properly. However, Lenin at the time believed that the essay was a 'very good one'[57] and Stalin was made the commissar for nationalities of the first Bolshevik government. (Early differences between Lenin and Stalin on the national question are detectable on a number of important issues, however, and will be discussed below.)

In the essay *Marxism and the National Question*,[58] his first and only book, Stalin saw the principal task of social democracy as being to protect ethnic minorities from the 'epidemic' of militant nationalism. What he means by this expression is not entirely clear, judging from the examples presented in the work; not only does he refer to Georgian, Ukrainian, Armenian and what he calls 'Polish chauvinism' but he also cites Zionism, pan-Islamism and anti-semitism as forms of nationalism.[59] Without any doubt, however, the most celebrated part of Stalin's essay is the schematic definition of what is a nation:

> A nation is an historically constituted, stable community of people, formed on the basis of a common language, territory, economic life and psychological make up manifested in a common culture.[60]

Language and units of economic life were already present in Kautsky's and Lenin's discussions on the subject. Community of territory is a derivative category of Lenin's theory of the right of nations to self-determination; for if self-determination means only secession and the formation of separate states, the territorial component is essential. The concept of 'psychological make-up manifested in a common culture' is derived directly from Bauer's definition of nations as 'communities of destiny formed into communities of character'.[61] By integrating this element into his definition of nations, Stalin is implicitly accepting Bauer's main contention that the nation is a historical community which is created through a common cultural, social and historical experience, and implicitly rejecting Lenin's argument about the two cultures in every nation. The problem for Stalin was that this last argument was precisely the point of contention between Bolsheviks and Austro-Marxists. Löwy and Davis rightly argue that the concept of 'psychological make-up' is not at all Leninist, because Lenin's argument is exclusively political. At least Stalin was aware of the one-sidedness of the exclusive emphasis on the political level.

It is possible to see in Stalin's work an acknowledgement that national communities are multifaceted phenomena, which cannot be satisfactorily explained by taking into account only political and economic development. In fact, Löwy's criticism of Stalin for using culturalist elements in his definition is a good example of dogmatism generated by the rigid Leninist appreciation of the national phenomenon: 'In fact, the idea of national psychology has more in common with certain superficial and pre-scientific folklore than with a Marxist analysis of the National Question'.[62] The main defect in Stalin's definition is that it excludes a large number of modern national communities. The German-speaking peoples would have been two, perhaps three nations; Italy would have become a nation only in the nineteenth century; the citizens of the Spanish state would have been one single nation, and so on. Moreover Stalin's criticisms of Bauer appear to be self defeating:

> Bauer sets up an impassable barrier between the 'distinctive feature' of nations (national character) and the 'conditions' of their life, divorcing the one from the other. But what is national character if not a reflection of the conditions of life, a coagulation of impressions derived from the environment?[63]

A page earlier, however, Stalin presents in criticism a quotation from Bauer which appears to be saying what Stalin thinks is his critique of Bauer!:

> a nation is nothing but a community with a common destiny which, in turn, is determined by the conditions under which people earn their means of subsistence and distribute the products of their labour.[64]

Stalin's understanding of the right of nations to self-determination resembles the argument of the Armenian Bolshevik Shahumyan and appears to differ from that of Lenin:

The right of Self Determination means that a nation may arrange its life in the way it wishes. It has the right to arrange its life on the basis of autonomy. It has the right to enter into federal relations with other nations, it has the right to complete secession. Nations are sovereign, and all nations have equal rights. [65]

In the same year that Stalin's monograph was published, Lenin wrote in the above mentioned letter to Shahumyan:

The right to self determination is an exception to our general premise of centralisation. This exception is absolutely essential in view of reactionary Great Russian nationalism, and any rejection of this exception means opportunism ... But exceptions *must not be too broadly interpreted*. In this case there is *not*, and *must not be anything more*, than the right to secede.[66]

In theory, Stalin's version of the right of nations to self- determination is far less rigid than Lenin's version; in practice, Stalin was less prepared to compromise his wish to achieve the highest possible centralisation of the Soviet state. In the same monograph, Stalin gives a clue as to what will be his behavior ten years later as Commissar of Nationalities:

The National question in the Caucasus can be solved only by *drawing belated nations and nationalities into the common stream of higher culture*. (emphasis added) [67]

By 'higher culture' Stalin probably means Russian culture. The evolutionary and hierarchical perception of national development which permeated the works of Lenin also had its impact on Stalin's understanding of the national phenomenon. When this is translated into the discussion of the Western European societies, Stalin replicates the pattern of the assimilated intellectual from a non-metropolitan society who is often too critical of his own society and uncritical of the 'progressive' nature of the metropolitan world. In discussing anti-semitism in Russia, Stalin argues that:

Russia is a semi-Asiatic country, and therefore in Russia the policy of 'encroachments' not infrequently assumes the grossest form, the form of pogroms ... Germany is, however, European, and she enjoys a measure of political freedom. It is not surprising that the policy of 'encroachments' there never takes the form of pogroms.[68]

The bitter irony of this perception sadly reflects the mediocrity of certain members of the colonised intelligentsia, who never lose the opportunity to inform the world of the 'superiority' of Western ways. Lenin clearly understood the nature of the problem when he warned in his last writings against the excesses committed by Stalin and Dzerzhinsky.

> I think that Stalin's haste and infatuation with pure administration, together with his spite against the notorious 'nationalist-socialism', played a fatal role here ... I also fear that comrade Dzerzhinsky, who went to the Caucasus to investigate the 'crime' of those 'nationalist-socialists' distinguished himself by his truly Russian frame of mind (it is common knowledge that people of other nationalities who have become Russified overdo this Russian frame of mind).[69]

Nevertheless, Stalin was considered to be the Bolshevik expert on the national question. His contribution to the Bolshevik debate should not be underestimated, in spite of his important theoretical differences with the work of Lenin on the subject.

In assessing the Bolshevik contribution to the Marxist debate on the national question, it would be fair to say that the main achievement of the Marxist-Leninist tradition was successfully to articulate the class contradictions of classical Marxism with the national contradictions of the imperialist era. In breaking with epiphenomenalism in order to explain the specific unevenness of the process of development in Czarist Russia, the Marxist-Leninist tradition managed to understand the political dimension of the national question, and the potential it has for the revolutionary movement outside Europe.

However, 'putting politics in command' in Löwy's phrase (following Marx) was also the main weakness of the Bolshevik approach to the national question. The class reductionist understanding of the political arena required the evaluation of the political nature of national communities within the paradigmatic field of class determination. For Lenin, the national question should always be looked at from the angle of the working class – an instrumentalist perception that obscures certain fundamental features of the phenomenon under observation.

The Marxist-Leninist tradition was unable to come to grips with cultural and ethnic aspects of national existence, and was blinded to their impact on the resilient constitution of national communities. It is, in fact, a regrettable irony that the only Marxist

theoretical analysis of the national question which could have provided Lenin and Stalin with insights into culture and ethnicity was
precisely the one which they set out to criticise with characteristic
self-righteousness: the theory of Otto Bauer.

From the political point of view, Marxist-Leninism's taxonomical periodisation of the national question required the identification of a bourgeois dimension in every national movement. This
effectively prevented a theoretical appreciation of non-bourgeois
national movements, a problem which was later to be partially
solved by Antonio Gramsci and his concept of the national-
popular, to which we now turn before considering Bauer's contribution in detail.

4

Gramsci and the National Question

In a provocative article, Antonio Gramsci argued that:

> Today the 'national class' is the proletariat. The multitude of workers and peasants ... who cannot allow the dismemberment of the nation because the unity of the state is the form of the apparatus of production and exchange built by Italian labour, the heritage of social wealth that the Italian workers wish to bring to the Communist International. Only the workers' state, the dictatorship of the proletariat, can today halt the dissolution of national unity.[1]

As a founding member of the Italian Communist Party, Gramsci had always acknowledged his political loyalty to the principles of Marxism-Leninism and his intellectual indebtedness to the works of Lenin for expanding and clarifying fundamental aspects of Marxist theory. But to argue that the proletariat is the 'national class', and that the 'workers state' is the only safeguard against the dissolution of national unity, is simply contradictory to the basic tenets of the Marxist-Leninist theory on the national question.

Gramsci seems to imply that the proletariat has a direct and immediate interest in the national movement. Does this mean that he broke with the class reductionist dimension of the Marxist-Leninist tradition? The answer must remain inconclusive. Gramsci's writings represent a transitional phase in the development of the Marxist tradition, and to understand the strains his work creates it is necessary to perceive his simultaneous continuity and fundamental, if unacknowledged, rupture with Marxism-Leninism. There is an unresolved tension – if not a downright contradiction – which in many ways colours the originality of the Gramscian thought and which has led to contradictory interpretations of his work.

Interpretations of Gramsci's Writings

Perry Anderson has mapped[2] the Russian social democratic and Marxist-Leninist continuity in the use of the concept of hegemony, locating Gramsci's usage of the term at the end of that continuum. This gives the impression that Gramsci employed the concept of hegemony 'for a differential analysis of the structures of bourgeois power in the west', while maintaining a formal continuity of essential meaning, namely, that of proletarian class alliances entered into under specific historical circumstances. This is the case even if the discursive presentation of the argument permitted an 'imperceptible transition to a much wider theory of hegemony than had ever been imagined in Russia'.[3] For Anderson, the notion of a class alliance is crucial for understanding the concept of hegemony, from its first Russian usage to the more sophisticated Gramscian understanding.

From a very different perspective, the work of Laclau and Mouffe[4] opens the way for a more creative reading of the concept of hegemony. The unity of meaning is achieved by emphasising Gramsci's break with class reductionism in his discontinuous use of the idea of class alliances, providing a conceptualisation of hegemony that radically departs from the original Russian notion.[5] In this interpretation, the value of the concept of hegemony resides precisely in its radical methodological break with the Leninist tradition, rather than in Gramsci's adaptation of the concept to the Western situation. The break is achieved by presenting a non-class reductionist analysis of the reconstitution of the political arena.

It will be argued here that it is only through this latter reading of Gramsci that the novelty of his analysis of the national question can be ascertained. If the notion of the proletariat as the national class is not to be regarded as a theoretical incoherence, it requires a conceptualisation of the national arena outside the paradigmatic field of class determination, and here lies the originality of the Gramscian concept of national-popular.

It should be noted, however, that both class reductionist and non-class reductionist readings of Gramsci are equally plausible from the point of view of the continuing discussion on the national question. But the class reductionist interpretation is at best a sophisticated reinterpretation of the old problems of Marxism-Leninism, as is evident in Anderson's article, and it fails to go beyond the questions and problems generated by the Leninist tradition.

The non-class reductionist reading discloses an imaginative – but nevertheless partial – attempt to find new solutions to the perennial Marxist problems of interpreting social order and political power beyond the strait-jacket of economism. This particular interpretation is concerned with Gramsci's critique of all forms of economism through the expansion of the notion of the state (the integral state), and also with the rejection of teleological and trans-historical notions of human essence, to make room for a conceptualisation of a multiplicity of socially determined historical subjects, a necessary condition for understanding the multifarious nature of the national phenomenon.[6]

To understand the meaning and significance of the Gramscian concept of national-popular – Gramsci's main contribution to the conceptualisation of the national question – it is necessary first to discuss briefly the importance of the concept of hegemony, through the original Gramscian analysis of what he called the historical bloc, and the all-important role of the intellectuals in consolidating and giving shape to the national community.

The notion of hegemony has its origins in the Russian socialist literature. For Lenin, it was a theoretical device to allow for the political intervention of the avant-garde party in a combined developmental situation. In the Gramscian use of the term, an initial level of analysis closely follows the Leninist conceptualisation. In his work on the Southern Question, Gramsci argues that the proletariat can become the dominant class to the extent that it succeeds in creating a system of alliances which allows it to mobilise the majority of the working population against capitalism and the bourgeois state.[7]

The tactical discussion on the Southern Question closely resembles Lenin's argument on the need to create an alliance between workers and peasants.[8] If one follows the Leninist logic, the analysis of the hegemonic situation is strictly confined to a political arena configured by class relations, and the concept of hegemony appears to name a system of class alliances in which the alignment is purely conjunctural. The hegemonic group is still one of preconstituted sectorial interests, a conceptual framework that does not contradict the notion of class alliances.[9] This is the source of the class reductionist interpretation of the Gramscian concept of hegemony.

In terms of this analysis, the only innovative aspect of Gramsci's argument would have been an adaptation and refinement of the Leninist position to the political conditions of Western Europe, and the extension of the concept to include the logic of domination of the bourgeoisie. Hegemony is then a 'dominant ideology'[10] and fundamental issues of coercion and consent remain as problematic as they are in the Marxist-Leninist tradition.[11] Central to this interpretation is a transcendental understanding of class identity. It requires the perpetuation at the political level of the fundamental identity of the class leading the hegemonic relation throughout the hegemonic process. If the political class identity of the participants remains unchanged through the hegemonic relation, then those sectors located in a subordinated position in this relation have either to be coerced or they must consent to the leadership of the dominant class.[12]

However, if it is possible to show that the Gramscian concept of hegemony implies not a perpetuation but a dissolution of political class identities, and a reconstitution of the participant elements in the hegemonic whole into an autonomous political unit, then the restraints of class determination are broken and the concept of hegemony is freed from the limits of class reductionism. In relation to the analysis of the national question, the class reductionist interpretation adds very little to the Leninist political and strategic discussion outlined in Chapter 3.

The key to appreciating Gramsci's transformation of the concept of hegemony is his perception of human identity emerging out of the process of historical development. The realisation of the human condition lies in understanding and locating oneself in the context of the relevant historical process. The point of reference is a historical humanism, but this term must be carefully defined outside the realm of teleology. There is no predetermined essentialist perception of human nature underpinning Gramsci's analysis. Historical humanism is not a Hegelian definition of the essential characteristics of human nature, but a rigorous attempt to understand the plural nature of the process of historical constitution of the identity of the human species. For Gramsci, human nature is not a homogeneous and trans-historical attribute, but a set of historical characteristics, related to specific temporal circumstances.[13]

The same logic applies to all forms of human consciousness. In abstract terms, there is no false or real consciousness, because there is no essential matrix to stand as a referent. This represents a break with the neo-Hegelian perceptions of human nature that had characterised other Marxist traditions and it is crucial for a pluralist understanding of the process of historical development because it supersedes the essentialist class reductionism implied in the notion of a *telos*, and therefore it is capable of grasping the pluralist nature of the national question.

The Gramscian definition of humanity combines the ensemble of present relations with a synthesis of past experiences. Gramsci calls this combination organic, because it links a series of discrete elements into a higher order coherent unit. Humanity is defined by a complex of social relations unique to every historical period and any comparison between human beings of different epochs is impossible because, according to Gramsci, 'we are dealing with different, if not heterogeneous objects'.[14]

People are both the originators of the will to change through their relation to present conditions and simultaneously the synthesis of past experiences. Both dimensions are organically linked and generate a specific moment, for which no a priori conceptual relation of causality could be established in the abstract to explain the particular link between the historical and contemporary elements. It is from this understanding of the development of humanity that the specific nature of the national-popular is derived. Far from the hierarchical developmental logic which characterises Marxist-Leninism, the Gramscian methodology permits the conceptualisation of the specificity of a plurality of historical and contemporary events, which in turn allows us to think of the national community as a unique, that is to say a historically particular synthesis. In Gramsci's words:

> ... the internal relations of any nation are the result of a combination which is 'original' and (in a certain sense) unique: these relations must be understood and conceived in their originality and uniqueness if one wishes to dominate them and direct them.[15]

In order to understand the implications of this discussion for the Marxist theory of the national question, however, another original Gramscian concept, that of the historical bloc, becomes significant. A protracted and controversial discussion has been generated over the precise meaning of this term. The problem results from the fact that the notion of historical bloc addresses itself to one of the most delicate areas of class reductionism, that of the relation between what Marx called, in that unfortunate metaphor, the 'base' and 'superstructure'.[16] The difficulty is compounded by the fact that while Gramsci made extensive use of the term, he only provided a schematic conceptualisation.[17]

In the same way as Gramsci argues that historical and contemporary experiences are organically linked in every human identity, he also insists that the historical bloc represents the organic link of the base with the superstructure. The historical bloc is the concrete expression of specific historical situations, in which the material conditions – the base – are organically linked with the superstructure – the ideological and political order. On a number of occasions Gramsci argues that it would be a mistake of 'incalculable political consequences' to privilege one of the elements of the organic relation. The exaggeration of the role of the base Gramsci calls economism, that is the according of supremacy to the base over the superstructure in a mechanical way.[18]

The importance of this formulation lies in the fact that it frees the discussion of so-called superstructural phenomena from narrow discussions concerning the nature of the process of determination. From Gramsci onwards, the notion of historical bloc has opened new avenues for the understanding of the relations between the social and political arenas by enabling the debate to go beyond the narrow parameters of class reductionism. The other important aspect is that the historical bloc itself is the locus for the formation of national identities. But before discussing this point, it is necessary briefly to evaluate Gramsci's analysis of the role of the intellectuals in the historical bloc.

Every social group which performs an essential function in the process of production creates, according to Gramsci, a group or stratum of intellectuals which gives homogeneity and awareness of its own function not only at the economic levels, but also in social and political fields.[19] This is a significant departure from earlier perceptions of intellectuals, which invariably located them as part of the upper classes, resulting from the classical Marxian division between manual and mental labour.[20] Gramsci suggests a reassessment by distinguishing the intellectual aspect inherent in every form of human existence from the intellectual function. In concrete societies, what distinguishes intellectuals from non-intellectuals is what he calls 'the professional function of the category of intellectuals'. This distinction results from the historical location of the intellectual function.[21] Intellectuals form a social stratum related to one of the fundamental social classes.

The organic intellectuals of fundamental classes represent the ideas and aspirations of their respective class, and in the case of the leading class in the hegemonic relation they constitute what Gramsci calls the 'ideological bloc'.[22] This is the site where the intellectuals of the subordinated classes are won over to the hegemonic system, creating a medium through which the intellectuals of the leading class become examples and orientators for the intellectuals of the subordinated classes.

However, Gramsci acknowledges that every new class or intellectual stratum finds cultural and intellectual categories already in existence. These appear to delineate the formal continuity of the society in question, regardless of any changes introduced by the newly arrived class or intellectual stratum.[23] The bearers of these old cultural and intellectual categories Gramsci calls traditional intellectuals; the example he gives in the Italian case is that of the Catholic priesthood. The organic intellectuals of the leading class assert their 'intellectual and moral leadership' by incorporating the traditional and organic intellectuals of the subordinated classes into the historical bloc through a process which he calls *transformismo*. This is usually a two-stage process in which the values and interests of the intellectuals not organically linked with the leading class are firstly disarmed of their contradictory or antagonistic positions vis a vis the historical bloc, and secondly integrated as much as possible into the broad positions of the historic bloc.[24] The hegemony of the leading class is secured, by defusing and incorporating to the hegemonic group the subordinated strata, via the incorporation of their intellectuals.

However, if the historic bloc is to be successful in the task of integrating the intellectuals of the subordinated strata, it must broaden its image so that it becomes acceptable to the widest possible audience. It must broaden the 'narrow corporative interests' of the leading class or the existing hegemonic group to the point at which it inspires popular support and is understood to be representing the aspirations of the community as a whole. At this point Gramsci introduces an original analytical category that allows the conceptualisation of the identity of the expanding historical bloc beyond the confines of the individual identities of the participant strata. This new concept is also of cardinal importance for Gramsci's conceptualisation of the national arena: collective will. This he presents as a point of practical articulation, creating a higher order unit of the non-antagonistic social forces that transcends and dissolves the economic corporate interests of the participant strata. This is the national identity.

> Any formation of a national-popular collective will is impossible unless the great mass of peasant farmers bursts *simultaneously* into political life. That was Machiavelli's intention through the reform of the militia, and it was achieved by the Jacobins in the French Revolution. That Machiavelli understood it reveals a precocious Jacobinism that is the (more or less fertile) germ of his conception of national revolution. All history from 1815 onwards shows the efforts of the traditional classes to prevent the formation of a collective will of this kind, and to maintain 'economic corporate' power in an international system of passive equilibrium.[25]

Leaving aside the historical arguments for the moment, here Gramsci is arguing simply the dissolution of fundamental aspects of class reductionism at the level of the political arena and, at the same time, identifying a set of political protagonists that operates outside the field of class determination. It is through the actions of these diverse political actors cemented into a collective will and in the context of a historically specific framework called historical bloc that processes of political transformation take, or do not take, place as in the case of the example above. In other words, the fundamental locus of political activity is not simply determined by class divisions. The economic field is only one among others and there is no discernible reason to accord privilege to its influence in the political arena.

If the interpretation of hegemony as class alliances is accepted, then the historical bloc is merely a political replication of the outcome of the relation between classes at a given conjuncture, and the intellectuals induce either forms of false consciousness or a scientific understanding of reality. The socialist component of the collective will is then the expression of higher levels of class consciousness as represented in the enlightened dimension of that classical Marxist dichotomy, class in itself, class for itself, and in the various schools of Hegelian Marxism. The Gramscian imaginative richness and diversity in conceptualising the political arena is then lost to the dogma of an increasingly irrelevant orthodoxy. It reduces the national-popular to a mere conjunctural strategic device which will be ditched as the hegemonic proletariat achieves higher levels of class consciousness.

If, on the contrary, a non-class reductionist understanding of the Gramscian concept of hegemony is adopted, then it is possible to grasp, with the help of the concepts of historical bloc and collective will, how historically specific elements can be successfully incorporated into an analysis of an international-state situation. In the context of the historical bloc, and through the activities of the organic intellectuals, the hegemonic force develops a collective will that cements, leads and changes the political arena, transforming its corporate character in the process. However, it is clear that, in the work of Gramsci, the leading force in the hegemonic relation must always be one of the fundamental classes. This severely limits the flexibility of the concept, because the hegemony of the fundamental class is not the result of the circumstantial relation of social and/or political forces, but has an ultimate ontological foundation[26] in the privileged position of the process of production. The hegemonic unit is restricted to be led by either the bourgeoisie or the proletariat. This limitation perhaps renders Gramsci's theory of hegemony less fruitful than the concepts of historical bloc and collective will.

We must now turn to the Gramscian conceptualisation of the national question, locating the origin of the notion of national-popular in the context of the Italian state's historical development.

The Gramscian Conceptualisation of the National Question

There can be little doubt that the centrality of the so-called Southern Question to the Italian state, as well as Gramsci's own Sardinian origins, played a crucial role in his thinking on the national question. Tom Nairn argues that:

> It is always important to recall this early phase of Gramsci's astonishing biography. He is the greatest of western Marxists. But it cannot be without significance that he was also a product of the West's most remote periphery, and of conditions which, half a century later, it became fashionable to call 'Third World'. No comparable western intellectual came from such a background. He was a barbed gift of the backwoods to the metropolis, and some aspects of his originality always reflected this distance.[27]

A notion which runs like a thread through Gramsci's historical work is the manifest failure of the Italian bourgeoisie, from the Risorgimento onwards, to develop the newly centralised Italian state into a homogeneous national community. According to Gramsci, the northern industrial bourgeoisie subjected southern Italy to the status of 'exploited colonies',[28] creating a deep division and antagonism which effectively precluded the crystallisation of an Italian national identity. This division between north and south not only resulted in the exploitation of the southern peasant masses, but also created an attitude of rejection and prejudice among the workers of the north and a stagnant society and culture in the south. This resulted from what Gramsci calls

> a monstrous agrarian bloc which as a whole acts as an intermediary and overseer for northern capital and the big banks. It sole aim is to preserve the status quo. Inside there is no intellectual

light, no programme, no urge towards betterment and progress.[29]

Gramsci is critical not only of the reactionary nature of the 'agrarian bloc' in southern Italy, but also of the inability of sections of the northern working class to overcome their 'corporative hangovers' and prejudicial attitudes towards the southern peasant society.[30] He is particularly critical of the support given to the southernist views by leading members of the Italian Socialist Party. This view shows remarkable similarities with the concept of orientalism evaluated by Edward Said, a concept created in the discussions of some Western 'experts' on Middle Eastern societies. These arguments are usually presented in the guise of a culturalist analysis and invariably present the 'backward' oriental culture as the causal factor for underdevelopment.[31] This ideology also impregnated the works of Bernstein and other revisionists leaders, and it is probably through the revisionist writings that the Italian socialists became acquainted with these ideas. According to Gramsci, this southernist view was also influential in the political orientation and general ideology of the proletariat itself, through the multifarious forms of bourgeois propaganda among the masses of the north. The essential arguments of the southernist position are defined by Gramsci thus:

> the southerners are biologically inferior beings, semi-barbarians or complete barbarians by natural destiny; if the South is backward, the fault is not to be found in the capitalist system or in any other historical cause, but is the fault of nature which made the southerner lazy, incapable, criminal, barbarous, moderating his stepmother's fate by the purely individual outburst of great geniuses, who are like solitary palms in an arid and sterile desert ... the Socialist Party gave its blessing to the whole 'southernist' literature of the clique of the so-called positivist writers ... who in articles, sketches, stories, novels, books of impressions and memoirs repeated in various forms the same refrain; once again 'science' had turned to crushing the wretched and the exploited, but this time it was cloaked in socialist colours, pretending to be the science of the proletariat.[32]

While the Turin communists reacted energetically against this ideology, there is no doubt that these views remain influential even today. The double entendre phrase quoted by Gramsci as characteristic of the hatred against workers of the north by southern immigrants – 'Italy is divided into Northerners and filthy Southeners'[33] – continues to be used in contemporary Italian. This sharp north-south divide prevented the consolidation of a historical bloc which, Gramsci argued, must be able to transcend the 'prejudices and corporative demands' of the working class and constitute a higher unit capable of representing the desires and aspirations of the community as a whole.

The Italian working class would not be capable of constituting the historical bloc through which the hegemonic unit will come into existence until it transcends these prejudices and constitutes a cultural community through which the subordinated peasants and the southern masses will be integrated into the national culture. In other words, the working class must construct a new historical bloc that must take the form of the national community, something that the Italian bourgeoisie conspicuously failed to do.

For Gramsci, the hegemonic unit constituted by a fundamental class is an international phenomenon insofar as it represents the development of a particular mode of production. The historical bloc is a national phenomenon insofar as it is the result of a unique historical situation, and it becomes the locus for the formation of a community of culture in a context delimited by historical and, at times, geographical factors. In this sense the cultural aspect is of crucial importance:

> Culture, at its various levels, unifies in a series of strata, to the extent that they come into contact with each other, a greater or lesser number of individuals who understand each other's mode of expression in differing degrees, etc ... From this one can deduce the importance of the 'cultural aspect', even in practical (collective) activity. An historical act can only be performed by 'collective man', and this presupposes the attainment of a 'cultural social' unity through which a multiplicity of dispersed wills, with heterogeneous aims, are welded together in a single aim.[34]

Common culture is a necessary condition for the crystallisation of a community. In Gramscian terms, no hegemonic unit will emerge in any given society without claiming to represent the society as whole. A fundamental class becomes the organiser of a hegemonic unit when, in the context of the historical bloc, the intellectuals and popular masses establish an organic link in which culture in the intellectual sense (knowledge) develops a connection with culture in its anthropological sense (shared experiences).

The organic intellectuals of the working class must not only know but also understand and feel the link with the popular masses.

If the relationship between intellectuals and people-nation, between leaders and led, the rulers and the ruled is provided by an organic cohesion in which feeling-passion becomes understanding and thence knowledge (not mechanically but in a way that is alive), then and only then is the relationship one of representation. Only then can there take place an exchange of individual elements between rulers and ruled, leaders (dirigenti) and led, and can the shared life be realised which alone is a social force – with the creation of the 'historical bloc'.[35]

The constitution of a historical bloc implies a radical and novel reconstruction of the relational nature and identity of different units of the social formation under consideration. It implies firstly the constitution of an organic link. This link in turn constitutes a higher order grouping in which participant units merge their cultural identities, forming a higher order shared culture which becomes the common denominator of the historical bloc. Consequently, in the same way that for Gramsci a class does not take state power but becomes the state,[36] the historical bloc does not take over the nation but becomes a new national community.

To understand how this process takes place, Gramsci reverts to analysing the French Revolution, in which he sees a successful case of the formation of a national-popular historic bloc, and the case of his contemporary Italy, where he argues that the bourgeoisie had failed to constitute this bloc.

France ... experienced a great popular reformation in the eighteenth century with the Enlightenment, Voltarianism and the Encyclopaedia. This reformation preceded and accompanied the Revolution of 1789. It really was a matter here of a great intellectual and moral reformation of the French people, more complete than the German Lutheran reformation, because it also embraced the great peasant masses in the countryside and had a distinct secular basis and attempted to replace religion with a completely secular ideology *represented by the national and patriotic bond*. (emphasis added)[37]

The bourgeoisie in France emerged as a fundamental class at the economic level, but did not achieve political power directly as a result of this. It gained political power only because it was capable

of constituting itself as the leading class of the emerging hegemonic grouping before the actual revolution took place. The bourgeoisie attained its hegemonic position because it transcended its
immediate corporate interests and presented itself as the representative of the Third Estate. In terms of its political discourse, the
bourgeoisie transcended its economic corporative interests by constructing the notion of popular sovereignty which gave other subordinated strata a sense of representation. Consequently national
sovereignty and popular sovereignty became interchangeable
terms, because the national community became the sovereign
through the concept of popular representation.[38] The emerging
historical bloc constituted the national community and this was
acheived by creating an organic link between the intellectuals and
the popular masses:

> More than any other national literature there exists in French
> philosophical literature treatments of 'common sense': this is
> due to the more strictly 'popular national' character of French
> culture, in other words, the fact that the intellectuals ... tend
> more to approach the people in order to guide it ideologically
> and keep it linked with the leading group.[39]

The responsibility for the development of the national-popular
link between the organic intellectuals of the bourgeoisie and the
popular masses fell upon the Jacobins. Before the revolution the
Third Estate was not, according to Gramsci, a homogeneous
stratum. Gradually a new intellectual elite emerged, not concerned
only with the sectarian interests of the bourgeoisie, but tending to
construct a political image of the bourgeoisie as the hegemonic
force of all subordinated strata. The principal tasks of the Jacobins
were to annihilate the counter-revolutionary forces and, more
importantly from the point of view of the national question, to
enlarge as much as possible cadres of the political grouping led by
the bourgeoisie. This meant identifying the specific requirements
of all forces that were not in contradiction to the leadership of the
bourgeoisie, in order to unite them under the patriotic banners of
the revolution, creating a cultural-patriotic link which represented
all popular forces, including large sections of the peasantry.[40] The
Jacobins managed to absorb into the revolution most sectors not
directly connected with the *ancien regime*. There was, however, one
important exception: the ethno-national minorities. Certain areas
within the French state inhabited by non-Parisian-French speaking
communities resisted their incorporation into the culture of the

emerging French nation under the leadership of the Jacobins. This was particularly the case in the area today called Euzkadi North and in Brittany. The Breton Question proved to be more important than the drive to create 'a single and compact' French nation.

> The resistance of the Vendée properly speaking is linked to the national question, which had become envenomed among the peoples of Brittany and in general among those alien to the slogan of the 'single and indivisible republic' and to the policy of bureaucratic-military centralisation – a slogan and a policy that the Jacobins could not renounce without committing suicide.[41]

The implications of this analysis for the ethno-national minorities will be examined below. In terms of the Gramscian discussion of the role of the Jacobins in consolidating the French Revolution, their main achievement was to develop a national patriotic collective will. In the Gramscian terminology, Jacobinism defines a political movement capable of creating a collective will which transcends the notion of pure class alliances, to constitute a form of political subjectivity that, as such, has no necessary class belonging. Gramsci illustrates this point by arguing that during the French Revolution the Jacobins were more 'advanced' than the French bourgeoisie, creating irreversible 'fait accomplis' and driving the bourgeois forward with 'kicks in the backside' ('*a calci nel sedere*').[42] Notions like 'La Patrie', and the sense of belonging to the French nation became crucial elements in the formation of the new historical bloc. The energetic actions of these intellectuals created the strongest possible links, paving the way for a stable hegemonic grouping under the leadership of the bourgeoisie.

> For not only did they organise a bourgeois government, i.e, make the Bourgeoisie the dominant class – they did more. They created the bourgeois state, made the Bourgeoisie the leading hegemonic class of the nation, in other words gave the new state a permanent basis and created *the compact French Nation*. (emphasis added)[43]

The Italian case presented a different picture. The historical inheritance of the peninsula only allowed the formation of an Italian nation at a relatively late period; the local bourgeoisie was weak and had to forge alliances with cosmopolitan elements such as the Catholic church, who 'sabotaged' the formation of a national-popular historical bloc. The ideological cause for this retarded formation of the Italian nation was the 'unfortunate fact' that the Italian peninsula was both the centre of the Roman empire and the spiritual and political home of the Catholic church.[44] At the time of the French Revolution, the cosmopolitan ideology of the church dominated those parts of the Italian peninsula not under the control of foreign powers. This resulted in a cast of intellectuals which, unlike its French counterpart, was not attached to the national popular culture.

> The Italian intellectuals did not have a popular-national character, but one that was cosmopolitan on the model of the church; it was a matter of indifference to Leonardo whether he sold the designs for the fortifications of Florence to Duke Valentino.[45]

The Italian intellectuals responded to the humanistic and cosmopolitan nature of the Graeco-Roman tradition. These intellectuals were oriented towards 'encyclopaedic' notions of culture, 'that invariably put them in a position distant from that of the popular masses'. At the political level, once the process of Italian unification started, the bourgeoisie was too weak to create a Jacobin party modelled on the French experience. 'In Italy, a Jacobin Party was never formed', creating instead a historical bloc with the Catholic church and thereby greatly diminishing the possibilities for the formation of a national-popular historical bloc.[46] (Gramsci devoted a great deal of attention to an analysis of the reasons for the non-existence of a national-popular bloc in the Italian peninsula, since he believed that the ensuing national cultural division was partially responsible for the emergence of fascism.[47])

Gramsci argues that the working class must succeed where the bourgeoisie failed. Because of the cosmopolitan nature of the bourgeois Italian intellectuals, because of the failure of the bourgeoisie to constitute itself as the national class, the working class alone occupies the role of the national class. Here lies the meaning of the quotation at the beginning of this chapter. The working class is called upon to be the fundamental class that builds a hegemonic grouping with the peasants and other subordinated strata, which will make possible a 'national-popular historical bloc' and crystallise a 'national collective will' through the activities of the new Jacobins – the Communist Party. As Eric Hobsbawm observes,

> Gramsci's strategy follows from his concept – quite original in Marxism, of the working class as part of the *nation*. Indeed, I

believe that he is so far the only Marxist thinker who provides us with a basis of integrating the nation as an historical and social reality into Marxist theory. He breaks with the habit of seeing it as 'the national question', something external to the working class movement, towards which we have to define our attitude.[48]

The new Jacobins of the Communist Party (PCI), as heirs of Machiavelli's insights and through their role as organic intellectuals of the working class, are the only ones in the Italian context capable of bridging the gap between national and popular culture, between culture as knowledge and culture as the collective experience of the community. They are also the only ones capable of reconstituting the dispersed collective wills of north and south, peasant and worker, and the intellectuals with all the rest, into a higher order national-popular will, a newly created political subject that transcends the class location of its participant elements.

This is the non-class reductionist reading of Gramsci's work on the national question. Only through such a reading is it possible to derive from his a theory on the specificity of the national community. If a class reductionist position is maintained, then the national-popular historical bloc is only an instrumental and strategic alliance of forces, intentionally designed to secure the leadership of the party of the proletariat in a system of class alliances determined by the positions of the participating classes. Both interpretations are equally possible, but the non-class reductionist position allows for an understanding of the specificity of the national phenomenon at its cultural and political levels. It also provides an image of a more coherent Gramsci, particularly in relation to the theoretical understanding of concrete national movements, since the characterisation of national-popular equally applies to historical blocs that make possible different forms of leadership of the hegemonic grouping. This conceptualisation is incoherent in a class reductionist discourse because all superstructural elements must have a class belonging.

It appears that Gramsci had successfully transcended the paradigmatic limitations of classical Marxism in evaluating the national phenomenon. A number of difficulties remain, however, and are best exemplified in the way in which he relates to the ethno-national and linguistic minorities in both the French and Italian states. The Gramscian conceptualisation of the national community has a major advantage over the analyses developed by the theoreticians of the Second and Third Internationals (Austro-Marxists excluded) in that it is capable of comprehending the political importance of the cultural dimension as well as conceptualising a form of autonomy for the political realm – in itself not an insubstantial achievement. However, by overcoming one form of reductionism – that of economism – Gramsci appears to be privileging another dimension – the political arena – instead of constructing a non-reductionist analysis of the national phenomenon. He tends to search for mechanisms that will consolidate the cultural uniformity of the national state, rather than attempting to evaluate the plurality of cultural and national existence. The nation and the national-popular are important only insofar as they are vehicles for the formation of a new form of political subjectivity: the national-popular collective will. Similarly culture, in its various meanings, is only analysed in its functionality to the political dimension. For Gramsci, national state, national language and the organisation of culture are all different aspects of the same process: 'The problem of the intellectual and moral unity of the nation and the state is to be found in the unity of language'.[49]

He castigates the Italian bourgeoisie for the same reason that he praises the French Jacobins: the consolidation of a single national-popular collective will in the form of one nation in one state. Despite his first-hand experience of the perils of national oppression in his native Sardinia, an oppression adequately documented in the writings on the Southern Question, Gramsci then praises the Jacobins for their energy and action in consolidating the French nation and state, choosing to ignore that this consolidation also took the form of a ruthless suppression of national and linguistic minorities.

The Jacobin slogan for a 'one and indivisible' republic, and the related zeal for the elimination of 'les patois' – Breton, Catalan, Occitan, Euzkera as well as other languages which vanished without trace – generated a ruthless repression exercised against those mainly landless peasant peoples who spoke a different language from the Parisian French. 'Aux Armes Citoyens!', was the battle cry against not only the nobility and reaction, but also those unfortunate national minorities who wished to maintain a separate language and cultural heritage. In Chapter 1 the pernicious effects of the Jacobin model on Marx and Engels' conceptualisation of the national phenomenon was discussed. It is sufficient only to recall the Jacobin *Report on the need to destroy rural dialects (patois) and universalise the use of the French language.* The net effect of the Jacobin policy was to create a tradition of intolerance and state centralisation which caused the almost total cultural obliteration of the non-Parisian-French speaking national minorities.[50]

To be fair, Gramsci shows some inconsistency on this issue. On the one hand, he argued (without elaborating) that for the Jacobins to compromise the slogan of 'a single and indivisible republic' to the demands of the Vendée was like 'committing suicide'.

> Except for certain marginal areas, where the national (and linguistic) differentiation was very great, the agrarian question proved stronger than the aspirations to local autonomy. Rural France accepted the hegemony of Paris.[51]

On the other hand, in the Italian case he gave signs of being aware of the ethnic plurality of the population of the Italian state, denouncing the drives towards centralisation of the Socialist Party. In a letter written in 1923 to *L'Unità*, he argued that Italy should become a 'Federal Republic of Peasants and Workers', and in 1925 he delivered a letter from the Krestintern[52] to the congress of the Sardinian Action Party (PSdA) which ended with the slogan 'Long Live the Sardinian Republic of Peasants and Workers in the Italian Soviet Federation!', and the Sardinian national slogan 'Forza Paris'.[53]

At the level of theory, however, Gramsci's work on the national question is primarily geared towards formulating an analysis of the process of consolidation of the cultural and political unity of a national state, in order to conceptualise the conditions for the formation of a national-popular collective will capable of leading the nationally united social formation into a stable socialist system. Within this conceptual framework there is little room for national and cultural-linguistic pluralism inside the boundaries of the state.

As we have seen, Gramsci attaches great importance to national culture. The historical specificity of the national community is the determinant of its cultural uniqueness. The capacity of the hegemonic grouping to lead the national community is crucially related to its ability to incorporate this national uniqueness into its world view, that is to say to constitute itself as the most complete expression of the identity of the national community. While for Gramsci the leading position in a hegemonic grouping is always played by an international fundamental class, the internal relations of a nation (state) are 'original' and 'unique'.[54] But from this emphasis on the national dimension, Gramsci distinguishes between national and nationalism, a distinction that probably emerged out of the specific conditions of fascist Italy. While half a century later it is no longer necessary to elaborate a conceptual distinction between nationalism and fascism, Gramsci's observation remains relevant. Criticising an article by Julien Benda in the journal *Nouvelles Littéraires*, repeating the question asked by an earlier writer: 'N'est-ce pas en se nationalisant qu'une littérature prend une signification plus universelle, un intérêt plus humainement général?',[55] Gramsci replies:

> For Benda, taste which is universal, is best served by being as particular as possible. But one thing is *to be particular*, another is to *preach particularism*. This is the mistake of nationalism, and on the basis of this mistake it often pretends to be universalist ... to be national is therefore different from being a nationalist. Goethe was a German 'national', Stendhal a French 'national', neither were 'nationalists'. An idea is not effectual if it is not expressed in some way, artistically, this is to say, in a particularistic form. But is wit particular insofar as it is national? Nationality is a primary particularity, but great writers particularise themselves again among their fellow nationals and this second particularisation is not an extension of the first. Renan, as Renan, is not at all a *necessary* consequence of French spirit; he is in relation to this spirit an original, *arbitrary* (as Bergson says) unpredictable event. Still Renan remains French, as man because he is man remains a mammal, but his value as that of man, resides precisely in his difference from the group into which he was born.[56]

For Gramsci, then, the critique of nationalism as an all embracing transcendental category cannot be based on an equally transcendental cosmopolitan (non-national) universalism. National locations are historically given attributes, but as such they say little about subjective individual characteristics. Thus far his observation is not questionable. However, Gramsci appears to imply that national culture and subjective individuality are unconnected; he reasons that ideas are national in form but their content transcends nationality. While at a high level of generalisation this may be correct (but, as will be shown, not for the reasons sustained by Gramsci), the form – or to be more precise the signifier – is not irrelevant to the condition of the signified or the referent. However, as contemporary post-structural linguistics remind us, relations between signifiers, signified and referents are not fixed; there is a constant flux through the subversion of boundaries between meaning and content. The fact that signifiers are unfixed does not mean that they are irrelevant to the condition of the signified. Consequently the expression of abstract ideas is not irrelevant to to the national-cultural conditions through which they are expressed, even if that connection is precarious and circumstantial and meanings are constantly subverted. It is this constant unfixity of meaning that explains the transcendentality of the ideas referred to by Gramsci, not any intrinsic, transcendental universal condition attached to them, as he seems to suggest.

At the same time, Gramsci acknowledges the different referential meaning in different languages of the concepts of national and popular, demonstrating a certain sensitivity for the historically conditioned subversion of meanings.

It must be noticed that in many languages 'national' and 'popular' are synonyms or almost (this is so in Russian, in German where 'volkisch' has a more intimate, racial meaning, the same as in the slavic languages in general; in French 'national' has a meaning in which the concept of 'popular' is already more politically elaborated, because it is linked to the concept of 'sovereignty'. Popular sovereignty and national sovereignty have the same value, or they had it in the past). In Italy, the term 'national' has a very restricted ideological meaning, which in any case does not coincide with 'popular', because in Italy intellectuals are remote from the people, this is to say, from the 'nation'. They are instead linked with a tradition of caste, which has not as yet been broken by a strong popular movement from below.[57]

Gramsci obviously was aware of the historical determination of the different forms of conceptualising the boundaries of the national community. An understanding of the specificity of national existence is clearly derived from the different ways of comprehending the relationship between the national and the popular, creating a conceptual space in which to encapsulate the political specificity of every national community. For Gramsci, the national-popular appears to be determined by both a universal dimension, in the form of the international mode of production and the class that leads the hegemonic grouping, and a particular dimension, in the form of the historical and cultural specificity that becomes the foundation of the historic bloc.

The question of whether Gramsci broke with the class

reductionism of the Marxist-Leninist tradition cannot be answered conclusively. It is, however, possible to say that his contribution to the development of Marxist theory is a set of analytical categories that enables us to devise a conceptual framework that breaks with class reductionism – but Gramsci himself fell short of this break. The notions of historical bloc and collective will permit a conceptualisation of the political arena outside the limitations of class determination, given that their configuration is not ultimately reducible to the determination of any of the fundamental forces in the process of production. This also allows a conceptualisation of the national phenomenon outside the restrictions of class reductionism in the form of the national-popular collective will, and an understanding of the heterogeneous forms of national existence at both the political and cultural levels. This two-dimensional understanding is limited, however, by Gramsci's commitment to a consolidation of a national state that provides the conditions for a process of expansive hegemony. Here, the leading force in every hegemonic situation is a fundamental class – the bourgeoisie or the proletariat – and the reasons for this ontological privilege have little to do with the conjunctural analysis, but are the direct result of an epistemologically defined process of class determination – the essence of class reductionism.[58]

So, the interpretation of the work of Gramsci could be located in either a class reductionist or a non-class-reductionist perspective, since both elements coexist (in a tense and contradictory way) in his work. In terms of the discussion on the national question, a class reductionist perspective makes some marginal advances in relation to the conceptual and methodological achievements and problems of the Marxist-Leninist tradition. The analysis is focused on Western-style democratic states, and the strategic importance of the national arena for the avant garde party is duly established. But the connection of the working class to the nation continues to be an insurmountable problem.

However, a non-class reductionist interpretation offers the possibility of conceptualising the centrality of the national arena in defining the field of political activity for both the working class and the hegemonic grouping. The strategy for the construction of a new historical bloc is designed to convert this historical bloc into the national community, so that it could be the basis for an integral state and an expanding hegemonic process. But this last aspect points towards one of the most important limitations of the Gramscian discussion of the national question. The national community is significant only insofar as it forms a vehicle for the creation of a new political subjectivity, the national-popular collective will. The national phenomenon is important only to the extent that it becomes the basis for the formation of a cohesive national community capable of sustaining a national state. The Leninist traces are evident. Gramsci's conceptualisation of the national-popular is a decisive and momentous advance on Lenin's theory of the right of nations to self-determination because of its novel conceptualisation of culture and the intellectuals, but at the same time it remains trapped in the Leninist bias towards statism – the achievement and consolidation of a single state encompassing one single national community. If the non-class reductionist perspective is accepted, Gramsci achieved a significant break with key aspects of class reductionism, at the cost of giving the political arena a privileged position.

The logic of the Gramscian theory is to conceptualise the multidimensionality of the political arena, and its ultimate goal is to construct a stable foundation for a historical bloc that sustains a socialist and democratic, but not necessarily plural hegemonic grouping. The logic of political unity requires an organic fusion of the elements of the historical bloc, which in most cases means the assimilation of the culture of the minorities[59] into that of the majorities. Pluralism is lost in the process of organic fusion. Thus traces of Marxist-Leninism are to be found in Gramsci's blindness to those aspects of the national phenomenon that are not connected with the urge to form a cohesive national state, as it is in the case of the ethno-national minorities that exist in every Western state. This blindness to pluralism is evident in Gramsci's essay with the suggestive title: 'Hegemony of Western Culture over the whole World Culture'.

> Even if one admits that other cultures have had an importance and significance in the process of 'hierarchical' unification of world civilisation (and this should be admitted without question), they have had a universal value only in so far as they have become constituent elements of European culture, which is the only historically and concretely universal culture – in so far, that is, as they have contributed to the process of European thought and been assimilated by it.[60]

Even Antonio Gramsci – 'Antonu su Gobbu' from the backwoods – could not transcend the Western European narcissistic fascination. No theory of the national phenomenon could be sensitive to the diversified aspects of national existence while remaining trapped by the 'insights' of the quotation above. We will now turn to a Marxist theory of the national phenomenon that offers a better understanding of the pluralistic dimensions of national existence: that of Otto Bauer.

5

The Background to Bauer's Theory: Multinationalism and neo-Kantianism

The acute nationalities conflict in the turn-of-the-century Habsburg empire was clearly a crucial factor in directing Otto Bauer's reluctant attention to the national question, as he himself acknowledges in the preface to the 1907 edition of his monumental work.[1] While the nature of the national problem faced by the socialist movement in Austria was clearly a decisive factor in motivating Bauer to conceptualise the national question, the theoretical appraisal that resulted from this conjunctural analysis transcends the specific configuration of the Austrian situation to become a major contribution to the general development of Marxist theory in this area.

In order to discuss Bauer's ideas it is necessary first to situate historically and contextualise the nature of his momentous but partial break with economism. In this chapter we will evaluate the three most important historical and theoretical influences on Bauer's analysis of the national phenomenon: the nationalities problem in the Austro-Hungarian empire, the nationalities programme of the All Austrian Socialist Party (Gesamtpartei), and the Austro-Marxist response to the neo-Kantian intellectual offensive against orthodox Marxism.

The Nationalities Problem in the Twilight of Austro-Hungary

On the eve of World War One, the Austro-Hungarian empire was a dual monarchy with a total population of 53 million of more than 15 different nationalities, occupying an area smaller than either South Australia, Texas or the Iberian peninsula.[2] In 1866 the Habsburg empire was militarily defeated by Prussia and as a result was decentralised through the Ausgleich or compromise of 1867, which remained the constitutional basis of the multinational empire until its dissolution in 1918. This agreement stipulated that the empire should be divided into two autonomous halves: one had the curious name of the kingdoms and countries represented in parliament[3] (Austria) and the other was the lands of the crown of St Stephen (Hungary).[4]

While foreign affairs, defence and finance were common concerns, both parts of the empire had a very large degree of autonomy, best exemplified by the fact that there was no joint parliament. This situation in effect consolidated the domination of the most centrally located ethno-national community in each of the two parts, the Austro-Germans and the Magyars. The former side was simply referred to as Austria and the latter half as Hungary. Karl Stadler argues that the main settlement was paralleled by minor compromises which resulted in a complicated mosaic of ethno-national and class alliances. Otto Bauer summarised the position thus:

> The 'Compromise' is an understanding among the ruling classes of the historic nations (German, Magyar, Poles, Croats), against the mass of their fellow nationals (whom the curial franchise excludes from power) and against the newer nations (Czechs, Slovenes, and Ruthenes in Austria, and Slovaks, Serbs and Rumanians in Hungary).[5]

While the Austro-Germans and the Magyars were each the most numerous nationality in their respective parts of the empire, they were far from being the majority of the population. In 1910 the Austro-Germans formed 23.9 per cent of the total population of the dual monarchy and 35.6 per cent of the population of Austria only. The Magyars comprised 20.2 per cent of all the people in the dual monarchy and were the largest single group in Hungary, but not the majority. The Czechs, who, according to Bauer, lost out in the constitutional arrangement, were the second largest national community in Austria, with 23 per cent of the population there and 12.6 per cent of that of the dual monarchy as a whole.[6]

To strengthen their political grip, the Austro-German rulers conceded administrative autonomy to the Poles of Austrian Galicia. State officials in that crownland were to be Poles and the Polish language was to be used instead of German in Galician schools.[7] This situation alienated the Yiddish-speaking Jews and Ruthenians (Ukrainians) of Galicia, who in 1900 together constituted 54 per cent of the total Galician population.[8] This concession to the Poles also deeply antagonised the Czech nationalist leadership, since the main demand of their movement was to recover for Bohemia the status of historical kingdom (Staatrecht), with a similar degree of political and national autonomy as the Magyars had in Hungary or the Austro-Germans had in Austria.

The coalition between Austro-Germans and Poles effectively neutralised the political influence of the Czechs. The problem was also complicated by the fact that within Bohemia there was a large German-speaking minority, while a substantial number of Czechs resided outside its historical boundaries. The Czech nationalists resented the German presence in Bohemia, considering the Bohemian Germans as colonists, even if their presence in Bohemia dated back several centuries. On the other hand, the Bohemian pan-Germanic (Deutschnational) activists considered themselves as the 'Herrenvolk' (master race) and according to Pauley regarded the Czech language as 'a mere dialect suitable only for peasants and servants'.[9] The result was that the Czech nationalists were often blocking and filibustering legislation in the Austrian parliament, and the pan-Germans were equally bent on obstructing the provincial diet in Prague. When in 1897 it was decided that all civil servants in Bohemia should be bilingual, bitter complaints were voiced by the Germans who felt discriminated against by this legislation as a large number of Czechs were conversant in German, but not vice versa.

Moreover this decree on bilingualism in Bohemia rekindled similar demands by other national communities, particularly the Ukrainians in Galicia.[10] To complicate matters further, towards the end of the century Austria experienced a process of rapid industrialisation and related social change. By the turn of the century, the industries of lower Austria and Bohemia reached a stage of development similar to those in Britain and Germany. Austrian coal production increased at a phenomenal rate and on the eve of World War One the country stood in sixth place in the world production of iron.[11] During 1903–13 the rate of industrial growth was higher than in Great Britain or Germany at the same period, but this apparently high rate of growth concealed greatly differential industrial development, which coincided with a long process of agricultural decline, causing a large internal migration to newly industrialised areas, in particular to parts of Bohemia and to the capital, Vienna. This process exacerbated further the unresolved ethno-national tensions, for it diluted the territorial concentration of the conflicting national communities.

It would, however, be incorrect to say that industrialisation was the cause of national tensions since the difficulties pre-dated the process of industrialisation. The upheavals of differential development only aggravated a problem that already existed. The

Bohemian case provides a good example of this. In 1851 in Bohemia there were five towns with over 10,000 inhabitants; by the turn-of-the-century there were forty-three. This process of urbanisation and industrialisation had, predictably, a profound effect on the ethno-cultural composition of Bohemia.

Early in the 19th century, Germans and Czechs lived side by side in sharply defined and separate settlements. The Czechs held with the exception of the towns, the central districts; the Germans surrounded them in an arc running through the border territories of Bohemia and Moravia. That situation changed with the growth of the local industries which made no national discrimination in its demand for labour; it was calculated that in 1900 Czech labour was three times as mobile as German. In the Czech districts, the urban population became mainly Czech, and the balance started changing even in the German border areas.[12]

In Vienna, population changes were equally dramatic. In 1857 the population of the capital was 476,220; in 1910 it was 2,031,498. In other words, the population increased more than four times in fifty-three years.[13] As Oxaal argues, economic expansion and liberal democratic reform were at the root of this massive migration, which had its symbolic expression in the destruction of the inner-city walls in 1858. With the migration of peoples from all four corners of the empire, Vienna was converted into a lively and cosmopolitan city. Towards the end of the nineteenth century, the city experienced an intellectual, artistic and aesthetic development with few comparisons in the history of European culture. The names of Strauss, Schoenberg and Mahler in music; Gustav Klimt and Oskar Kokoschka in painting; Otto Wagner and Adolf Loos in architecture and town planning; S. Zweig and R. Musil in literature; Sigmund Freud,[14] the founder of psychoanalysis, Ludwig Wittgenstein and Ernst Mach in philosophy; Otto Bauer and Max Adler in Marxist theory – give just a brief indication of the extraordinary legacy of intellectual and cultural diversity of turn-of-the-century Vienna.[15]

But turn-of-the-century Vienna also witnessed the erosion of the progressive values which paved the way for this extraordinary cultural renaissance. The development of the multi-ethnic and multi-cultural environment that made possible this cultural and intellectual development was deeply resented by conservative pan-Germans incapable of adapting to the changing pace of life and nostalgically yearning for a 'pure' German past. This nostalgic backlash took the form of bitter controversies over schools instructing in languages other than German (particularly Czech) and over bilingual notices and place names. Viktor Adler, the veteran socialist leader and founding member of the All Austrian Socialist Party, was moved to say that, 'In Austria, the question of names of railway stations had become one of principle of the most important kind'.[16]

For the pan-Germans, the presence of ethnic minorities in 'their' Vienna was a constant irritation and a source of psychological insecurity.[17] Their frustrations and nostalgia were displaced in the form of a pathological hatred of the less cohesive and politically weakest ethnic minority: the Viennese Jews. The multicultural environment of Vienna moved a young pan-German from the Austrian provinces, Adolf Hitler, to say: '*Deutschösterreich muss wieder zurück zum grossen deutschen Mutterlande ... Gleiches Blut gehört in ein gemeinsames Reich*'.[18]

This sense of ethnic insecurity in relation to both the multicultural environment of late imperial Vienna, and the then recently united German state, was to become later, in the words of Stadler, 'the original home of a particularly virulent and cruel brand of Nazism'.[19] Long before the emergence of the Nazi party, however, Austrian politics witnessed the emergence of a nostalgic and racist party in the Christian Social Movement,[20] which was to become the main political rival of the socialist Gesamtpartei, the only truly multinational political organisation in late imperial Austria. The virulent anti-semitism which characterised the Christian Social Movement was, according to Boyer,

> an exceedingly complex defense mechanism against unwarranted social change, but one which functioned in very different ways depending upon the actor group involved. It was not the only issue which brought ultimate victory to Lueger and his party in 1896, even if it did provide a useful initial principle of organisation and cohesion in the early days of the movement.[21]

As Oxaal's study shows, the Jewish population of Vienna was culturally, occupationally and residentially diverse. There was a profound cultural gap between the intellectual and German-speaking strata from which major leaders of the Socialist Party emerged, and the recently arrived Yiddish-speaking traditional Jews from the Eastern crownlands, Galicia and Bukovina. There was no Jewish ghetto as such, Jews lived in different parts of the city, and in occupational terms,

> For every one Jew so employed [as money-dealers] in Austria in 1900 it appears that four Catholics were engaged in a trade which was fundamental to the perpetuation of the Jewish stereotype ... The data on Jewish occupations in Vienna, far from suggesting that they were unique and unrepresentative indicate that many of Jews held positions which were typical of the occupational structure of the city.[22]

In other words, Jewish homogeneity only existed in the minds of the Viennese anti-semites and the emerging Zionist movement.[23] The fact that a large number of prominent leaders of the Austrian Socialist Party were of Jewish extraction (including Bauer himself), had an impact in the contradictory anti-semitic stereotyping. At times Jews were depicted as greedy capitalists and on other occasions as godless revolutionary socialists.[24] Anti-semitism has not disappeared in contemporary Austria even if the Jewish population is very small; the Waldheim affair is eloquent proof of this.[25]

The young Hitler detested the multicultural environment of turn-of-the-century Vienna. He often referred to it as 'Rassenbabylon' and 'Stadt der Blutschande' (City of incest), which, Stadler comments, shows Hitler's lack of competence on the subtleties of the German language, since the term 'Blutschande' (incest) denotes the very opposite of what he meant – 'the shameful pollution of German blood with foreign'.[26]

The Specificity of Austrian Socialism

Given this situation of intense ethnic hatred and national confrontation, it becomes clear why the Socialist Party had to devote a great deal of intellectual and political resources to dealing with the problem. An added difficulty for the Austrian socialist movement was that (as was shown earlier) Marx and Engels developed, in the course of the 1848 revolutions, a crude, misinformed and uncompromising stance on the nationalities problem of the Habsburg empire. They professed, to put it mildly, some antipathy towards the Czechs, Croats and other Slavic national communities lumped together in an imaginary unit called Southern Slavs. They considered that the cultural identity of these peoples was not 'worth surviving' the democratic revolutions of 1848. The solutions offered by Marx and Engels to these unfortunate peoples was either to be totally assimilated into the 'superior' German or Magyar nations with 'democracy as compensation', or to be 'obliterated' in the course of the democratic struggle.[27]

The paradox facing Austrian socialists at this time was that the solutions to the nationalities problem in the Habsburg empire proposed by Marx and Engels circa 1848 were strikingly similar to the positions held by their bitter opponents, the pan-German movement. A radical reappraisal of the nationalities problem in Austria was required and was initially achieved, as described below, in the party congresses of Vienna-Wimberg and Brno (Brünn).

Socialism in Austria did not begin with the formation of the Gesamtpartei. In German Austria the socialist movement grew out of the 'Arbeiterbildungsverein': societies for the cultural improvement of the working class. This characteristic of the embryonic socialist movement had, according to Rabinbach, a profound impact on the subsequent development of the party, since it never abandoned its pedagogical and educational role.[28] At the same time, a number of socialist organisations emerged among the Czech workers and other non-German national communities, who were nevertheless suspicious of the German socialist organisation, given existing national antagonisms. The process of rapid industrialisation experienced by several Austrian regions provided fertile ground for the formation of an All Austrian Socialist Party, but nationalist and ideological dissensions, coupled with repressive measures of the Austrian regime, only permitted the formation of a united party in Hainfeld, a sleepy village south of Vienna, in 1889, and this thanks to the intense efforts of Viktor Adler.[29] The Socialist Party was defined as whole Austrian (Gesamtösterreischen), or, as it was later called, Gesamtpartei (whole party), in order to indicate the multinational nature of the organisation. With the possible exception of the army and bureaucracy, the Gesamtpartei was the only truly multinational entity in the final years of the Austro-Hungarian empire. It was also, according to Kann, the only example in Austrian history of the emergence of a major political party that came into existence beyond national loyalties.[30] In the course of its first decade of existence the party became an important parliamentary force, after the abolition of restrictive ordinances and the establishment of universal male suffrage in 1896.[31]

From the moment of its formation, however, the party had to cope with the difficult problems of ethno-national divisions within its ranks. In particular, the Czech socialists resented the high profile of the Germans within the party and demanded the establishment of their own trade union commission.[32] Initially the demands of the Czech sections of the party were resisted by the respected leader Viktor Adler, but by 1897 the situation became unsustainable and the party as a whole began to recognise that the resolution of the national question could not be postponed until the victory of the working class; therefore there was a need to delimit clearly the position of the party vis a vis the national question.[33] The taxing nationalities problem of late imperial Austria impelled the party to relinquish the economic reductionism prevalent in most turn-of-the-century socialist parties, and to adopt a position more sensitive to national demands.

In 1897 the biennial congress of the Gesamtpartei took place in the Wimberg Hotel in Vienna. Following Czech demands, the party decided to transform itself into a federative organisation of six national parties (Ukrainian, Czech, Polish, German, Italian and Slovene), with a common executive committee.[34] This new organisational arrangement gave way to an intense and prolonged discussion of the theory and strategy of the nationalities question, which culminated two years later in the biennial historic 1899 congress in the Moravian city of Brno (Brünn).

At this congress, an unusually thorough theoretical and strategic debate on the national question took place, culminating in a number of unprecedented theoretical and organisational decisions which subsequently sent shock waves through the international socialist movement. The protocols of the conference make fascinating reading,[35] since in terms of the economic reductionist logic then prevalent in the socialist movement it made no sense to devote almost the entire congress of a working class party to discussing the national question. However, given the political circumstances of Austria this was the main topic of the conference, and the discussion represented a serious attempt to understand the political, cultural and theoretical dimensions of the national phenomenon. The tension between economic reductionism and the wish to come to grips with the elusive national problem is best exemplified in the opening speech of the official speaker on behalf of the executive committee of the Gesamtpartei, J. Seliger. He initially argued that it was an 'apparent contradiction' for the congress of 'International Social Democracy in Austria' to try to find a 'theoretical solution' to the nationalities problem in the multinational empire,[36] but he then went on to argue that the party's interest in the nationalities question was wholly legitimate. It was 'the workers who suffered most as a result of national strife', and those conditions of national strife 'prevented the workers from uniting against the bourgeoisie'.[37] In the congress itself there were three detectable positions on the national question.

The first was the class reductionist position maintained by Prähauser, a delegate from Salzburg, the most ethnically homogeneous German city in Austria. Prähauser supported Rosa Luxemburg's position that the origin of national strife is economic, a dispute among the different sections of the bourgeoisie, and as such is of no importance for the workers' movement which must concentrate on class issues. He was supported by the Italian delegate from Trieste, Gerin, who argued that the only task of social democracy is to 'continue the class struggle' and not to indulge in discussions on the national question. On the language issue, Prähauser argued that German would continue to be the language of 'culture and communication' regardless of the opinions of the 'Czech comrades'.[38] This, however, was a minority view and of no consequence for the final resolution.

The second was the view sustained by the Slovenian delegate Etbin Kristan from Trieste. Kristan argued for the complete separation of the concept of nation from any form of territorial organisation – 'The executive demands autonomous national territories, we demand national autonomy regardless of territory'[39] – a position almost identical to that expounded by Karl Renner under the pseudonym of Synopticus in a booklet published in Vienna that same year.[40] This position was known as the personality principle;[41] it demanded the organisation of national communities regardless of the place of residence, with a strong emphasis on cultural institutions, coupled with non-national forms of territorial organisation. It was on the whole supported by delegates from ethno-national communities that were territorial minorities. Also, according to its proposer, this form of national organisation accounted for the widespread geographical mobility of workers within the boundaries of the Austrian state, resulting from the process of differential industrialisation. This viewpoint was influential beyond the borders of Austria. It was later adopted by the Jewish Bund in Czarist Russia, since it best suited the minority status of Jewish communities. It was the principle of national cultural autonomy, so severely attacked by Lenin and Stalin, who wrongly believed that it was the final resolution of the socialist congress at Brno.

Viktor Adler opposed the motion, arguing that while he believed it was a 'very ingenious idea', the practicalities of implementing such a complex two-tier organisational principle would be a bureaucratic nightmare. He also believed that the resolution presented by the Slovenian delegate was contradictory, because it demanded a federal state and federalism could only by organised on the basis of territory. The motion was put to a vote and rejected.[42]

The third position on the national issue at the congress was presented by the executive committee of the Gesamtpartei, which demanded, in essence, that Austria become a democratic federation of autonomous national states. This was the position that was finally adopted, after the incorporation of a number of amendments introduced by the Czech delegates concerning the German language. The Czechs objected to the original executive proposal that German should be considered the common language out of practical necessity, because they were unwilling to grant any special status to German. The final resolution read:

1   Austria should be transformed into a democratic federation of nationalities (Nationalitätenbundestaat).
2   The historic Crownlands shall be replaced by nationally delimited, self-governing areas in each of which legislation and administration should be entrusted to national chambers elected on the basis of universal suffrage.
3   All self-governing regions of one and the same nation shall jointly form a single national union which shall manage the national affairs on the basis of complete autonomy.
4   The right of minorities should be protected by a special law.
5   We do not recognise any national privilege and therefore we reject the demand for an official language. Parliament will decide as to whether and in what degree a common language is necessary.[43]

From this it is possible to see how Lenin and Stalin were so wrong about the Brno programme. The decision of the conference was to campaign for the formation of an autonomous and multinational federal state, rather than to implement the concept of national cultural autonomy. (Ironically, the Brno programme appears to be closer to the letter of the Soviet constitution than to any other existing form of state organisation.)

The source of the Bolshevik confusion was the so-called programme of national cultural autonomy. This was based on the minority motion of the Slovene delegate Kristan, and was masterminded by Karl Renner, who with Otto Bauer was later recognised as the main theoretician of the national question for the Gesamtpartei. In spite of the programmatic similarities, there are a number of significant differences between Bauer and Renner. Not only did Bauer belong to the left wing of the party, while Renner aligned himself with those closest to a revisionist position, but Renner's project was directed towards conceptualising the constitutional rights of national communities in multinational states, while Bauer's work was directed towards the historical and theoretical conceptualisation of the national question.[44] Renner only officially joined the socialist party after the Brno congress, and because he was a civil servant barred from political activity he published his early works under the pseudonyms of Synopticus and Rudolf Springler. In his book *The Right of Nations to Self-Determination* (not to be confused with Lenin's pamphlet of the same title) he considered it his main task:

> to explore and present this internal state order and supranational order of law, which should replace the political struggle of the nationalities for power with the orderly procedure of court and parliamentary transactions ... [the purpose is to] materialise the legal concept of nation, first within the narrow framework of the nationalities state, and thus present an example for the future national order to mankind.[45]

Renner's main object was not to conceptualise the nation as such but, as Agnelli argues, to find a solution to the constitutional problems of Austria on the basis of a strictly federalist position, carefully separating the territorial state from national identities.[46] At the congress of Brno, his ideas were supported only by a minority.

In summarising the positions of pre-Bauer Austrian socialism on the national question, it is possible to say that the class reductionist Marxist analysis prevalent in the socialist world of that time found its echo among the leaders of the Austrian socialist movement. But the deep-rooted national confrontations of the dual monarchy and their paralysing impact on the Austro-Hungarian political life, together with the profound impact of nationalist ideals on large sections of the socialist rank and file, forced the leadership to move out of the traditional socialist terrain of the political dimension of the class struggle to the theoretically virgin and politically unknown national arena. This was done reluctantly, to judge from the utterances of a number of leading Austrian socialists. There was a kind of impatience, almost an angry reaction to their bad fortune in comparison with other more fortunate socialist parties, particularly in Germany. The Austrian socialists deeply resented that they were obliged to devote their precious intellectual and revolutionary energies to a problem which, in their perception, had little to do with the stated goals of working class politics. As N. Leser argues,

> Austrian socialists like all other, were primarily concerned with the emancipation of the working class, but their day-to-day political work compelled them to acknowledge the overwhelming importance of the nationality issue within the context of the Habsburg empire. To the bulk of the population these questions were at least as real and of equal immediate concern as the tactics of the class war.[47]

There is a profound irony in this. From the Austrian Socialist Party's reluctant engagement in an intellectual and political debate with nationalism, and from their no less reluctant but concerted effort in coming to grips with the national phenomenon – instead of the more 'normal' issues of working-class politics – a theoretical and political analysis of unparalleled sophistication emerged. While the conditions of combined and uneven development produced in Czarist Russia innovative ways to conceptualise the political struggle in the Marxist tradition, the political nightmare of the national struggles in the collapsing dual monarchy produced some of the most theoretically sophisticated Marxist discussions of the national question. This was not the result of unqualified support for the national causes, as the Bolshevik detractors were quick to argue – there was, in fact, no love lost between the Austrian socialists and nationalist movements. Rather the socialist party of Austria (Gesamtpartei) realised that without tackling the national question head on, without developing a thorough political and intellectual understanding of the national phenomenon – an understanding that was so conspicuously absent in the classical Marxist tradition – they were condemned to political paralysis and oblivion under the rising tide of nationalism.

In coming to grips with this problem, Austrian socialism prepared the ground for the development of a theory of the nation in the work of Otto Bauer, a theory of the nation that transcended the political and intellectual limitations of the nationalist bickering of the decaying Habsburg monarchy to become the patrimony of the universal heritage of the Marxist tradition. In order to develop a theory that encapsulated the multidimensionality of the national phenomenon, Bauer had implicitly to break with the fundamental canons of economism. In the introduction to his work he argues:

The national community is one of the most complex social phenomena, with a vast array of different social manifestations. For
this reason, to understand how membership of the national
community shapes the will of the working class on struggle, it
becomes essential to consider the problem from different angles.
If we do not wish to relinquish such a task, we must risk ventur-
ing beyond our narrow disciplinary boundaries.[48]

It is clear that, for Bauer, the political impossibility of locating the
multidimensional national phenomenon in terms of the traditional politics of turn-of-the-century Marxist socialist movement,
as well as the intellectual impossibility of conceptualising this
elusive phenomenon in terms of the canons of Marxist orthodoxy,
created the condition for a decisive but never explicitly acknowledged break with all forms of economism. In order to understand
the intellectual conditions for the development of this break, a
brief discussion of the Austro-Marxist debate with neo-Kantianism
is required.

The Theoretical Impact of Austro-Marxism[49]

The theoretical development of Austro-Marxism was another interesting paradox taking place in late imperial Vienna. For as Sully
argues,[50] in Vienna a curious combination of cultural and intellectual creativity symbiotically coexisted with an obsolete and decaying social and political order. Bauer locates the emergence of the
Austro-Marxist tradition in the response developed by a young
generation of intellectuals and political activists to the theoretical
criticism of classical Marxism in Austro-Hungary at this time.[51] In
this sense it is very important not to confuse Austro-Marxism with
the Austrian Socialist Party, since the development of the two does
not coincide. During the formative years of the party the most
influential current of thought was Kautsky's orthodox interpretation of classical Marxism, a position shared by the majority of
socialist parties affiliated to the Second International.[52] The emergence of Austro-Marxism as a distinct intellectual approach within
the Marxist tradition must be understood equally as a generational
reaction against the ossification of Kautsky's orthodoxy; as a critical reaction to Bernstein's revisionism and the powerful intellectual critique of orthodox Marxism from the neo-Kantian ethical
socialists of the Marburg school, and as a response to the criticism
of Marxist economic theory from the Viennese Marginalist school

of economics. The leading Austro-Marxists grew up in the socialist student movement of the university of Vienna, from where they engaged in the political activities of the Austrian Social Democratic Party.[53] Bauer locates the origin of the school in the activities of

> A group of young Austrian comrades active in scholarly research ... They were united not so much by a specific political orientation as by the particular nature of their scholarly work. They had all grown up in a period when men such as Stammler, Windelband, and Rickert were attacking Marxism with philosophical arguments; hence they were obliged (felt the need) to engage in the controversy with the representatives of modern philosophical trends ... living in the old Austria rent by national struggles, they had to learn *to apply the Marxist conception of history to very complicated phenomena which defied analysis by any superficial or schematic application of the Marxist method.* Thus there developed within Marxism a narrower (spiritual) intellectual community (Geistesgemeinschaft) which has been called 'Austro-Marxism'. This name is intended precisely to distinguish its members on the one side from the (previous) generation of Marxists represented above all by Kautsky, Mehring and Cunow, and on the other side, from contemporary schools of Marxism in other countries, above all the Russian and the Dutch schools. (emphasis added)[54]

The Austro-Marxists operated as an influential theoretical and political grouping within the party up to World War One. After the war Otto Bauer became the general secretary of the party and the members of the group took different positions in the continuing debates within the socialist movement.

In 1903 Max Adler and other members of the group constituted, in the educational tradition of the Austrian Socialist Party, the 'Zukunft-Verein', an educational academy for workers. The Austro-Marxist group also began to hold regular meetings in the Café Central. In 1907 Bauer and Renner founded the journal *Der Kampf* to give expression to the innovative views of the Austro-Marxist 'Geistesgemeinschaft'. The publication of *Der Kampf* also denotes a political and theoretical distancing from the editorial policies of Kautsky and the *Neue Zeit*, since all members of the group had been regular contributors to that journal. This distancing was later to be reflected in Kautsky's polemics with Bauer over the national question. Above all, however, it was in the Marx-Studien series, edited by Max Adler and R. Hilferding, that most influential works for the theoretical development of Marxism were published. In volume 1 Max Adler's *Causality and Teleology* and Karl Renner's *Social Functions of Juridical Institutions* were published; volume 2 was Bauer's *Nationalities Question*; volume 3 was Hilferding's *Finance Capital*; volume 4 was Adler's *The Marxist Conceptualisation of the State*. What characterises Austro-Marxism is not so much a homogeneous approach to the development of Marxist theory, but a concerted attempt to tackle difficult theoretical and political issues that defied monocausal or one-dimensional explanations.

The second important characteristic of Austro-Marxism was that it attempted to engage in a serious debate with non-Marxist political and philosophical schools, such as the Austrian Marginalist school of economics and the neo-Kantian philosophical tradition. The third characteristic was its rejection at the political level of the dichotomy reform–revolution as exhausting all categories of political activity. It is possible to see in Austro-Marxism a discussion of the complexities of the political arena which necessarily leads to a break with class reductionism, and which is only paralleled in the Marxist theory in the work of Gramsci.[55] As will be shown below, the debate with the ethical socialism of the revisionists and socialist neo-Kantians was central in this endeavour. As Ananiadis argues:

> What constitutes the originality of Austro-Marxism is the supercession of the theoretical configuration (economism, instrumentalism) that informed the themes of pre war debates and fixed their terms in oppositional couplets (reform/revolution, parliamentary democracy/dictatorship of the proletariat). It is this restructuring of the theoretical terrain that made it possible for the Austro-Marxists, in the light of the new experiences of the labour movement, to pose the problem of the relation between socialism and democracy in novel terms.[56]

The Austro-Marxist debate with neo-Kantianism was crucial in providing critical categories of analysis which permitted Bauer to develop the novel conceptualisation of the national phenomenon developed in his book on the national question. In many ways, Adler's vigorous debate with neo-Kantianism in *Causality and Teleology*[57] paved the way for the conceptual framework of Bauer's discussion. To contextualise Adler's arguments, it is necessary to review briefly the neo-Kantian criticisms of classical Marxism.

The Neo-Kantian Critique of Marxism and Adler's Response

The turn of the century witnessed a powerful intellectual and political attack on classical Marxism. The key characteristic of this attack was that it came not from reactionary forces but, on the contrary, from groups that were in part genuinely interested in socialism and saw in the socialist idea a desirable political project. Within the organisational forms of German socialism, Bernstein's revisionism challenged the central tenets of historical materialism,[58] and at a more sophisticated level, outside the organisational framework of the socialist movement, the works of the ethical socialists of the neo-Kantian Marburg school[59] also emerged as an influential critique.

The neo-Kantian tradition emerged in Germany in the late 1880s. The movement grew rapidly in size, to become the 'nouvelle vogue' of German philosophy and the basis for philosophical training in German universities. The different schools in this tradition had little in common besides a reaction against irrationalism and materialism, and the idea that philosophy could acquire a scientific status if it returned to the methodological premises of Immanuel Kant. After World War One, the movement rapidly declined, defeated in part by the emerging tide of romanticism and other critics of rationalism.

In terms of the critique of Marxism and the Austro-Marxist response, the Marburg school and the so-called Southwestern or Baden school developed the most influential arguments. While most members of the Marburg school professed a form of ethical socialism which made them sympathetic with some of the goals but not the practice of the socialist movement, this was not the case with the Baden school. The latter, however, professed a greater interest in the historical and cultural sciences than other branches of neo-Kantianism, and were a major influence on Max Weber and his sociological tradition. This made the encounter with Austro-Marxism unavoidable.

The Marburg school was initiated by Hermann Cohen and his disciples, P. Natorp, R. Stammler – whose work is discussed by Adler and Bauer – and E. Cassirer. Following the Kantian tradition, they understood history and politics as a process of education guided by reason and the moral idea of 'free men' exercising rights and responsibilities in a constitutional state.[60] They were bourgeois humanists and rationalists, and therefore opposed to violent revolutions, believing in human 'good nature' and reformability.

The group proposed a form of democratic evolutionary socialism and as such had a certain appeal to revisionist intellectuals. Cohen's work was directed to prevent the subordination of consciousness to what he called undifferentiated experience and to protect the 'free individual' from all forms of 'monism and determinism'[61] of which historical materialism was one of its most important forms. He believed that truth was always in agreement with reason and that the laws of reason are independent from experience. As Willey argues, 'being' is transformed into the problem of validity, metaphysics is replaced by logic, and the realm of being is replaced by the realm of values.[62] Cohen's theory of knowledge is the core of his humanism because the conditions for producing general human culture are found in logic. According to his student, E. Cassirer, what distinguishes critical thought from dogmatic thought, for Cohen, is the fact that the former never expresses itself in a merely static way. It is a 'living and dynamic effort that must always be prepared for a new start'. Thought is not 'gegeben' (given) but 'aufgegeben' (propounded). It is not an immovable centre of our intellectual universe, but a continual process and endeavour.[63]

Both Marburg and Baden neo-Kantians agreed on the priority of the ethical 'ought' over the phenomenal 'is'. One of Cohen's most influential disciples, Rudolf Stammler, became a leading legal philosopher in the German world and his philosophy of law was criticised by Adler and Bauer. For Stammler, ethical philosophy begins with the Kantian separation of 'is' and 'ought', but he argues that the goals of the 'ought' are no less real because they cannot be known in experience. They are like 'the polar star that guides the mariner'.[64] Willey argues that the neo-Kantians went beyond Kant by giving ethical ideas a 'quasi-ontological status'.

For Cohen, moral law has two meanings: the idea of humanity and the idea of socialism. In sharp distinction to Marxist socialism, Cohen argued that these two ideas have no determinate content since they possess the character of purpose. Humanity and socialism belong to the 'ought', they exist as a mission for 'man's moral will'. The essence of socialism is to be found in the integrity of persons and their purposeful role in unfolding moral order. 'Society itself is a moral idea' is the reforming guide and principle of world history. Socialism thus becomes, in the Kantian fashion, a postulate of practical reason, indispensable to the coexistence of humans in industrial societies.

The discrepancy between social reality and moral existence is thus only overcome through the aim of achieving socialism.[65] Cohen's profound divergences from Marxism thus become apparent. He and the neo-Kantians in general deplored what they called 'Marx monism', since historical materialism ignores the all-important separation between the 'is' and the 'ought'. Since in orthodox Marxism human beings do not strive for ethical goals, but act on behalf of their class interests, Marxism represents for the neo-Kantians a 'flat denial of moral freedom', an odious anathema to their core values. For Natorp, a disciple of Cohen, 'Socialism cannot be produced by fiat'; it is only through spiritual and social education aimed towards the 'free' development of the individual spirit that socialism will be achieved. In a clear reference to avant-gardist theories, Natorp argued that the building of socialism cannot be the monopoly of any special elite but it is a process involving the organic community, of which each individual is an integral part.[66]

Cassirer described Cohen's rejection of Marxism in a way that is highly representative of the Marburg school's general critique of historical materialism:

He [Cohen] had the deepest sympathy for the working class; he was aware of its needs and he defended its claims. In this respect he was always a 'socialist', even at a time in which a profession of socialism was very dangerous at a German university. But he could never adopt an 'orthodox' socialism. His whole philosophy was in strongest opposition to the fundamental views of Marxism, to 'economic materialism.' 'Who could ever have thought', he remarked in one of his papers, 'that the great political party which fights out the social problem in all its consequences, should regard materialism as its true basis and principal dogma? *This program and this party grew from the soil of idealism.* Historical Materialism is the strongest contradiction to that ethical idealism in which socialism has both its theoretical and historical roots.'[67] (emphasis added)

This criticism of orthodox Marxism had, in spite of claims to the contrary by Kautsky, a genuine appeal to many Marxists, given that the Marburg neo-Kantian tradition hoisted the banner of social justice in what it vaguely defined as ethical socialism. This was particularly the case among those disenchanted by the lack of fulfilment of the epiphenomenalist prophecy of the impending and necessary collapse of capitalism. True, Marburg neo-Kantians were denounced as 'petty bourgeois ideologues' and 'metaphysical idealists', but it was only in the works of the Austro-Marxists that a serious counter-criticism beyond stereotypes and cliches was attempted. [68]

In sharp contrast with the Marburg school, the Baden or Southwestern neo-Kantian school had almost no interest in concrete socialist problems and their involvement in political issues was kept to a minimum. In spite of this, their methodological discussions had a substantial impact on the future development of history and the social sciences, particularly in major methodological and epistemological issues that subsequently became the point of departure for the Weberian tradition in sociology. The school's founder was Wilhem Windelband, who became the most eminent historian of philosophy in the German world of his time. The other important figure was Heinrich Rickert, the great systems builder of the school, who became Windelband's successor in Heidelberg. In his previous appointment, in Freiburg, he had developed a long and intellectually influential friendship with Max Weber. The main concern of Windelband and Rickert was to develop a theory of values that will delineate the boundaries between what in German are called 'Naturwissenschaft' and 'Geisteswissenschaften'. [69] However, Windelband himself referred to what in English are normally called natural sciences as 'nomothetic sciences'; and the humanities and social sciences he called 'idiographic sciences'. As opponents of historicism and relativism, he and Rickert argued for the universal nature of values.

In producing guidelines for historians, Windelband states that the historian should ask: 'Through what impulses of thought in the course of historical movement are the principles, which we use today to understand and judge man and his world scientifically, brought to consciousness and improved?'. [70] This question is designed to dispel the influence of the Hegelian logos in historical analysis, by developing a form of empathetic understanding, and it shows remarkable similarities with Dilthey's 'Verstehen' method. In spite of important similarities, however, the Kantian rationalism of the founders of the Baden school prevented full agreement with Dilthey over this issue. Both Dilthey and the Baden neo-Kantians believed that a methodology of history first required a critique of consciousness, and they also agreed that the historian seeks meaning and significance in the events under historical analysis. But there is an important difference of emphasis: for Dilthey 'meaning' is the fundamental category, so he attaches great importance to 'Verstehen'; for Rickert and Windelband 'valuing' is the fundamental category.

For the Baden neo-Kantians the conceptualisation of universal values is of primordial importance, and a careful analysis of the role of value ('wert') is required. In their discussions, the concept assumes a double function: it is the principle that defines both the unity of all scientific knowledge and, at the same time, the scope of the meaning of that scientific knowledge. A system of values not only reflects the presuppositions of the sciences, but also their goal.[71]

Windelband goes on to argue that, within the framework of what we may today call social sciences, historical and human facts are not only singular and unique, concerned with unrepeatable phenomena; they are also teleological. They always relate to meaning and purpose because as single, never recurring events they posses inherent value. The task of human sciences is not to explain human facts but to understand them in terms of the motives and experiences of the human beings concerned. This last idea had a profound impact on the work of Max Weber. Max Adler in *Causality and Teleology* subsequently criticised Windelband's arguments about the teleological nature of the historical sciences. Kolakowski argues that, according to Windelband and Rickert, the teleological viewpoint applies to natural sciences too, but in a more restricted sense.[72] Crucial to the arguments of the Baden school was the idea that all knowledge involves the adoption and rejection of judgements, the attainment of 'truth' being the supreme objective. Against all forms of relativism, Rickert argued that to recognise truth is also to recognise general obligation. The value of 'truth' does not derive from science but, on the contrary, is a precondition of it. Rickert's work was also of great intellectual influence on Weber, particularly on the arguments about meaning and value. He defined cultural values thus:

> In regard to values considered in themselves, one cannot ask whether they are *real*, but only whether they are *valid*. A cultural value is either actually accepted as valid by all men, or its validity ... is at least postulated by some civilised human being. Furthermore, civilisation or culture in the highest sense must be concerned not with values attached to objects of mere desire, but with excellences which ... we feel ourselves more or less 'obliged' to esteem and cultivate for the sake of the society in which we live.[73]

In *Causality and Teleology* and other works on the epistemology of the social sciences, Adler criticises both the works of the neo-

Kantians of the Marburg and Baden schools as well as the orthodoxy of classical Marxism. His criticisms are developed at two
levels: one directed against the economism of the Second
International and, in the later works, of Marxism-Leninism; and
the other against the transcendental idealism of the neo-Kantians.
He uses the Kantian 'critical' methodology to criticise epiphenomenalist notions of economic determination and reject classical
notions of historical materialism. At a second level of analysis,
Adler criticises the idealist transcendentalism of the neo-Kantians
by sustaining the non-reducible specificity of social processes; in
particular by arguing that the fundamental neo-Kantian concepts
of 'truth' and 'value' are meaningless outside an a priori socialised
existence. Adler's work represents a major contribution to the
development of Marxist and sociological theories; it is regrettable
that no English translation is available.[74]

The point of departure for Adler's analysis is what he considers
to be the neo-Kantian misinterpretation of Marxism as a form of
materialist economic history. He rejects Rickert and Stammler's
accusation of 'one sided materialism' and that 'historical materialism conceives ideological phenomena as a by product of economic
relations', by arguing that Marxism by virtue of being a science
('Wissenschaft') rejects every form of essentialism. Marxism is a
sociological theory, meaning a theory of the social processes, and
as such is incompatible with any form of 'materialist metaphysics'
– a position that privileges material over social relations.[75]

For Adler, Marxism has nothing to do with materialism as a metaphysical system. He thought this a misunderstanding which
resulted from the unfortunate use of the term historical materialism and because Marx himself developed a 'certain tactical alliance' with eighteenth century materialism, against the abuses of
idealistic speculation.[76] Adler firmly believed that every essentialist
definition of the social arena, be it materialist or spiritual, is arbitrary and teleological, because neither matter nor spirit in themselves can be known outside the realm of socialised experience. He
further argued that experience is not an a priori, because it is
unthinkable outside socialised existence and therefore stands in a
relation of dependent causality from social relations. Adler turns
the original accusation of 'philosophical monism' against the neo-
Kantians, by maintaining that they themselves are falling into the
forms of essentialism which they supposedly criticise in Marxism
when they try to separate the problem of objective validity from
the reality of experience allowing 'validity like a new sort of
Platonism to shine upon the world from an inaccessible beyond'.[77]

Adler's assertion of the irreducibility of social forms is of enormous importance to the debate about the Marxist analysis of the national question, since it is the basis for Bauer's subsequent discussion of the specificity of national existence. For Adler, social experience is a transcendental condition of human existence because it is based on a form of human cognitive capacity whose formal existence is not amenable to causal explanations. A non-societalised individuality is meaningless because individuals always require social referents to assume autonomous existence. Forms of individuality are inherent to the form of the social and the formal relation between the two cannot be deduced causally, in the same way as no causal explanations can clarify general notions of time and space.[78] What emerges from Adler's argument is that the arena of the social implies always a form of relationship between the individual and the collective, and the formal configuration of this relationship is not reducible to what he calls scientific laws of causality.

Bauer found in Adler's debate with neo-Kantianism a useful point of departure for the formulation of a multidimensional theory of the national arena in two important respects. Firstly, through the consistent use of a Kantian critical methodology, Adler rejects any a priori positional privilege in the process of social causality. Neither 'the process of production' nor 'the national spirit' are in themselves valid starting points. Secondly, the notion of the irreducibility of the forms of the social acts to limit theoretically the relation of the national identity of subjects, or national community. In the analysis of the social arena, Adler begins neither with 'abstract individuals' nor with 'society', which he considers 'empty abstractions',[79] but with what he calls 'societalised men', that is the idea that the basis for all sociation is to be found in individual consciousness. That individual consciousness is not a transcendental abstraction but an indivisible aspect of the existence of the social arena. It could be argued (as Bauer does) that ethno-national identities are just one of the many individual manifestations of that societalised subjectivity.

Adler's second critical path is directed against all forms of economic reductionism of the Second and Third International. In later writings it was also directed against the reductionist nature of Marxist-Leninist discourse. Adler found Lenin's philosophical criticism of the works of Avenarious and Mach,[80] philosophically deficient and to have 'a musty aroma of philosophical and theoretical necromancy'. For Adler, materialism in Lenin's hands becomes a dogmatic world view in which 'dialectic is a mere sham and cover for unresolved problems'.

It is no longer possible in this fashion, as habit, opinion or philosophical standpoint may dictate ... simply to begin with either spirit or matter, nor can the so-called external world just be set up independent of our consciousness without falling, as Lenin did, into precisely what he accuses the idealists of, namely 'the most thickheaded fideism'[81]

The specific configuration of the nationalities problem in Austria, the original response of the Socialist Party and the productive theoretical debate that resulted from the neo-Kantian critique of historical materialism, were all contributing factors in the development of the nationalities theory of Otto Bauer.

6

Otto Bauer and the National Question – part one

For classical Marxists, the nation was a temporary phenomenon located at a precise stage of the development of the forces of production, and as such it was predetermined to fade out with the abolition of class societies. In contrast, Bauer asserts that not only will nations not disappear with the abolition of class societies, but the very consummation of the socialist project will require an expansion and differentiation of national communities.

> So in a socialist society, no new element of spiritual (*geistig*) culture will be able to gain access to a nation without fusing with the culture of that nation, and without being influenced by it. The autonomy of distinctive national cultural communities will necessarily mean a growing differentiation between the spiritual (*geistig*) cultures of nations, despite the levelling out of material differences.
> Integration of the whole people in their national cultural community, full achievement of self-determination of nations, growing spiritual (*geistig*) differentiation of nations – this is the meaning of socialism.[1]

Bauer's stand on the national question contradicts the conventional wisdom of classical Marxism. In the stifling idiom of class reductionism, national existence cannot transcend considerations of class position. In the class reductionist paradigm, socialism is required to transcend and abolish the process of class determination in all forms of societalised existence. From this perspective, socialism and national existence are clearly incompatible.

A Gramscian analysis accords with Bauer's argument only to the point at which this 'growing spiritual differentiation of nations' results from the presence of a politically hegemonic force which coalesces the national community with the aid of a strong 'Jacobinian' collective will. The aim of this is to articulate the national with international dimensions of cultural and political existence. Other European Marxist traditions will see in Bauer's

142

argument a 'sell-out' which jeopardises the premises of Marxist internationalism.

Does this mean that the work of Otto Bauer provides a definitive break with class reductionism in the analysis of the national question? In this chapter and the next it will be argued that Bauer develops a rich, incisive and far reaching discussion of the topic. His theory permits the conceptualisation of the national question outside the paradigmatic field of class determination – an almost unique event in the Marxist tradition. However, the clarity and consistency of Bauer's analysis is undermined by his unsystematic and uncritical use of terms and analytical categories derived from mainstream class reductionist Marxism. This results in a contradictory argument that weakens the impact of Bauer's insights.

The Context of Bauer's Work

The nationalities theory of Otto Bauer has been unjustifiably omitted from many contemporary discussions on the theoretical and empirical aspects of the process of national formation. Until recently, his work has been almost completely ignored in the English-reading world.[2]

While Bauer's book *Die Nationalitätenfrage und die Sozialdemokratie* is considered of paramount importance in the unfolding of the Marxist theory of the national question, so far it has not been translated into English, except for some subsections of paragraphs 10 and 30.[3] The book has been recently translated into French, and some chapters have been published in translation in the excellent reader *Les Marxistes et la question nationale*.[4] It is also only recently that the Spanish-reading audience has had the opportunity to read a translation.[5] There is also a partial translation into Hebrew.[6] However, not only is Bauer's work not available in English, but most contemporary works on nations and nationalism either ignore or make only passing references to it, which, as Kolakowski argues, are 'generally incorrect'.[7]

Despite the challenge to contemporary Marxism posed by the recurrence of nationalist movements, the highly original contribution of Bauer appears to have been forgotten. The omission is all the more puzzling when the prominence of his arguments in the debates around the turn of the century is taken into account.[8] Some contemporary writers acknowledge the exceptional quality of Bauer's work: Kolakowski considers Bauer's work to be 'the best treatise on nationality problems to be found in Marxist literature and one of the most significant products of Marxist theory in general', while H. B. Davis states that Bauer's book remains to this day 'the most pretentious Marxist treatise in the field'.[9] Melvin Croan argues that 'if Bauer finds a permanent place in the annals of the history of political thought, it may only be on account of his contribution to the theory of nationalism ... Bauer's *Nationalitätenfrage und die Sozialdemokratie* represent a brilliant application of Marxist theory to a problem which Marxists up to that time had conveniently glossed over.'[10]

In the light of these comments, Bauer's absence from contemporary theoretical debates is unwarranted. However, while he is ignored in the West, perestroika and recent unprecedented changes in communist states, have rekindled Soviet interest in Bauer's nationalities theory and Austro-Marxism. A number of works have recently been published in Russian on these topics.[11]

So why was Bauer forgotten? This form of theoretical amnesia, appears to be related to the problems of the Marxist tradition in trying to come to grips with the national question. It is possible to detect three causes. First, Bauer's theories are perceived by some historical commentators as devoted primarily to the discussion of the nationalities problem in the context of Austro-Hungary. Consequently they cease to have any relevance after the collapse of the dual monarchy. Even if, of 600 or so pages of Bauer's work, roughly half is devoted to the analysis of the development of national communities within the context of Austro-Hungary, the theoretical conceptualisation goes beyond the empirical limitations of the Austrian case.

Second, Bauer's main programmatic proposals relating to the Habsburg state (the notion of cultural national autonomy) are confused with his theoretical analysis, to the point where the failure of the programme of national cultural autonomy is considered tantamount to the failure of Bauer's theory. This is the line of argument taken by most Marxist-Leninist critics of Bauer, who are anxious to criticise the notion of national cultural autonomy because it contradicts Lenin's theories of both 'democratic centralism', and 'the right of nations to self-determination'. The Jewish Bund and other social democratic parties of oppressed national minorities in Czarist Russia were inspired by the programme of national cultural autonomy in their demands for self-rule. Given that the Bolsheviks opposed the demands for national and political decentralisation sketched in the 'cultural autonomy' programme, it was for them a matter of great political urgency to refute these arguments.[12]

This understanding of Bauer's position is incorrect in a number of ways. The Austrian *Gesamtpartei's* main programmatic proposals on the national question (the Brno programme) must not be confused with Bauer's theoretical analysis, and the project of national cultural autonomy should not be attributed to Bauer.[13] The confusion results from the Bolshevik debate on the national question in the context of Czarist Russia. It was Karl Renner who originally developed the programme of national cultural autonomy, and it was first discussed in the Brno congress of 1899 when Bauer was too young to attend. It is also important to keep in mind that the Brno programme is not a theoretical analysis, but a programmatic position developed in the context of the bitter national struggles of the Austro-Hungarian empire. Bauer himself was critical of aspects of the programme, as Lenin was always quick to note. Mommsen in fact argues that the impact of Bauer's work on party cadres resulted from the inability of the leadership of the Austrian Socialist Party to revise the Brno programme.[14] Bauer's reservations related to the position of the workers' organisations vis a vis national organisations and to the rights of non-territorial national minorities.[15]

The third element which contributed to Bauer's unpopularity with classical Marxists had to do with the rigidities of class reductionism. In Chapter 5 it was argued that in the course of his double debate with neo-Kantianism and classical Marxism, Max Adler asserted that the forms of the social cannot be ascertained through mediating causal laws. Bauer's *Nationalitätenfrage* represents, as will be shown below, a concrete elaboration of these postulates in the analysis of the national question. An economistic epistemology can hardly encapsulate Bauer's conceptualisation of the national phenomenon, since he deviates from the postulates of economism on the crucial issues of the non-reductibility of forms of the social which in classical Marxist theory 'belong' to the superstructure. Given the paralysing impact of economism in the theoretical development of the Marxist tradition, it is not surprising that the 'heretical ideas' of the Austro-Marxists were consigned to oblivion. In recent years, serious attempts have been made to rethink economistic categories of analysis and to sensitise the Marxian tradition to non-economic agents and to the plural nature of the social process of causality. In view of the recent collapse of Marxism-Leninism, this would appear to be an appropriate time to awaken the Austro-Marxist tradition from its undeserving hibernation. It may be useful to examine the insights that Bauer offers to the understanding of that elusive and recurrent problem called nationalism.

The Conceptualisation of Nations in Bauer's Work

In sharp distinction to most Marxist discussions of the national question, Bauer does not begin his work with the evaluation of the role of the bourgeoisie, the mode of production or the class struggle. Also, in an attempt to avoid ready made and prescriptive formulae, he does not provide an initial definition of the national community, and in his introduction to the 1924 edition warns readers that the definition which he will subsequently provide is not the important part of his conceptualisation of the national phenomenon:

> In fact, the main focus of my theory of the nation lies not in my definition of a nation, but in the description of the integrative process out of which the modern nation emerged. If my theory can claim any merit, it is that it derived that process of integration for the first time from economic development, from the changes in the social structure and from the articulation of classes in society.[16]

Bauer's purpose in embarking on his detailed analytical discussion is to try to understand the national community as a discrete unit resulting from a complex and multidimensional ensemble of social forces, and to elaborate a theory which is both argued from a Marxist standpoint and capable of grasping the nature of the national phenomenon as a dynamic process of transformation and continuous change.[17] In Mommsen's view, the most innovative aspect of Bauer's analysis lay in the attempt to develop a theoretically sensitive and politically practicable theory of the national question which Bauer characterised as a social morphology ('soziale Formenlehre'). A very important influence here was Max Adler's dual debate with neo-Kantianism and Marxist economism which, as shown already, had been very influential in earlier discussions of the national question.[18]

To achieve his goal of presenting a systematic analysis of the national question, Bauer begins from what he considers to be the 'concrete expression' of the existence of the national community in each individual member of the nation. This is what he calls the 'national character':

> The question of the nation can only be explored on the basis of the notion of a 'national character'. If we were to take any

German to a foreign country, e.g., to sojourn among the English, he would immediately realise that these people are different, with a different way of thinking and a different way of feeling ... provisionally we shall call the set of physical and spiritual features that distinguish one nation from another its 'national character'.[19]

This concept does not, according to Bauer, exhaust all the possibilities of grouping human beings. Besides national characteristics, all human beings have a common sense of humanity, while classes, professional groups, interest groups, oppressed groups, and so on have common characteristics which transcend national differences. He also acknowledges in the spirit of Marxism that ties of solidarity unite workers from different nations, but carefully differentiates this solidarity from the notion of national character. For Bauer, the question of cultural bonds between the working class and the bourgeoisie of any given nation is not connected with the question of the attitude of workers to their own bourgeoisie, or to the workers of other national communities.[20] This is an ethical and political issue, unconnected with the alleged intensity of the national community of character.

One of the main difficulties with the concept of national character is that the term has been so successfully monopolised by ethnocentric and racialist theories, to the point that in many contemporary discussions the concept simply becomes a code word to justify the superiority of one ethnic or national group over another. Most discussions of the national question, particularly those which take place within the Marxist tradition, studiously avoid any positive use of this term, thereby perpetuating its conceptual monopoly by racialist and ethnocentric theories. Yet the curious fact remains that historians,[21] as much any branch of the social sciences, including Marxism, constantly refer to the concept. The terms 'French Structuralism', 'German Marxism', 'Austro-Marxism', 'British Labourism', 'American Jingoism' have a precise national meaning which is often put to use by people who at the same time will strenuously deny any significance to national characteristics.

The term 'character', however, is distinctly polysemic (that is, it denotes several meanings), as Metzger shows in his interesting but somewhat dated article. In German scientific discourse, the term 'Charakter' generally refers to a sum of traits, and sometimes to their configuration.[22] In English, in addition to this, it could show either a high degree of individuality (s/he is a great character) or a collective generalisation closely connected with willpower ('strong' or 'weak' character).

In classical Marxism, the idea of the character of the working class is used to conceptualise the configuration of traits and characteristics which result from the common position of the proletariat in the capitalist mode of production. When classical Marxism proclaims that 'workers have more in common with each other than with the bourgeoisie of their respective nation', it is not to deny the specific character of the working class or the national community, merely to assert as an ontological certainty the *necessary condition* that one set of character traits derived from an economic position supersedes others derived from national and cultural existence. This argument is as indemonstrable as its ontological mirror image, the equally absurd notion that national identity always transcends class loyalties. To borrow terminology from Max Adler, both assertions portray a static metaphysical essentialism incompatible with the dynamic specificity of the social arena. It is against both forms of essentialism that Bauer's theory is directed.

To avoid what he considers to be 'transcendentalist distortions' in the usage of the concept of national character, Bauer argues that it is always necessary to locate this equivocal notion in a historical perspective:

> Above all, the national character has unjustly been ascribed a durability which can be refuted by historical evidence. It cannot be denied that German tribes shared a great number of characteristics at the time of Tacitus. These common characteristics distinguished them from other peoples, e.g. from the Romans of the same period. Equally, one cannot deny that the Germans of our time have certain common characteristics which differ from the characteristics of other peoples. This is true irrespective of the way in which these characteristics might have developed. However, no educated person will contest that a contemporary German has more in common with other contemporary civilised peoples (Kulturnationen) than with the Germans at the time of Tacitus.[23]

National character is understood, then, not as an abstract metaphysical essence but as a historically modifiable characteristic which culturally links the members of a national community over a given historical period. What links one generation with another is not the immutable transference of a mythical national spirit but the fact that contemporary generations do not operate in a vacuum, rather they enter a social arena shaped by the historical circumstances of previous epochs. As with any other social characteristic, the national character is *modifiable* by historical forces, but it cannot simply be referred back to previous generations because contemporary experiences change beyond recognition the nature of the phenomena under consideration. Both dimensions, the historical and the contemporary, are an essential ingredient for determining the logic of the present configuration of the national character. The national character is a discrete unit of contemporary and historical forces, none of which can be seen in isolation as a determinant factor, while both kinds of forces are always present in forming national identities.

For Bauer, another important source of the misinterpretation of the concept of national character is that even explanations which accept the historical relativity of the term refer to it as a causal explanatory concept:

> When we describe the national character, we do not thereby explain the causes of any given actions, but we only describe the common characteristics of a great number of actions ... this is not at all a causal explanation but a mere recognition of already observed common features of different individual actions.[24]

The important consequence that Bauer derives from this argument is that national character is not the causal factor in national existence but, on the contrary, the concrete, descriptive expression of the latter. A national character is a historical construct and, as such, the empirical expression of national existence at a given historical period. It is not the point of departure for the analysis of the nexus that links the national community, but the concrete embodiment of such a nexus. It is not an explanation, but the very element which must be explained, if one is to understand the elusive nature of the national character.

> The concept of national character is not an explanation, but rather something to be explained. By identifying the diversity of national characters, science (Wissenschaft) has not *solved* the problem of the nation, it has merely *formulated it*.[25]

The community of character is emphatically not what constitutes the cultural specificity of national communities, but is only a concrete, empirical expression of the latter. Once the set of empirical characteristics considered to be causal factors of what

Bauer calls the *community of character* ('Charaktergemeinschaft') are identified, the task of trying to understand the nature of the national community begins. For Bauer, a correct understanding of the historical and contemporary processes which delineate the specificity of concrete national communities requires the formulation of causal explanations of the empirically observable elements constituting the national character.

In Bauer's formulation, it is possible to detect the impact of Max Adler's dual debate with neo-Kantianism and classical Marxism. Crucial to Adler's critical stance was a spirited argument in support of the irreductibility of the forms of the social[26] and a strict rejection of any essentialist stance in the identification of forces that give *content* to the social arena. The neo-Kantian distinction between 'is' and 'ought' is refuted by Adler through a strict reference to relations of causality, thereby rejecting any teleological inference in the analysis of the social arena. The iron laws of necessity of classical Marxism are rejected through the same logic, because they postulate unacceptable forms of what Adler calls metaphysical essentialism. Relations of causality are to be ascertained through what we today recognise as a strict deconstruction of the social phenomena under consideration, rather than through ontologically privileged relations of determination.[27]

Following Adler's logic, Bauer is on firm ground in his attempt to demystify the notion of national character by strictly relativising and contextualising its existence. However, he runs the risk of falling into the opposite form of essentialism, that of transparent epiphenomenality – not in the concrete manifestation of epiphenomenalism referred to in the present discussion of Marxism and the national phenomenon (the transparency of economic forces) but in the more general sense of negating any form of autonomous existence to a social construct. To account entirely for the existence and character of any empirically given social phenomena in terms of strict relations of causality, implies seriously undermining the scope for autonomous existence of the phenomena under consideration.

The requirement constantly to identify the causal dimension of the national character implies not only its lack of autonomy, but also its intrinsic status as a vehicle for the expression of something else, namely the elements that shape the historical dimension of national existence. Thus the concept of national character as defined by Bauer appears to lack any autonomous existence, and this may create some ambiguities in the use of the concept.

The difficulty arises at two levels: firstly, Bauer does not indicate clearly the difference between 'national character' and what is called today 'national identity', meaning the positional subjectivity of national agents.[28] Secondly, the initial relation of causality between national existence, national identity and national character is often subverted by a polysemic configuration of the elements. While in some cases it is possible to see paths of causality to previously observed concrete features of national character, in view of their dynamic interplay with other aspects of social existence, these features cannot always be referred back to the causal agents. To provide a brief example: even if one is to accept the likelihood that the centuries-long colonial encounter was one contributing factor in the configuration of the Anglo-British and French national identity before World War Two, it would an erroneous simplification to argue that because of this, both the Anglo-British and French national characters are irrevocably moulded to enter into relations of domination.

Bauer's attempt strictly to relativise and contextualise what he calls the national character is not yet sufficient to explain its fluidity. It is also important to recognise the permanent *unfixity* of relations of causality between national existence, national identity and national character, and the likelihood of an autonomous configuration of the elements involved. This includes the need to redefine the relation between the elements in such a way that permits the development of an analytical logic which transcends the originally defined relations of causality. In contrast, Bauer's discussion of the national character is based on the description of strict relations of causality, restricting the observation of autonomous features of the national phenomena and impairing the understanding of its multidimensional existence.

Bauer also criticises the view that national character is a tangible manifestation of the 'spirit of the people' ('Volksgeist'). This idea is derived from the Hegelian tradition which, as was shown earlier, divides national communities into 'historical' and 'non-historical' nations, according to the abilities of their respective national spirits to build independent national states. As was argued in Chapter 1, Marx and Engels took on board the logic of this idealistic and metaphysical consideration, transforming the concept of national spirit into the more materialist but no less metaphysical notion of the ability of the national community in question to enter the capitalist mode of production. Bauer argues that the national spirit cannot be used to explain the national community because it is nothing but the transformation of the national character into a metaphysical essentiality.[29] But while categorically rejecting the causal validity of the notion of the 'spirit of peoples', Bauer nevertheless accepts, as a point of departure for his analysis, the Marxian dichotomy between 'historical' and 'non-historical' nations. This he does while strictly qualifying Marx and Engels' position, using the notion of 'the historical awakening of nations without history'. This will be discussed below.

For Bauer, then, the common national character is not what constitutes the national community, but is only its concrete expression. The national character is one of the expressions of 'societalised' existence, it is the expression of the representation of social reality in each national subject. What distinguishes a national community is that its members are the result of the same historical forces operating in each individual member of a given society. [30]

Once the national character has been identified, Bauer argues that it must be explained in terms of the social and historical conditions that lead to its emergence. To do this, he narrows the descriptiveness of the term by arguing that the national character is a determining factor in the sphere of what he calls 'will' ('Wille'). For Bauer, will is exteriorised in every cognitive process through which a plurality of subjects commonly perceive certain characteristics of a given observable phenomenon, attaching importance only to commonly perceived characteristics, and ignoring or giving secondary importance to others.[31] 'Will' is the concrete expression in every individual subject of the 'societalised'[32] quality of human experience.

Once this definition of the sphere of 'will' has been established, Bauer proceeds to conceptualise the notion of national character in a less descriptive manner. The idea that this character is the set of physical and spiritual connotations which characterise co-nationals is then enlarged by the idea that the mechanism which permits the presence of the national character in every member of the national community is the common orientation of 'will'. Consequently the empirical generalisation called by Bauer 'national character' is the tangible expression of a collective 'will' resulting from the historical experience of the national community, and exteriorised in each member through a societalised selective perception of external reality. This, according to Bauer, is what explains the fact that different national communities have different perceptive criteria, develop different forms of morality, of law, different aesthetic criteria, different ways of perceiving religion, and even different ways of understanding scientific thought.[33]

In the introduction written for the 1924 edition of the

Nationalitätenfrage, Bauer expands this notion of the perceptual differences of various national communities. After arguing that it is not difficult to understand the 'strong resistance' that his use of the notion of national character generated in the Marxist tradition – given the abusive and 'shameful' use made of the concept by nationalists during the war – he goes on to justify the use of the idea with a number of examples. For this purpose, he relies heavily on what he describes as a 'highly stimulating' book by the anti-republican, devout Catholic and conservative French philosopher of science, Pierre Duhem,[34] *La Théorie physique: son objet, sa structure.*[35] Bauer argues that in this book Duhem compares the way in which the most important 'English' (British) and French physicists conduct their research and finds, in Bauer's words, 'remarkable national differences'.

According to this thesis, the French are interested in coherent, clear and non-contradictory systems. They develop verifiable hypotheses from fundamental laws through a deductive method. In opposition to this, Bauer argues – following Duhem – the English develop mechanical models from which they deduce a conglomerate of empirical laws. They are not too disturbed if the hypotheses they use to construct their empirical models are not connected, or even if they contradict each other. For the English, the goal is to grasp the research in a comprehensive, understandable and graphic way. For the French, the goal is to understand in a clear and orderly way. Quoting Duhem, Bauer argues that the French have a 'superior capacity' for abstraction and generalisation; the English for representing graphically complex equations and to explain them through simple and clear representations.[36]

Duhem also argues that there are differences in the way in which French and English physicists use algebra. For the French, physical theory is a logical system and algebraic equations are only an auxiliary device to put in evidence the fundamental hypothesis. For the English, algebraic calculus is like a mechanical model, it exactly reproduces the movements of the researched phenomena; they are not too concerned with establishing a narrow equivalence between the idea and the algebraic symbol. They leave that to intuition. They have, however, a 'superior capacity' to understand very complex combinations in a fast and graphic manner and are very efficient in using condensed methods of calculus. The French use classical algebra, while the English use modern algebraic symbols with numerous intermediary operations, but which require a large number of symbols and complex rules.[37] Duhem himself suggests that the differences in formulations of physical theories are the result of what he calls the 'spiritual diversity' of both nations, which according to Bauer (and presumably Duhem), can also be found in other branches of spiritual sciences ('Geisteswissenschaften'), such as the development of French philosophy from Descartes and the development of English philosophy from Bacon.

Bauer argues that Duhem also found differences of national character in literature. The heroes of Shakespeare and Corneille, reflect different national models. The attitudes of Auguste and Rodrigue differ significantly from those of Lady Macbeth and Hamlet.[38] The same logic is used by Duhem to explain the difference between English and French law. In France civil law is systematic, based on 'abstract but clearly defined concepts'. English law is less coherent, but more in tune with the needs of every day life.

Bauer then states that capitalism has 'levelled the material and cultural content' of the different national communities but, in spite of this, 'national specificities remain influential' in the way in which those national cultures appropriate new developments. The same criteria applies to the working-class movement:

> The same working class movement emerges in all industrialised states, but when confronted with the same facts of capitalist exploitation, the Italian working class reacts differently from the Scandinavian. This is what I have in mind when I refer to the *'national character'*. I do not mean by it those fallacious images of nationalist demagoguery which discovers only heroes among its own people and only traffickers among others. I rather wish to express those diversities only accessible to a far more sophisticated psychological analysis which appear in the basic spiritual structure, in intellectual and aesthetic taste, in the manner of reacting to the same stimuli – in all those things we take into account if we compare the spiritual life of different nations, their science and philosophy, their poetry, their music, their fine arts, their social and public life, their life-style and habits.[39]

He goes on to argue that what he calls 'the nationalist interpretation of history' is based on the idea that national characters are the 'essential substances' which determine historical content.

> We cannot overcome that nationalist conception of history by negating either the incontestable fact of national peculiarities, or the equally incontestable fact of the diversity of 'national

characters'. Only if we strip the national character of its substantive appearance, in that we show that the prevailing 'national character' is nothing but a precipitate of past historical processes which will be further modified by the following historical processes, will we be able to overcome the nationalist conception of history.[40]

From this Bauer defines his main task as being to explain and derive national specificities from the very history of the national community.[41] He proceeds to a narrower definition of the national character: it is not only the physical and spiritual connotations of nations but, more fundamentally, the similarity in the orientation of will. The national character is a commonality of 'volitive orientation' that results from societalised subjectivity. The various historical conditions, the differing forms of social organisation as well as the diverse geographical and physical conditions of existence are linked together to produce the specificity of national existence. Thus the historically determined conditions of existence create the causal variables that give shape to a specific national community.

However, the national community is not only the result of the historical determination of the conditions of existence; it is also above all a form of both *'common'* and *'communitarian'* experience emanating from the latter. This aspect is crucial for understanding Bauer's conceptualisation of the national community. In order to explain it, Bauer introduces the conceptual elements that will shape his definition of the nation. To capture the contemporary dimensions of historical legacies that have shaped the various national communities, he introduces the idea that the nation is a *'community of fate'* ('Schicksalsgemeinschaft').[42]

This concept was not invented by Bauer; it was used by Nietzsche and by Eduard von Hartmant to denote a series of events not actively sought or desired, but which take place outside or beyond the wilful action of a group of subjects who are nevertheless influenced by its outcome.[43] For Bauer, the term has a related but different meaning, it equally implies the presence of a set of historical circumstances which precedes and influences subjective awareness and is consequently given to subjects, over which they can nevertheless exercise a form of transformative control that results from their contemporary experiences.

In order to clarify the concept, it is necessary provisionally to embark on separate evaluations of its two interlinked dimensions: the path of historical determination and its projection to the future, and the somewhat idiosyncratic use of the term 'community'. The first aspect has already been touched upon in the discussion of the national character. On the second Bauer sharply distinguishes two related concepts, that of *community* and that of *homogeneity*, illustrating the difference with a historical example. England and Germany faced, in the nineteenth century, a similar process of capitalist development. The same historical forces crucially influenced the collective experiences of both national communities, but despite similar experiences England and Germany remained separate national communities. The term 'homogeneity of fate' implies a set of social agents being subjected to the same historical forces without necessarily interacting with each other. Bauer uses the example of the working class to clarify this point. Wherever the capitalist mode of production becomes dominant, an industrial proletariat emerges which experiences *the same* conditions of exploitation under capitalism, regardless of national location. Displaying the naive optimism of turn-of-the-century Marxism, Bauer argues that 'the proletariat of every capitalist nation' has a 'homogeneous character'. The same class location conferred upon them a type of character which is expressed in the same commitment to struggle, 'the same revolutionary mentality, the same class morality, the same political will'. But in this case it is the *homogeneity of fate* and not the *community of fate* which generated the common character.[44]

Even if in certain circumstances the proletariat class could be considered a community, it is certainly *not*, in Bauer's terminology, a community of fate. To be part of such a community is not the same as being subjected to the same fate. A community of fate signifies not only the experience of the same historical circumstances, but the experience of those circumstances in a situation of *common reciprocal interaction* ('durchgängige Wechselwirkung untereinander').[45]

A national community is a form of communitarian life that has a specific configuration, where the identity of the collective is constituted by the interactive relation of its members, which is in turn replicated in individual identities. The element of 'interactive reciprocity' is what distinguishes a community of fate from any other form of communitarian life. In this sense, the concept of 'Gemeinschaft' Bauer uses is of Kantian origin, denoting two different dimensions of community life. One is that of 'common homogeneous characteristics' which is best denoted by the Latin word 'Communio', meaning a quality of equality of circumstances and homogeneity, and the second can be denoted by the Latin word 'Commercium' meaning a dynamic process of interaction.[46] While every Commercium is a Communio, not every Communio is a Commercium, and this is what Bauer has in mind when he distinguishes between community of fate and homogeneity of fate.

Following on from this discussion, Bauer conceptualises the nation thus:

> Consequently, it is possible to define the nation as a community of character that it is not born out of an homogeneity of fate, but out of a community of fate. This is also the significance of language for the nation. With the human beings with which I most closely interact I manufacture a language, and with the human beings with which I have a common language I most closely interact.[47]

In this unusual way of understanding the concept of community, Bauer is influenced by the work of Max Adler on causality and teleology, particularly on the notion of the irreducibility of the forms of the social. For Adler, social links logically precede the existence of individuality and society, without which both notions are strictly unthinkable. Consequently, it is the very process of interaction that determines the configuration of the social arena as well as the constitution of subjective identities. Bauer argues that the process of common reciprocal interaction lived in a permanent reciprocal relation generates the national community and expresses itself in an inter-subjective bond that shapes each 'individual national identity'.

> the nation constitutes a social phenomenon. It is not a sum of individuals, but each individual is the product of the nation; the fact that they are all the product of the same society makes them into one community. Those qualities that appear as distinguishing features of individuals are, in reality, a social product – and indeed for all members of the nation, a product of one and the same society – that is what makes a collection of individuals a nation. In this way nations do not exist as creatures of a formal [legal] convention (*Satzung*), rather they logically, but not historically, pre-exist every formal convention.[48]

From this it is possible to infer that for Bauer the question of how the boundaries between national communities come into existence is quite different from the question of how the national community is constituted. Historical and/or political circumstances can link or separate groups of people, and the explanations for these are to be found in a more comprehensive analysis of the historical conjuncture, not in the theory of the formation of nations. Also from the ensuing discussion it is possible to notice that Bauer's use of the concept of community is substantially different from the way in which it is used in mainstream sociology, following Tönnies. Bauer knows and rates highly Tönnies' *Gemeinschaft and Gesellschaft*, but he nevertheless gives the concepts of community and society a different meaning.

In his usage of these terms Bauer explicitly follows Adler's critical discussion of Stammler's neo-Kantian legal terminology. For Stammler, 'the essence of society' is the process of cooperation of human beings under an external formal convention ('*äussere Satzung*'). In sharp distinction, however, the essence of the community (in the sense of commercium) is that the individual, in his/her physical and spiritual being, is the product of the numerous interactive relations with other individuals, and therefore expresses in his/her individuality concrete manifestations of the communitarian character. Consequently, what distinguishes the nation from all other communities of character (in the sense of communio), is that the nation is not a mere homogeneity of fate, it only comes into existence and develops as a community of fate (in the sense of commercium). Bauer immediately qualifies this statement by arguing that, communities of fate cannot emerge unless a given 'external formal convention' delimits their boundaries. This is to say that the boundaries of the national community are set by an external framework and the explanation as to how that external framework comes into existence is different from the question of what constitutes a national community. The separation, however, is not as clearcut as Bauer appears to suggest.

If, say, the Finnish language is the formal framework which constitutes the boundaries of the Finnish nation as an interactive community, and the Argentinian state is what constitutes the formal framework through which the Argentinian nation as an interactive community comes into existence, Bauer is right in saying that the interactive relation in both cases could be conceptualised outside the framework that brought both national communities into existence, since the interactive relation is replicated in each 'subject position'. However, in the long run, the subjective positions will tend to disintegrate in the absence of a framework that makes possible the existence of an interactive community. Both communities can only continue to exist on condition that the framework which delimits their interactive relation is maintained, replaced or reproduced. While it is possible to think of an Argentinian cultural community outside the framework of the Argentinian state, and a Finnish cultural community that exists outside the framework of the Finnish language, both subjective positions will eventually disintegrate and be transformed into something else unless an external framework is found to preserve the specific form of interactive relation.

The Role of Language

Bauer neglects one of the most important external frameworks in forming national communities: the state. While it is possible to separate the interaction from the framework that generates it, the interactive relation will eventually cease to function outside that framework. According to Bauer, in the case of the national community this function of external framework is often given by language.[49] However, in keeping with his non-essentialist stance, he argues that it would be misleading to hold that language is the causal factor in the formation of national communities. This puts him on a direct collision course with Kautsky, whose key argument in his theory of the national question is that language is the determinant factor in the formation of nations. In a critical review of Bauer's book in the *Neue Zeit*, Kautsky argues that 'the crucial mistake from which all others are derived [is that he] refuses to recognise the strongest link [between members of the national community which is] evident for everyone to see: their common language.'[50]

To this criticism Bauer responds in a later article by arguing that at a superficial level there is no disagreement between Kautsky and himself – empirically observable nations are communities of language. However, the observation that every nation uses a common language is not yet sufficient to provide a conceptualisation of the national phenomenon:

> I may rather ask, why precisely this particular group of human beings and not another, or indeed, why does not a narrower group make use of the same language? The question of which force delimits the boundaries of communication leads to the concept of community of communication, and if we wish to determine causally the boundaries of communication we will eventually reach the concept of 'community of fate' through the concept of community of culture.[51]

The central theoretical chapter of Bauer's book represents a meticulous attempt to provide an answer to this question.[52]

As a consequence of his emphasis on the process of interactive relation as the basis for the formation of the national community, a careful discussion of patterns of communication is a key dimension of Bauer's work. In spite of Kautsky's assertion to the contrary, for Bauer language is the principal medium of communication through which the national community is constituted:

> even if there are patterns of interaction that link German and English workers, they are much more diffuse than the patterns of communication that link the English worker with the English bourgeois. Both live in the same cities, both read the same posters, the same newspapers and participate in the same sporting or political events ... Language is the instrument of interaction. If there were stronger links of interaction between English and German workers, they would have the same language in common, and the community of language would not be between the English bourgeoisie and the English working class.[53]

Language is the 'great medium of interaction', the need for interaction generates common languages, and when the linguistic patterns of interaction disintegrate so does the national community, for it is 'unthinkable' for a national community to maintain its cultural commonality without a common language.[54] Up to this point it seems that Bauer is replicating Kautsky's arguments. However, in the introduction to the 1924 edition Bauer attempts to dispel the Kautskian idea that the community of language is the concrete expression of the process of economic development and the constitutive causal factor in the formation of national communities:

> the community of language is the product of a very complex process of integration and differentiation. The dissolution of the community of fate leads to a cultural, and consequently, linguistic differentiation; the articulation of a community of fate leads to cultural and consequently, linguistic integration. The community of language is only a partial manifestation of the cultural community and a product of the community of fate.[55]

If a common language is an important factor for the unity of the national community, it does not mean, as Kautsky argues, that language in itself generates the process of cultural and national unity, but that language is the consequence of a complex process of articulation of the other cultural, social and political factors which configurate what Bauer calls the community of fate. While he accepts that most national communities cannot in the long run subsist without a common language, this last is not in itself sufficient to constitute a national community. This is certainly so in the case of those different national communities that share the same language.[56]

The main difference between Bauer's argument and the position taken by Kautsky and Lenin on the role of language is that for Bauer language is not the causal variable which configurates the national community, but rather it is the channel or medium through which the interaction that shapes the national community takes place. If, however, this process of communication could take place outside language, and if an alternative medium of communication could be found through which the national community is constituted, then it is possible to think of a national community lacking a common language.

If, for example, in the case of Switzerland it can be shown that the centuries-long experience of living under a very distinctive form of decentralised state apparatus creates a stronger bond of communication than a common language, it is possible to argue that the Swiss are a national community without necessarily having a common language. This may also be the case, according to Bauer, of Jewish communities in medieval Europe. Following Marx's analysis of the Jewish question,[57] Bauer argues that the strict residential segregation imposed upon Jews, and their confinement to monetary occupations in a non-monetary social order, created a strong interactive link between various Jewish communities. This link developed although Jews were not concentrated in one geographical area and despite the lack of a common language for day-to-day communication.

> the link through economic exchange that related the Jew with the peasant was much weaker than the more intimate communitarian interaction with other Jews. The difference between the culture of monetary economy and that of natural economy was incomparably stronger than the commonality produced by the mutual interaction which took place in completing a purchase, a sale or a loan. In this way, the Jews remained a separate nation in the midst of other peoples.[58]

However, the development of the capitalist mode of production dramatically changed the position of Jews in society. A part of the Jewish population joined the industrial bourgeoisie. This change in the class position of a part of the Jewish population gave way to a revolutionary change in lifestyles, the new Jewish bourgeoisie began to distance itself from the traditional Jewish population, and found a closer affinity with 'their fellow christian class members' ('christlichen Klassengenossen').[59] While Bauer's discussion of the Jewish question in Eastern and Central Europe is not without some interesting insights, he is at times inconsistent in his overall theoretical discussion, as Stalin was quick to point out.[60]

In summarising the discussion of the connection between language and the development of the interactive process that constitutes the national community, the two examples presented above indicate that in exceptional circumstances language is not an essential factor in the formation of national communities, while in most cases it becomes the interactive medium through which the national community is constituted. Language alone is not an indicator of the presence or absence of a national community.

Bauer's Definition of National Communities

Having discussed various aspects of the process of national development in Bauer's theory, it is possible now to see how the various dimensions of the problematic of national formation are put together in his definition of the nation. It is important to remember that the aim of the earlier work of Adler in the Marx-Studien series was directed towards rejecting the forms of essentialism present in both class-reductionist Marxism and the transcendentalist essentialism of the neo-Kantians. Bauer's emphasis on understanding the formation of the national community as a process rather than a classification derived from what he calls the 'materialist' or the 'spiritualist' theories of history, is a direct result of this Adlerian task, which became (in more than one way) the hallmark of the theoretical distinctiveness of the Austro-Marxist tradition.

Refusing to accept any essentialist principle in his conceptualisation of the national question, Bauer opened the way for a multidimensional understanding of the national community. This is perhaps another important reason why the theory has been so consistently misinterpreted. A superficial reading of Bauer's theoretical chapter in his voluminous work is not enough to understand the intellectual aim of his analysis. There are no cliches and ready made formulae applicable to every circumstance, Bauer's definition of the nation as 'the totality of human beings bound together through a community of fate into a community of character'[61] is meaningless if one does not follow the painstaking process of reviewing the different dimensions of the complex, resilient and not well-understood process of national formation.

Bauer locates his work in direct opposition to the three main currents of thought which dominated the conceptualisation of the national question: what he calls the metaphysical theories, a term derived from Adler's work on *Causality and Teleology* which includes what Bauer calls 'national materialism' and 'national spiritualism'. The second current of thought he terms psychological theories, meaning those theories 'that seek to discover the essence of the nation in the consciousness of, or the will to, solidarity'.[62] These are the so-called voluntaristic theories of the nation with which Bauer is mistakenly associated in a number of important works on nations and nationalism.[63] The third group of theories that Bauer analyses and rejects are the empirical theories, that is those that theoretically enumerate the essential elements of a nation and decide whether concrete national communities fit the pattern through the presence or absence of the enumerated elements.[64]

In discussing these theories Bauer argues that 'common descent and common culture' are basically derivative categories of the notion of shared history in the process of constructing the national character. A common territory is an important condition only insofar as it allows for the conditions of interactive relationship to take place. Territorial separation disrupts the unity of the national community because the intersubjective process required to develop the community of fate cannot take place.

However, 'in the age of printing, the post, telegraph, steamships this is much less the case than formerly'.[65] In view of the phenomenal contemporary expansion of all means of communication it is possible to infer from the logic of Bauer's argument that the territorial dimension is even less important. Yet the common territory becomes significant in a different way in that it forms the basis for a related important phenomenon: the national state. This will be discussed below. A shared language, for the reasons discussed earlier, is 'a second order means'. It is the medium through which the community of culture is maintained, re-creating the national community in each subjectivity through common interaction. In an interesting footnote, however, Bauer qualifies this understanding of the role of language to dispel any possible interpretation that language is a neutral medium:

> Language, of course, is not simply a means of transmitting a culture, but is itself an element of culture. A Frenchman does not differ from a German only because his language conveys a different culture, but also because the language itself is a cultural element which has been transmitted to him and determines, by its specific qualities, his speech, thought, and character. The difference between French and German rhetoric is due in part to the difference of language.[66]

The critical review of the different theories that attempt to explain the nature of the national community allows Bauer to present the originality of his argument. *The nation cannot be understood by enumerating a set of categories or by referring to some essential quality.* The national community is the end result of a systemic process in which different dimensions are brought together through a common historical development in dialogue with the main facets of contemporary experience. This is the meaning of Bauer's definition of the national community as 'human beings bound together through a common fate into a community of character'. Subjective positionality is the expression of societalised existence, the content of societalised existence results from the structural linkage of a process of common reciprocal interaction and that of historical development.

> For us society is not a mere addition of individuals, but each individual is the product of society. In the same way, for us the nation is not an addition of individuals that enter into a mutual relation through a common language, but the individual him/herself is the product of the nation. His/her individual character did not emerge in any other way than through a continuous interaction (*Wechselwirkung*) with other individuals, in the same way as the character of those individuals emerged from the continuous interaction with him/her.[67]

The national community, therefore, exists independently from national consciousness, which is the result of the awareness of the existence of other nations, since the subject becomes conscious of his/her national dimension by comparison with others. This is why national consciousness became a generalised perceptive mechanism only as a result of the process of modernity. The last aspect acquires great importance in the political arena. Given that the national community manifests itself in the 'individual character [of every member of the national community,] every attack on my national community is like an attack upon myself and every glory of the national community is like my own'.[68]

While Bauer is on firm ground in arguing that national consciousness is not a necessary ingredient of national existence, the second part of his argument stands on very slippery ground. Although it is true that national sentiment is often associated with 'basic sentimental representations' of great importance to individual identity, as Bauer argues in an ironic style reminiscent of the nostalgic verses of a famous Argentine tango,[69] it does not follow that this link is automatically translated into the political arena in a single ideological format. The political understanding of the role of the national sentiments described by Bauer is best served if they are perceived as 'floating ideological forms' capable of being articulated with concrete ideological positions. Nationalism in general, it has been argued, is associated with neither the political left nor right, while all concrete forms of nationalism can be located in a conventional political spectrum, opening the way for an understanding of the political dimension of national existence as an ideologically contested field.[70]

It is clear that Bauer understands the development of national communities as a multifarious process in which the various dimensions are linked, not in a fixed manner but in a dynamic relation which permits an understanding of the nation as a process rather than a fixed one-dimensional relation of causality.

A multidimensional understanding of the national community is essential to dispel the deforming influence of economism. Does this mean that Bauer decisively broke with all forms of economic reductionism? Unfortunately this is not the case. While he is indeed close to such a break in the discussion of the national community, he relapses into classical Marxist categories of analysis in conceptualising another important aspect of national development, the historical dimension of national formation. Bauer tries to formulate universal laws of national development which are closely connected with the various stages of development of the productive forces, described by the evolutionist theory of classical Marxism. The argument can be best illustrated in his treatment of the theory of national evolution; the use of the dichotomy of historical and non-historical nations, and the connection he draws between nation and state. This will be discussed in the following chapter.

7

Otto Bauer and the National Question – part two

Bauer's Theory of National Evolution

When discussing the historical dimension of Bauer's work, and particularly, when evaluating the validity of generalisations he makes from his case studies, it is important to take into account the historical and political context in which he embarked on his study of the national question. As was shown in Chapter 5, the final years of the Austro-Hungarian empire were marred by heated national confrontations which consumed much of the political and intellectual energies of Austrian socialists. Because of their comparative success in the effort to transcend the bitter national differences of Austria-Hungary, the socialists formed the only political organisation in the troubled empire that truly reflected its multinational character.

Bauer's theoretical and historical discussion was directed towards making a decisive contribution to the debate over the national question and the resolution of the multinational tension. He believed at the time (as many other socialists did) that it was possible to save the multinational structure of the Austrian monarchy by radically transforming it into a decentralised democratic and federal state. It is important to keep in mind the attempts by the Austrian socialist party to come to grips with the national question, because Bauer's work through the Marx Studien series was initially a contribution to the continuing party debate to clarify the main historical and theoretical issues of the national question. Consequently Bauer's work must be also understood as an attempt to amend and improve the nationality policies of the Gesamtpartei.[1]

In his historical analyses, Bauer's main case studies were those of the Austro-German and Czech national communities, since much of the tension in Austria related to them. He also drew on other national communities in Austria and the Ottoman empire for examples, but the main thrust of his historical discussion was directed to the German and the Czech case.

What characterises Bauer's historical analysis of the national phenomenon is the assertion that in every historical nation there are two classes or two groups of classes. The first category truly participates in national life, creates and enjoys national culture and the process of national development takes place only within its ranks. These are the classes which hold political power and, more crucially, dominate the means of production. The second group, normally the subordinated classes, is excluded from national life although its toil sustains the lifestyle and culture of national classes.

There are two exceptions to this rather crude dichotomy. The first is what Bauer calls the 'primitive clanic communism of the German tribes'[2] and the second is the socialist society of the future. In both cases there is no private ownership over the means of production which, through the class mechanism, separates in all other cases the dominant national classes from the subordinate classes excluded from national life.

Bauer calls these subordinated classes 'Hintersassen der Nation'[3] (tributary classes of the nation), whose 'exploitation sustains the proud building of national culture from which they are excluded'.[4] Given that, for Bauer, what constitutes the nation is the cultural unity of the dominant classes, the history of the national community is then simply the history of the linear developmental succession of different dominant classes and strata with a parallel development of the tributary classes. Feudal landlords, manufacturing bourgeoisie and petty bourgeoisie comprise the first and serfs, free peasants, artisans and workers the second. As Garcia Pelayo argues, the validity of these analytical categories is doubtful even if they are confined to the German example used by Bauer.[5]

Bauer reaches two conclusions on this. Firstly, the process of national integration and separation can be explained through the developmental logic of the forces of production. In the German case, the separation of the Dutch tribe from the main Germanic group is explained through the process of sedentary settlement of the germanic inhabitants of the lowlands. The dominant classes of the Dutch tribes lost contact with other germanic peoples, thereby developing a separate community of fate. The second conclusion is a thesis about the progressive expansion of the national community. Through the process of linear historical development, different dominant classes incorporate groups or strata that were previously tributary to the national community, and during the capitalist period the working class will be progressively integrated into the national community through the army, the ballot box and the educational system.[6]

This process will culminate in the total integration of the population into the national cultural community with the emergence of socialism and the abolition of class societies. Here lies the meaning of the quotation on the first page of Chapter 6. The 'growing spiritual differentiation of nations' will result from the disappearance of the non-national tributary classes. There are also no tributary classes under primitive clanic communism because there is no surplus production to generate class divisions. This is not a national cultural community, but a mere community of descent. Under socialism, as happened under clanic primitive communism, the whole population will belong to the national community; the crucial difference is that, this time, it will not be a static community of descent but a dynamic cultural community resulting from the socialised enjoyment of the fruits of production. Thus, the main difference is that during the period of primitive communism the national community resulted from a biological community of descent, whereas in the socialist society the national community will result from the cultural integration of all members of the community into national life. The naivete of this historical formulation is truly puzzling when compared with the sophistication of Bauer's theoretical arguments evaluated in Chapter 6.

Another conceptual discussion directly relevant to Austria is Bauer's critical use of that Marxian dichotomy, historical and non-historical nations.[7] Bauer takes from Marx and Engels the main components of their conceptualisation of that dichotomy while drastically cutting back its deterministic slant. He incorporates the main Marxian argument into his historical evolutionary model while maintaining that modern capitalism had caused the 'awakening of non-historical nations'. With this conceptual tool he tries to explain the national revival of the Czech national community and other communities in Austria. Bauer also attempts to use this theory to evaluate the process of national awakening in late imperial Austria and to provide some theoretical and political ideas for discussion within the Austrian Socialist Party, addressing the politically explosive issue of national rights in that multinational state. In evaluating Bauer's use of this dichotomous characterisation of nations, it is crucial to keep in mind the debates within Austrian socialism over the nationalities issue.[8]

Commenting on the articles written by Marx and Engels in the *Neue Rheinische Zeitung*,[9] Bauer argues that they are not 'just ephemeral journalistic works' but display the 'historical vision' of their authors. However, it is important to note, he says, that these articles were born out of the 'storm of the revolution', and the authors failed to perceive that, as a result of 'circumstantial events', the non-historical nations were driven to the reactionary camp. This last situation was not, he argues, 'a permanent feature' but the result of transient revolutionary circumstances. Engels, however, thought it was the fundamental intrinsic feature of those unfortunate national communities and this, according to Bauer, is 'the fundamental error' of those articles. He concludes that Engels' opinion that 'nations without history have no future has proven to be incorrect'; on the contrary, the 'historical method of investigation thought out by Marx and Engels permits us today to understand the causes of the awakening of non historical nations to historical life under the influence of capitalism, democracy and the revolution.'[10] Later he goes on to argue that, precisely opposite to Engels' prediction, 'today the representatives of the nations without history had become revolutionary, while those of the historical nations became more conservative.'[11]

In Bauer's analysis there are two types of non-historical nations. The first comprises those national communities which lack a 'high culture' and consequently had never 'surpassed the primitive stage' of development. The second is comprised of those communities which achieved in the past a 'higher level of development' but as a consequence of the collapse or disappearance of their upper (national-cultured) classes, they had lapsed into a state of stagnation and 'lack of historicity'. In order to document this view, Bauer embarks on a detailed historical analysis of the main national communities that constituted the Austrian side of the dual monarchy. His main arguments are that at the beginning of the nineteenth century Cislethian Austria included three historical nations, the Germans and Italians who each had a nobility and middle classes, and the Poles who only had their own nobility. To demonstrate how a historical nation is transformed into a non-historical nation, Bauer first discusses the changes experienced by the Czech nation.

After the defeat of the Bohemian army at the hands of the Austrians, the Bohemian leaders were executed or fled abroad and the emperor's soldiers settled in Czech areas. The lands of the Czech nobility were confiscated and the nobility exterminated. The few remaining Czech nobles were promptly assimilated into the class of new settlers. After the Thirty Years War, the Czech population was reduced to a third of its original size. All that remained of this nation were a few craftsmen and a large peasant population. According to Bauer, these classes could not 'develop the Czech culture' and without a nobility and an indigenous middle class, 'the Czechs lost their culture and vanished from the historical stage'. The Czech language became a language of 'despised and exploited classes'. Everyone who advanced into the upper layer of that society, 'was ashamed to admit knowledge of the language of the unfree Czech peasants'. The national Czech culture 'died' and consequently the Czechs became a non-historical nation.[12]

The Slovenes are another example of a non-historical nation. According to Bauer, the Slovenian peasants did not form a cultural community. What united the peasant villages was 'the inertia of a peasant culture transmitted from generation to generation'. This is 'very different' from the dynamic development that characterises 'modern national communities of culture'.[13] In Cislethian Austria not only Czechs and Slovenes but also Ruthenians (Ukrainians) and Serbs were 'nations without history'. This situation was, however, dramatically changed by the revolutionary impact of the capitalist mode of production.

> This picture had been completely altered by the developments of the last 120 years. Capitalism and, in its wake, the modern state, effected everywhere a widening of the cultural community, in that they freed the masses from the fetters of an all powerful tradition, and called them to participate in the regeneration of a national culture. We refer to this process as the awakening of the non historic nations (*Das Erwachen der geschichtslosen Nationen*).[14]

The role of industrial capitalism has been to awaken non-historical nations to historical life. The bourgeoisie and their allied intellectual groups were, in Bauer's terms, the 'historical agents' of this regeneration. The development of industrial capitalism led to the popular spread of certain basic skills, and therefore, in terms of Bauer's argument about the progressive expansion of the national community, incorporated large 'tributary' sections of the population of historical nations into national life. This same process also 'awakes the non historical nations into historical life'. Bauer tries to show, through detailed historical analysis, how industrial capitalism was the most important cause for the 're-entry of the Czech nation into cultural life'. A new proletariat developed out of the Czech peasants, who hated the German bourgeoise and mistakenly included in this form of hatred the German working class. The Czech cottage industry and artisans were also affected by the development of industrial capitalism and joined the Czech workers in their hatred of Germans. A similar process takes place among other national communities. In Austria:

> All social antagonisms manifest themselves as national antagonisms because the dominant classes had long since become German. The ... hatred against bureaucracy, nobility and the capitalist class had to take the form of the hatred of Czechs against Germans.[15]

Initially, the Austrian state developed a few primary schools for the Czech peasants, but the main impulse for national revival came from the Czech intelligentsia, especially teachers and clergy, who began to revive the national language and culture.

The important side effect of this process was to intensify the national antagonisms, since with the development of industrial capitalism and its intricate relations between nations and classes, 'national hatred is a form of transformed class hatred'.[16] Given the dominance of German culture in Austria, German workers were better protected, educated and had at their disposal a 'more advanced' industrial organisation. This generated a hatred of 'the privileged German majority', which in turn generated the 'German hatred of the minorities'.

For Bauer historical nations are those that have 'normal' class structures, while non-historical nations are those national communities entirely located within certain subordinated classes or strata and whose segmental position differentiates them from others by class or political factors. Non-historical nations exist in multinational societies based on the coercive juxtaposition of different national communities, in which national existence is epiphenomenal to a subordinate class location. The development of capitalism requires the development of communicative cultural skills, and consequently the proletariat, the middle class and the new intelligentsia, 'revive' the national culture and 'awake' the national community into national life.[17] Bauer's analysis of the process of the awakening of non historical nations is considered by Herod as a 'valid historical model through which the fall and renascence of certain of the central European national groups could be intelligently explained',[18] and R. Rosdolsky argues that 'it conceptualizes in a very correct manner the situation of many oppressed populations in Central and Eastern Europe in the 18th and 19th century'.[19]

However, and in spite of this eulogy, if Bauer's conceptualisation of the awakening of non-historical nations is put together with the connected discussion on the exclusion of the tributary classes from the national culture, and the one-dimensional evolutionism of his historical conceptualisation of the national community, what emerges is a picture of a linear epiphenomenalist analysis of his historical case study. This picture stands in remarkable contrast with the perceptive multidimensional theoretical discussion of the process of national formation.

It seems that in Bauer's work there is an almost unsustainable tension between the imaginative analysis of the nation as a community of fate, and the narrow one-sidedness of the case study which is trapped in the class reductionist perspective dominant in the socialist movement of his time. In some ways it seems as if there are two Bauers writing this book: one Bauer fresh out of the intellectual environment of fin-de-siècle Vienna, with brilliant and innovative ideas matured through Max Adler's and his own debate with the neo-Kantians and classical Marxism; and another Bauer, the party man, loyal to the dogmas of economistic Marxism and severely restrained by the need to demonstrate his allegiance to the doctrinal teachings of Marx and Engels.

Nation and State in Bauer's Work

Before concluding this evaluation of Bauer's work, a brief review of another aspect of his ideas is necessary, that of the connection between the national community and the state. According to Bauer, the modern national state emerges out of the development of mercantile capitalism. However, he qualifies this statement in two ways. Firstly, it does not mean that every form of state organisation represents the domination of the bourgeoisie, for there are certain historical periods in which no class clearly dominates the state apparatus.[20] Secondly, and more directly relevant to the discussion on the national question, Bauer argues that there is no intrinsic reason for a capitalist (bourgeois) state to be 'national'.

National states, Bauer argues, are not the causal result of the development of the capitalist mode of production, but rather of a specific configuration of historical events in Western Europe. In order to substantiate this claim, he indicates that the modern state emerged in Italy, the country that could claim the 'oldest mercantile form of capitalist production'.[21] Here, in the rich Italian city states, for the first time, the dominant classes learned to use the state 'as an instrument to further capitalist interests'. Once established, one aspect was crucial for its survival, the ability to constitute a mercenary army to sustain its generally small area of dominance and extract the taxation which made the whole operation profitable. In this case, there was no reason for the state to become 'national'.

However, in 'the great western nations' the process of mercantile state development followed a different path – it became 'entangled' with the feudal state.[22] At this point Bauer develops a detailed historical discussion to substantiate the matter-of-fact argument that, in France, absolutism used the mercantile bourgeoise to eclipse the power of feudalism. In Germany, he argues, the situation was rather different and as a result the German nation was dismembered into a series of small states. The emergence of a national state in France and the fragmentation in Germany had nothing to do with mercantile capitalism as such, but was rather the result of a different historical configuration of class alliances within a collapsing feudal order.[23]

Now, the nineteenth century witnessed a dramatic change, which Bauer calls the nationality principle. This is the notion that every national community must have its own separate state. After lamenting that in 'modern political sciences' the concepts of 'nation' and 'state' are hopelessly confused, and after giving examples of the improper use of the term nation to designate the population of a state, Bauer rhetorically asks, 'Why it seems so 'natural', so 'rational' that every nation and only one nation, should form a political community?'[24]

He answers his question in two ways; firstly he argues that all movements for national emancipation are the result of a real or alleged fear of foreign domination. In certain cases this is undoubtedly correct. Many national independence movements overthrow a heavy foreign yoke and the emerging national state is a welcome advance on the previous state of affairs; 'this is a straightforward case and requires no explanation', Bauer argues. But in no small number of cases, the movement for national emancipation greatly advances the position of the upper classes of the oppressed national community under foreign domination, while the change makes little difference to the oppressed classes. Bauer reasons that only in very few cases is the struggle for independence perceived with indifference by the subordinated strata. He also quotes a number of cases when the subordinated strata were 'better off' under foreign domination than under the yoke of 'their own upper classes'. What causes this curious phenomenon of the popular masses struggling against foreign domination in cases where they have nothing to lose or to win?

> Petty bourgeois, peasants and workers are under alien domination in every state, including national states. They are exploited and oppressed by landowners, capitalists and bureaucrats. But this form of alien domination is not readily apparent but must be grasped conceptually. *However, foreign national domination is evident* [emphasis added], immediately visible. If the worker goes to a public service office, or attends a court hearing, s/he may not understand that the latter are an alien power ... they appear to be agents of his/her own nation. But if the judge or civil servant are from a different nation, if they speak a foreign language, the subordination to the alien power becomes clearly visible and consequently unbearable.[25]

This is the main explanation of the 'popularity' of national states: the fear, real or imagined, of foreign domination. A people being ruled by a foreign nation rapidly discovers that this makes oppression and exploitation 'evidently clear and therefore unbearable'. The conclusion that Bauer draws from this is that the desire to avoid foreign domination is the trigger of all movements for national-state emancipation during the nineteenth century.

There is, however, another dimension to widespread existence of national states, and it relates to the functionality of the national state apparatus for the development of the capitalist system. This is related to the centralising tendencies of capitalism, and here Bauer reproduces without any major innovation Lenin's and Kautsky's arguments. The consequence of this centralistic tendency, he says, is that 'powerful economic forces operate against the fragmentation of the economic area of the national community'.[26] Two powerful forces combine to give birth to that symbiotic creature called the nation state: a political desire to be free from foreign national rule, and the economic functional requirement of mercantile capitalism to enlarge as much as possible the area of a homogeneous market. If free trade were a widely accepted philosophy it would have been possible, according to Bauer, to tolerate the political fragmentation of the same national communities into autonomous states. However, in a world in which there are powerful trade barriers the national state is the best defence for the national mercantile classes.[27] So mercantile capitalism exercised a dual, contradictory, effect on the development of the national community: on the one hand, a centrifugal political effect based on the demand for democratic self-determination and the rejection of foreign rule, but on the other hand, a centripetal effect based on the economic requirements of a unified area of trade.

Bauer concludes that it is therefore important to understand the nationality principle (the idea of the nation state) as a historical construct generated by the bourgeoisie in struggle. In line with the classical Marxist view of the importance of the modern centralised state for the hegemonic success of capitalism, he argues that the triumphant bourgeoisie required a universally accepted principle to delimit the geographical area of the state. If the use of Gramscian terminology may be permitted at this point, what Bauer argues is that the triumphant bourgeoisie required a hege-monic principle which would allow the incorporation of all strata of the society into the newly created social order. But how will the borders of the new bourgeois state be delimited? And, more impor-tantly, what mechanism will generate the widest possible support for this new form of state? This is the point at which the national community enters the picture.

Before explaining his position, Bauer must dispel a misunder-standing arising from the class reductionist analysis of orthodox Marxism. He must explain why 'certain social forms' have autono-mous existence while others have not. Here Bauer makes a clear distinction between social forms which exist as external and inter-nal mechanisms. External mechanisms are in general formal organisations, often but not necessarily coercive, such as the state. These forms are not autonomous because they cannot survive outside a given juridical order which gives them meaning. The second type of social forms also originate in a specific economic and political conjuncture, but are nevertheless capable of tran-scending the original relations of causality. Since they constitute part of the subjectivity of the participating agents such forms do not exist as an external force, 'they survive because they are not alive in an external power, but in each individual'.[28] From this it is not difficult to discover Bauer's understanding of the nation as a community of fate. 'When the Czech leader Palaký states in a out-burst of anger that the Czechs were here before the Austrian state and will be here after the dismemberment of the Austrian state' or, if one is allowed use a more contemporary example, when a Palestinian leader states that 'Palestinians were here before the creation of the Israeli state and will be here after its dismember-ment', s/he is expressing an idea central to the nationality principle:

the community, which is an indestructible force operating in each individual, is, after its emergence, independent of every positive right and independent from every existing power. The national community is alive even if the state collapses, because it is alive in every single individual member.[29]

This is, according to Bauer, the potency of the idea of the national state. The state as an external power could be physically destroyed. The bourgeoise destroys the feudal or absolutist state, but the national community cannot so easily be destroyed because it is 'alive' in each individual member. So, the bourgeoise rapidly realised that the national community was the best possible substratum on which to implement its economic and political project. In a way which remarkably resembles Gramsci's thinking Bauer argues:

> When the revolutionary bourgeoisie wishes to annihilate and replace the traditional state hostile to its goals ... it confronts the hostile external power with the durable internal national community. In this way it appropriates the demand that the very internal community should be the holder of the external power and that the external power should protect the internal community. This is the root of the nationality principle.[30]

In other words, the effectiveness of the struggle of the bourgeoisie and, as Gramsci argues, the working class, is that in order to develop its political project it does not co-opt the national community, but simply *becomes* it by identifying the bourgeois state with the national community. Bauer qualifies this by arguing that it is not a general theoretical principle but a result of the relationship of the bourgeois state-national community at a given historical period in Western Europe. As much as the nationality principle was a 'powerful device' of state formation, it is not a universal principle as the existence of multinational states appears to indicate. This last point is initially directed towards understanding the history of Cislethian Austria and advocating the radical transformation of the Habsburg empire into a federal state of nationalities – along the constitutional lines suggested by Renner and the principles of the Brno programme.

Bauer's point is not entirely wrong because it is directed to legitimise the existence of that multinational state that subsequently ceased to exist. As Walker Connor rightly argues, in spite of the strength of the above discussed tendency to create national states, the vast majority of states registered as members of the United Nations are not national but multinational.[31]

The theoretical argument that Bauer developed after his lengthy discussion of the Austrian situation closely resembles Renner's ideas and bears a certain similarity to the Millet system in the Ottoman empire. Following the centralising principle initially developed by the absolutist state and taken over by the bourgeoisie, and whose politico-philosophical expression is to be found in Rousseau, state and society in contemporary states are an all-embracing centralised totality. There are two politico-juridical entities, one the individual and the other the sovereign 'vólònte general'. This is what Bauer and Renner call the atomistic-centralist structure of modern states. This totalising tendency fails to acknowledge a very important intermediate location, what we may today call the pluralistic structure of the civil society. In the case of the national question, the ethno-national identity of the dominant groups becomes associated with the state, to the economic, cultural and political disadvantage of national and ethnic minorities. To counteract this tendency, Bauer and Renner suggested a careful decentralisation of the state apparatus coupled with the juridical institutionalisation of the 'personality principle'. The idea was later vilified by the Bolsheviks under the name it took in Russia – the principle of national cultural autonomy. This political system guarantees certain cultural and political rights to every national community by organising autonomous national corporations of co-nationals regardless of territory of residence.[32]

Another important issue which must be resolved before attempting to summarise Bauer's argument is the question of national boundaries. What delimits a national community from another? Why is England and not Yorkshire or Lancashire a national community, or why Germany and not Bavaria, or indeed why are the people of Andalusia not considered a national community as are the people of Catalonia?

Bauer answers this question in two ways. Firstly, he says there is a tendency in each 'narrower community of culture' – such as the ones mentioned here – to become separate national communities. Each of these cases represent developmental stages in the process of national formation. However, there is a counter tendency to this process of differentiation, and it is related to the idea of the progressive expansion of the national classes. 'Modern Capitalism begins gradually to distinguish the lower classes of each nation sharply from each other, for they gain access to the cultural life of the nation and to the national language.'[33] In other words, the delimitation of one national community from another cannot be established in the abstract but only after the concrete evaluation of the process that led to the formation of the national communities under analysis. For the same reason, it cannot be theoretically established whether Yorkshire or Lancashire are separate national communities. It all depends if the community of fate that links Yorkshire subjects is stronger than the community of fate that links English people as a whole. All the mentioned groups are potential national communities; it is an empirical test to prove whether they are or not. This is not a convincing answer since the evaluation of the elements that constitute a community of fate, is a matter of contention. What empirical indicators would Bauer use to ascertain whether the population of the Valencian community in the Spanish state are Catalan or Valencian? This is a matter of debate among the Valencian people.

Bauer's *Nationalitätenfrage* and the Nationalities Conflict in the Soviet Union

Bauer's relation to the Soviet Union was neither hostile nor supportive. He rejected the bureaucratic dictatorial methods of the Bolsheviks and he was an ardent critic of Stalinism but, unlike Kautsky and other Western European orthodox Marxists, he advocated a greater cooperation between the reformist and revolutionary wings of the socialist camp. He argued that the dichotomy reform–revolution was misleading and saw in the Bolshevik Revolution a positive initial step towards the construction of socialism in that country, provided that genuine forms of democracy and pluralism could follow from the initial authoritarian Bolshevik uprising.[34] Bauer also believed that the process of industrialisation would necessarily push the Soviet Union towards a democratic road. In one of his most important works, 'Zwischen Zwei Weltkriegen?' ('Between Two World Wars?'), he argued:

> A sudden transition from the Soviet dictatorship to a democracy is certainly not possible ... (but) the gradual democratisation of the Soviet constitution will become necessary to the degree to which the Soviet people develop in the course of a rapid cultural climb to self-conscious citizens (Kulturmenschen) who are not prepared to obey bureaucratic absolutism, who demand personal freedom, intellectual freedom and the freedom of personal decision and self-government.[35]

In view of Bauer's position on the Soviet system, it is no coincidence that with the development of perestroika and the momentous changes taking place in Eastern Europe there is a renewed interest in his work in the Soviet Union and other Eastern European countries.[36]

When evaluating the impact of Bauer's work on the pressing nationalities problems in the Soviet Union, it is important to keep in mind that he was considered by the Bolsheviks to be their most formidable left-wing ideological opponent on the national question. The *Nationalitätenfrage* was translated into Russian before 1917. The book was widely read by the Mensheviks and left-wing socialists, and it exercised an enormous influence on the Jewish Bund and other socialist groups among the non-Russian nationalities. Given that it contradicts some important Bolshevik premises on the national question, Lenin and Stalin took upon themselves the task of strongly refuting Bauer's argument. As mentioned above, Stalin was sent to Vienna to acquaint himself with the Austrian position and to write a monograph to refute the main arguments of Bauer's *Nationalitätenfrage*.[37]

It is not surprising then that, before perestroika, the Soviet literature on Bauer was united in its rejection and vilification of his main ideas on the national question.[38] It was possible to detect, however – particularly in academic writings – a growing unease with the Leninist dogma that was choking, in more that ways than one, Soviet research on ethnicity and national culture. Important Soviet ethnographic studies tended implicitly to validate some of Bauer's arguments despite the stigma attached to him. Victor Kozlov of the Institute of Ethnography in Moscow observed in a pre-perestroika article that:

> In the course of ethnogenesis, various factors, including the specific natural features of ethnic territory lead to the emergence of common features of material and spiritual culture.[39]

This conception of communal national character is certainly closer to Bauer than to Lenin, as is another important attempt to redefine Stalin's old concept of 'psychological make-up':

> The old concept of psychological make-up of a nation if taken in its full sense, represents all the areas of social psychology and not just national peculiarities. Even if we confine the concept of psychological make-up to these peculiarities alone, we should find that they are embodied not only in the culture but also in

the consciousness, life style, ethics and traditions. Lastly, the psychological make up may be regarded as a supra class conception, which, however it cannot be in a class society.[40]

The Soviets' poor record on nationalities and the ever-growing threat of dismemberment of the Soviet Federation is a powerful encouragement to revise the old Leninist dogma on the national question. Perestroika appears to be creating the conditions for such a revision to take place. There is a desire to debate with, and learn from, Western socialist experiences and a renewed interest in what the Soviets consider to be the theoretical works of left-wing social democracy. The work of Bauer is a prime example. Shveizer, for instance, concludes his article on Austro-Marxism by arguing that many left wing socialists in Western Europe evaluate perestroika 'from positions characteristic of the last works of Bauer'. He also notes Bauer's concern about events in the Soviet Union and approvingly quotes Bauer's assertion that the [Stalinist] 'wave of terror has not only brought a loss of prestige to the Soviet Union but has in general caused a colossal harm to socialism'. He then congratulates Bauer: 'This position cannot but evoke respect for him'.[41] Ierusalimsky argues that one of the main achievements of Austro-Marxism was 'a serious working out of the national question'. While he states that Austro-Marxism has certainly not produced full and correct answers, 'the irony of history' bears out that 'if many clever revolutionary formulas and ideas of the first two decades of our epoch belong to the past, then these problems are today at the centre of attention of all socialist oriented forces'.[42]

The urgent national problems in the Soviet Union are propelling many Soviet academic and political analysts to re-evaluate Lenin's and Stalin's legacy on the national question. A. A. Prazauskas, a Lithuanian academic from the Institute of Oriental Studies, recently (1988) called into question 'the great attainments of Leninist national policy' after 1920. He characterised the basic elements of Stalinist national policy as 'supercentralisation of administration', 'compulsory learning of Russian', 'under-representation of non-Russians in the central apparatus', 'destruction of cultural autonomy' and 'mass deportations of some national communities'. This meant that Soviet federalism 'lost any significance' and that Soviet policies on the national question were coloured by 'Duplicity and cynicism'. The claim that the national question has been resolved was a slogan that did not reflect the real situation. Prazauskas then argues that:

The national question – this is the resolution of a question about the liquidation of national inequality ... depends directly and in the closest way upon the degree of development of democracy in a given society. Within the limits of a bureaucratic model of socialism in general, there were no mechanisms which would have expressed national interests and secured the timely resolution of problems.[43]

Class reductionism impelled the Bolsheviks to see in the national question a temporary phenomenon that will be superseded by the development of a socialist society. The Russian language was seen as a mere tool of communication and national sensitivities over this issue were overlooked. Internationalism was seen as the transcendence of national differences and not as respect for national diversity. The ideal of a post-national Soviet culture was never accomplished. Contemporary Soviet realities have proven the Bolsheviks wrong. As Bauer argued, national communities are not a temporary phenomenon and the positive recognition of national cultural diversity with equality of rights and opportunities at the political level is a precondition for the abolition of national oppression. Federalism requires not only political decentralisation but, more importantly, the decentralisation of the party structure. National equality also requires political equality of languages. Perhaps a critical review of the ideas of the Brno (Brünn) programme, free from past prejudices, could be the point of departure for a fresh approach.

No one can claim that the work of Bauer offers instant solutions to the very protracted national conflicts in the Soviet Union – in fact some of Bauer's arguments suffer from the same Bolshevik malaise: class reductionism. But a reassessment of his work in the light of present Soviet realities may inspire some Soviet analysts to break with the Leninist dogma and try some original solutions to one of the most drawn-out of Soviet problems: the national question.

Conclusion: is Bauer's Theory Relevant Today?

It is not difficult to agree with Kolakowski that Bauer's *Nationalitätenfrage* is 'the best treatise on nationality problems to be found in the Marxist theory', even when the distortive rigidities of the economistic model used for the discussion of the case study are taken into account. The theoretical conceptualisation he developed represents a fine attempt to come to grips with the multidimensionality of the national question. He analyses the national community as a developmental process which cannot be reduced to any single, ontologically defined mechanism of causality. While the term community of fate today seems dated and farfetched, the characteristics of the phenomena described by Bauer seem to reveal the national community as a continuing process.

His conceptualisation makes it possible to think of this national community as an intersection of the interactive relation of subjects through a given historical context, and provides the flexibility necessary to explain different dimensions of that elusive phenomenon called the nation. The notion of the national character, too, seems a useful point of departure for a discussion of the ideological dimension of the national imaginary. The idea of a national character has been neglected by most Marxist discussions to the extent that it became completely monopolised by ethnocentric discourses which perceive it to be the essence of some transhistorical and metaphysical quality. As Bauer rightly argues, if one is to demonstrate the falsity and the immorality of ethnocentric visions of the national character, it is crucial to maintain the validity of the argument by not falling into the opposite form of essentialism – the ontological and universal denial of the existence of national characters.

Bauer's account of relations of causality, however, must be treated with caution. In their zeal to dispel the teleological notions of social existence propounded by the neo-Kantians, Adler and Bauer at times take the discussion of causality too far, negating any transformative autonomy of the phenomenon under consideration.

In many ways, Bauer's discussion of the relations between nations and states is overshadowed by the Austrian socialist debate on the future of the Austrian empire. He neglects the role of the state in structuring the national community, because he was eager to suggest a political solution to the Austrian predicament in terms of a federation of nationalities. However, Bauer's argument about the historical relativity of the national state is worth pursuing. He is right in arguing that there is nothing intrinsically 'national' in the make-up of contemporary states, as there is nothing intrinsically 'etatist' in the make-up of national communities. The relation between the nation and state is a heuristic construct which needs to be explained in more detail, and Bauer's account of the European historical relativity of that relation is a useful place from which to start.

The Austrian socialist project for a multinational federal state is treated with derision nowadays. The ideology of the national state has become a normative yardstick in the analysis of the national community. In particular the doctrine that every national community is to have its own national state and that each national state should comprise a single and entire national community has created an unfortunate terminological ambiguity. The historical relativity of the ideology of the nation state is often neglected, and the close connection between the notions of 'nation' and 'state' is taken for granted; not only in the specialised literature, but also in most popular political discussions of the topic.

This hides the fact that the nation state is a modern construct which results from contingent and circumstantial events connected to the development of modernity in Europe. There is no obvious generic reason to support the idea that states should be 'national', nor that all national communities should have their own separate national states.

More ominously, the exclusivist ideology of the nation state has provided the breeding ground for violent conflicts and the most disturbing and destructive forms of ethnocentrism. Even among national liberation movements it is easy to find internal ethnic and national conflicts. It is no exaggeration to claim that the desire for homogeneous national states inevitably puts ethnic and national minorities in a vulnerable position. Persecution of ethnic and national minorities, expulsion and ostracism are common features of the political history of modern nation-states. Even the most aberrant forms of contemporary racism are connected to the paranoiac desire that every state should comprise an entire, exclusive and homogeneous nation. For if, as W. Connor argues, 92 per cent of all states registered in the UN are multi-ethnic and multinational, then the desire to correct the discrepancy between the theory and the practice of the national state becomes a permanent threat to ethnic and national minorities and an enduring source of intercommunal tension.

In terms of the Marxist tradition, the most strident critics of the nation state have also been the strongest critics of the importance and value of national existence. The pitfalls of economism did not permit classical Marxists successfully to deconstruct the relationship between the nation and the state. National communities were seen as functional to the state and economism led to the paradigmatic trap of understanding national identities in terms of the existence of national states. The rejection of the bourgeois state necessarily led to the rejection of the nation.

Here lies the contemporary value of the work of Bauer: the ability to deconstruct the duality nation–state and to develop a theory of the nation which analyses national communities in their own terms. The dual debate of Austro-Marxism with neo-Kantianism and classical Marxism sensitised Bauer's theory to the multidimensionality of the national question. It is puzzling that the same openness was not translated to the analysis of the concrete case study.

Bauer's work has a number of theoretical and historical limitations, some of which were outlined in the course of this and the preceeding chapters. It does, however, develop in an analysis which is a useful – if limited – point of departure for a positive rethinking of the national phenomenon beyond the limitations of the nation state, and a more sensitive understanding of the national arena. Without this, the national question will continue to be what Nairn calls 'Marxism's great historical failure'.[44]

Conclusion

The aim of this study of the classical Marxist European heritage on the national question has been to establish the causes for the recurrent intellectual and political inability of this tradition to explain the nature of the national phenomenon. In trying to account for this 'great historical failure'[1], it has been argued by some that European Marxism has no specific theory on the national question and in any case it is impossible to provide a coherent theory given the elusiveness of the phenomenon under consideration.

Contrary to this position, the aim of this work has been to argue that the most influential European Marxist discussions on the national phenomenon show a recurrent thematic unity and a relatively cohesive line of argument, despite important political and intellectual differences between them. The theoretical and epistemological bases of this thematic unity have been called *the Marxist parameters of analysis of the national question*. These are: a) *the theory of the universal evolution of the forces of production*: this is the position that understands the process of social transformation as universally explicable in terms of developmental laws, and capable of expression in universal and hierarchically defined stages of transformation; b) *the theory of economic reductionism* is the epistemological stance which defines the privileged causal status of the productive process and establishes that all meaningful processes of social change occur through changes in the process of production which is located in the economic arena (the Marxian metaphorical dichotomy base–superstructure represents a sharp conceptual distinction between causal factors and residual categories designed to secure the conditions of existence of causal factors); c) *the eurocentric bias in concrete discussions of the universal process of change*. This is the construction of developmental models which universalise observed categories of social transformation resulting from the distinctive and specific rationale of Western European societies.

These parameters of analysis are not specific to the discussion of the national question. Nor do they constitute a unified and explicitly conceptualised corpus of theoretical literature. They do, however, give meaning to the most influential European Marxist discussions of the national question reviewed in this work, constituting a paradigmatic strait-jacket which limits the ability of historical materialism to deal with the diversified forms of the national question. These parameters also represent an obligatory point of departure for various attempts to evaluate the political and class dimensions of national existence. The works of Bauer and Gramsci show a greater sensitivity towards the multifarious forms of national existence because of their ability partially to break with the limiting paradigms of classical Marxism.[2]

Marx and Engels

Contrary to the generalised opinion that Marx and Engels' discussions of the national question were ad hoc positions informed by circumstantial events, it has been argued here that there is a certain coherence and sense of purpose in their work. The apparent contradictions in their standpoint are expressed in their support for the demands for state independence of the Irish and Polish national movements on the one hand, and their adamant refusal to grant any such concessions to the Czechs and other Southern Slavs on the other.

In evaluating these positions it has been argued that, far from being contradictory, they represent a coherent expression of the analytical stance of Marx and Engels. What configured this in both cases was the perceived developmental logic of the forces of production within the capitalist system. Polish and Irish independence were at the time 'progressive' because they helped to unfold the historical transformation of the capitalist mode of production.[3] Czechs and other Southern Slavs required, in the judgement of Marx and Engels, the perpetuation of 'backward' developmental conditions, since neither could survive as an independent state in a system of capitalist production.

The use of the metaphysical Hegelian dichotomy of historical and non-historical nations was stripped from the mythical notion of Volksgeist but, at the same time, was reinvigorated by the unilinear evolutionist view of the development of the forces of production. This was conceptualised as the ability of national communities to enter into capitalist relations of production. This view represented an epistemologically coherent but profoundly insensitive and deterministic analysis of the national question. In a style reminiscent of the Calvinist dualism of Weber's Protestant ethic, this approach appears to argue that some national communities were afforded the privilege of entering the capitalist era while others were damned for ever. For Marx and Engels the modern nation was a coherent historical phenomenon; it represented a mechanism for consolidating and securing the conditions of existence of the bourgeoisie. Consequently the theory of non-historical nations is not a curiosity, a slip of the tongue or a regrettable mishap. It is, rather, the result of the formulation of rigid universal laws of social evolution which define the precise historical location of the modern nation and, by default, render obsolete the existence of national communities unable to fulfil this eurocentric criterion.

The second aspect of Marx and Engels' analytical stance was the requirement that every modern nation should form its own separate state, which made the formation of national states the only real and valid raison d'être for nationalist movements. National communities unable to form such states should be assimilated into more 'vital' and 'energetic' nations, with democracy as compensation. It was argued that the Marxian model of national development was that of 'large' Western European national states, particularly France and 'British England'. The latter was considered a successful case of assimilation of the Celtic fringe, with the important exception of Ireland – a historical nation deserving a national state. This conceptualisation of the national question constituted the nucleus of the misleading heritage of European Marxism, and informed the positions in the main debates of the Second and Third international on the national question.

The Second International

In his influential work on the historical development of Marxist theory, Kolakowski argues that during the period of the Second International Marxist theory was not codified as a rigid orthodoxy.[4] Contrary to this assertion, it has been argued here that the plurality of thinkers and debates in the development of the Marxist theory – including the national question – did not prevent its ossification. During this period the debates on the national question were both common and thorough, reflecting the importance of the subject for the fin-de-siècle socialist movement. But, with the important exception of the works of the Austro-Marxist tradition, they did not break with the parametrical rigidities imposed by the thought of the founding fathers. In evaluating the

most influential contributions of the competing Marxist schools of
the period, it is possible to recognise a genuine attempt to come to
grips with a problem perceived to have been insufficiently discussed by Marx and Engels. In the works of Kautsky and
Luxemburg, however, the very real possibilities of conceptualising
the national phenomenon in a novel and imaginative way were
silenced by the dogmas of economism. In spite of profound and
lasting disagreements over important conceptual and strategical
issues, Luxemburg and Kautsky were equally confined to a partial
and limited understanding of the national issue by the crippling
epistemological stance of epiphenomenalism. Thus an autonomous theoretical analysis of the national phenomenon became a
conceptual impossibility.

Not all political and theoretical stances of the Second
International were equally shaped by economic reductionism.
Bernstein, challenged the dominant discourse by attempting a
revision of the parameters of economic determination. He believed
that the most significant characteristic of Marxist theory was not
the conceptualisation of the economic determination of the forces
of production – the base and superstructure metaphor – but the
discovery of a developmental thought (Entwicklungsgedanken)
which allowed for a universal conceptualisation of the evolutionary process (Evolutionsbegriff) of the social arena.[5] Social transformation was not considered to be the result of an abrupt
revolutionary change, but the consequence of a universal process
of developmental evolutionism whose final goal could not be pre-
dicted because it is, too, subject to the same logic of mutation.
Developmental evolutionism was the natural condition of social
existence and it applied to the future socialist society as well as to
contemporary capitalism. The revisionist tradition not only criticised the classical Marxian notion of the inevitable collapse of capitalism, but was also highly critical of the idea that the social arena
would be finally polarised into two antagonistic and fundamental
classes.

However, the relative liberation from the strait-jacket of economism was compensated by an even stronger dependence on the
paradigm of social evolution which permeated classical Marxist
theory. Revisionism merely replaced the working class as the privileged agency of social change with another privileged agency – the
ethical and progressive human being emerging out of modernity.
The same teleological bias of classical Marxism in identifying a
privileged agency of social transformation, and bestowing upon it
a functional-causal status in the process of social change, was

maintained. The one-dimensional evolutionary paradigm which characterised the thoughts and ideas of the revisionist school are clearly detectable in Bernstein's conceptualisation of the national arena. The national community was identified with the national state and nationhood was essentially a political issue. The state was progressively transformed by the increasing political participation of the working class: it ceased to be the exclusive domain of the bourgeoisie and became a positive asset of the working population. The transformation of national state also reflected the developmental evolution of the social arena. If at the time of the *Communist Manifesto* the proletariat had no fatherland, this situation was dramatically changed by the progressive democratisation of the national state. All state affairs were legitimate socialist concerns, including colonialism. This developmental logic provided the rationale for Bernstein's uncritical acceptance of the progressive nature of industrial capitalism and for his rigid understanding of the process of social evolution in hierarchical and eurocentric terms. If the emergence and existence of national communities is to be located in Bernstein's universal-historical continuum, then there is no escape from a hierarchical interpretation of national development or from the argument that, given the uneven nature of the process of development, some nations are 'more civilised' than others. The optimistic revisionist belief in progress and civilisation resulted in a complacent and profoundly ethnocentric treatment of the national question. While the revisionist enthusiasm for colonial ventures was unique in the context of the Second International, it has been argued that it would be wrong to regard this position as an unconnected aberration. The unilateral notions of social evolution which permeated most classical Marxist works on the national issue were at least partly responsible for both the creation of an intellectual breeding ground for these ideas, and for what Kolakowski calls a 'rigid codification of a dogmatic orthodoxy'.[6]

In terms of the evolutionist notions which prevailed in the thoughts and actions of the leaders of the Second International, the October Revolution was an inconceivable event. It would be misleading, however, to argue that Marxism-Leninism broke with epiphenomenalism because it could not justify the Bolshevik Revolution. Rather, it was Lenin's and Trotsky's ability to break with the limitations of epiphenomenalism which allowed the Bolsheviks to sensitise Marxist theory to the social and political conditions of Czarist Russia, paving the way for the political struggle which successfully culminated in the Revolution.

The social and political structure of the vast and diverse country of Russia resisted the imposition of Western and Central European models of development. Above all, three aspects of what was later called Marxist-Leninist theory were considered crucial for the conceptualisation of the national question. Firstly, the expansion of the political field permitted Marxism-Leninism to conceptualise the political dimension of national phenomena free from the limits of the transparent relations of causality which characterised the discussion of Kautsky and Luxemburg. The relative autonomy of the national phenomenon allowed Marxist-Leninists the strategic use of national demands to advance the cause of the revolution. Secondly, the conceptualisation of the Revolution allowed Marxist-Leninism to argue that a bourgeois democratic revolution could be immediately followed by a socialist revolution, and that revolutionary situations display regional peculiarities. This permitted the conceptualisation of the right of nations to self-determination – a cardinal point in the Marxist-Leninist theory of the national question – as a bourgeois democratic demand to be supported by the proletariat in 'backward' situations: that is, situations in which bourgeois democratic revolutions had not yet been fully accomplished and where the avant garde party is aiming to transform the bourgeois democratic revolution into a fully fledged socialist revolution. Thirdly, the conceptualisation of imperialism and the motion of combined and uneven development paved the way for an understanding of the specific forms of oppression in the colonial world and for the articulation of the class contradictions of classical Marxism with the national contradictions of the imperialist era. In breaking with epiphenomenalism in order to explain the specific unevenness of the process of development in Czarist Russia, the Marxist-Leninist tradition managed to sensitise Marxist theory to the political dimension of the national question, and to the potentialities of the revolutionary movement outside of Europe. This position was vindicated by the revolutionary successes in China, Cuba and Vietnam.

However, putting politics in command was also the main weakness of the Bolshevik approach to the national question. The class reductionist understanding of the political arena required the evaluation of the political dimension of national communities from within the paradigmatic field of class determination. The national question in the Marxist-Leninist tradition was always looked at from the angle of the working class, an instrumentalist perception which obscured certain non-class features. The Marxist-Leninist tradition was unable to come to grips with the cultural and ethnic aspects of national existence because it was impossible to reduce the latter to the field of class determination. This blinded the Bolsheviks to the role of culture and ethnicity in the constitution and resilient existence of national communities. As Prazauskas, the Lithuanian member of the Soviet Institute for Oriental Studies, argues, the Marxist-Leninist approach to the national question led to the compulsory use of Russian language in the administrative apparatus, and to the lack of political mechanisms to express national or ethnic interests.[7] This perhaps explains some of the contemporary difficulties faced by the Soviet Union on the taxing nationalities problem.

Also, the taxonomical periodisation of the Marxist-Leninist analysis required the identification of a bourgeois dimension to every national movement. This prevented Marxist-Leninism from conceptualising the existence of non-bourgeois national movements – a glaring inadequacy for the ideology of a political movement which defines itself as the avant garde of the anti-colonial struggle in societies where, as a general rule, bourgeois classes hardly exist.

Gramsci

In view of the conflicting interpretations of the work of Gramsci, it has been argued that a class reductionist and a non-class reductionist reading of his work are equally possible. But from the point of view of the ongoing discussion on the national question, the originality and novelty in Gramsci's legacy resides only in recovering and expanding his partial break with class reductionism. The non-class reductionist interpretation of Gramsci discloses an imaginative and original – but nevertheless partial – attempt to find solutions to the perennial Marxist problems of interpreting the national issue beyond the restrictions of economism.

The concepts of historical bloc and national-popular represent an original way of conceptualising the specificity of the national arena. The constitution of a historical bloc implies a radical reconstruction of the relational identity of the elements which constitute the arena of the social. Classes are part of a historical bloc only insofar as they merge their specific identity with other classes or strata participating in that relation, thus creating a political will which constitutes a more inclusive social and political grouping. Gramsci argues that the historical bloc is a form of communality which attempts to become the national community; common culture is a crucial aspect in the crystallisation of a national community. For him, no hegemonic unit will emerge without claiming to represent society as a whole. A fundamental class becomes the organiser of a hegemonic unit when, in the context of the historical bloc, the intellectuals and popular masses establish an organic link in which culture in the intellectual sense (knowledge) develops a connection with culture in its anthropological sense (shared experiences). In the specific case of Italy, Gramsci called upon the working class and its organic intellectuals to lead the historical bloc that was to constitute the Italian national community, through a national-popular collective will – a task which the Italian bourgeoisie had conspicuously failed to perform.

The notion of this collective will captures both the political and cultural specificity of the national community, at the same time suggesting an organic link between intellectuals and popular masses for the purpose of creating the basis for a stable hegemonic formation. The significant novelty in the Gramscian approach is that the configuration of historical bloc and national-popular is not ultimately reducible to the direct determination of any of the fundamental classes in the process of production.

Gramsci's contribution to the development of Marxist theory is a set of analytical categories which enables us to think in a conceptual framework that breaks with class reductionism, but he himself fell short of this break. While the notion of national-popular collective will permits an understanding of the various forms of national existence at both the political and the cultural level, this two-dimensional understanding is limited by Gramsci's commitment to a consolidation of a national state that provides the conditions for a process of expansive hegemony.

The strategy for the construction of a new historical bloc is designed to convert this bloc into the national community, so that it can provide the basis for an integral state in an expanding hegemonic process. But herein lies one of the most serious limitations of the Gramscian discussion of the national question. The national community is important only insofar as it becomes the vehicle for the formation of a new political subjectivity in the form of the national-popular collective will. The national phenomenon is only important to the extent that it becomes the basis for the formation of a cohesive national community that will be able to sustain a national state. The Leninist traces are evident. Gramsci's notion of the national-popular is a decisive advance on Lenin's theory on the right of nations to self-determination because of the novel conceptualisation of culture and the intellectuals, but at the same time it remains trapped in the Leninist bias towards statism – the achievement and consolidation of a single state encompassing one single national community. Important traces of economic reductionism are to be found in Gramsci's inability to conceptualise those aspects of the national question not connected with the urge to form a cohesive national state – as in the case of the ethnonational minorities that exist in every Western state. The ethnonational plurality of the national arena and the problematic connection between the nation and the state remain outside the Gramscian formulation of the national-popular, blinding this otherwise insightful theoretical analysis to important plural dimensions of national existence.

Otto Bauer: the Way Forward?

To grasp the momentous but partial breakthrough of Otto Bauer, it is necessary to appreciate how the sharp nationalities conflict in the context of late imperial Austria was a crucial factor in directing the reluctant attention of the All-Austrian Socialist Party (Gesamtpartei) to the national question. While the conditions of uneven development in Czarist Russia produced innovative ways to conceptualise the political struggle, the political nightmare of the national struggles in the cracking Habsburg empire produced some of the most thoughtful Marxist discussions of the national phenomenon. This was not the result of an outright socialist support for nationalist causes – there was, in fact, no love lost between the Austrian socialists and nationalist movements. Rather, the Gesamtpartei realised that without tackling the national question head on, without developing a thorough political and intellectual understanding of the national phenomenon, they were condemned to political oblivion under the rising tide of nationalism. It was, above all, political urgency which generated the most serious questioning of the economistic conceptualisation of the national question.

Another important contribution to the originality of Bauer's thought was the emergence of that unique intellectual and political community which subsequently took the name of Austro-Marxism. What, above all, characterised the Austro-Marxist tradition was, as Bauer argues, the growing awareness of the complex nature of the social arena – a world that defies monocausal explanations. In terms of the emerging theory of the national question, Max Adler's critical engagement[8] with neo-Kantianism and revisionism on the one hand, and with classical Marxism on the other, was crucial in providing the new categories of analysis which permitted Bauer to make a break with economism and to develop the novel conceptualisation of the national phenomenon discussed in the *Nationalitätenfrage*.

The main advantage of Bauer's work in comparison with all of the other attempts to conceptualise the national issue is the analysis of the national community as a developmental process not reducible to a single, ontologically defined mechanism of causality. The characteristics of the phenomenon described by Bauer as community of fate are useful in understanding the national community both as a multidimensional and as a developmental process. The definition of national character is rescued from what Bauer calls the 'metaphysical essentialism' of nationalist ideologies, to become a historically specific characteristic of national communities.

In spite of this, Bauer's conceptualisation of the relation between nation and state is overshadowed by the old Austrian debate. He denies any role to the state in structuring the national community because he was eager to suggest a political solution to the Austrian predicament in terms of a federation of nationalities. He is right, however, in arguing that the form of the state does not functionally require a 'national' content and, likewise, that there is nothing intrinsically 'etatist' in the existence of national communities. The relationship between the two is a heuristic construct that needs not to be taken for granted, rather it must be historically explained. Bauer's argument is then a useful initial step in the process of deconstructing the relationship between nation and state.

However, the unilinear developmental character of the case study in Bauer's work is in sharp contrast to the perceptive and multifarious theoretical discussion of the process of national formation. It seems that there is an almost uncomfortable tension between the innovative theoretical analysis and the case study, which is enmeshed in a class reductionist outlook. It has been argued that in some ways it seems as if there are two Bauers writing this book: one Bauer fresh out of the intellectual environment of fin-de-siècle Vienna with brilliant and innovative ideas matured through Max Adler's and his own debate with the neo-Kantians and orthodox Marxism; and another Bauer, the party man, loyal to economistic Marxism and constrained by the need to demonstrate allegiance to the position of the socialist party.

In trying to establish the causes for the recurrent inability of the

European Marxist tradition adequately to conceptualise the national question, the separate and joint influences of economic reductionism, evolutionism and eurocentrism have been identified in each and every analysis of the national issue discussed in this work. Bauer and, to a lesser extent, Gramsci came closer to a more sensitive conceptualisation of the national arena only in those aspects of their respective works which involve a departure from economic reductionism and evolutionism. These departures went some way towards sensitising Marxist theory to the diversified forms of national existence.

But if the Marxist tradition is to leave behind once and for all what Nairn called the 'great historical failure', it must attempt to conceptualise the elusive and recurrent national phenomenon firmly outside the parameters of analysis which informed the European classical Marxist debates on the national question.

Notes

INTRODUCTION

1. C. Castoriadis, *The Imaginary Institutions of Society* (Cambridge: Polity Press, 1987) pp. 168–9. See also J. Thompson, 'Ideology and the Social Imaginary', in J. Thompson (ed), *Studies in the Theory of Ideology* (Cambridge: Polity Press, 1984) p. 21.
2. 'Evolution', in C. D. Renning (ed), *Encyclopaedia of Marxism, Communism and Western Society* (New York: Herder & Herder, 1972–3) p. 241.
3. T. Nairn, *The Break up of Britain* (New Left Books, second expanded edition, 1981), p. 329.
4. See for example S. Zubaida, 'Theories of Nationalism', in G. Littlejohn *et al.*, *Power and the State* (London: Croom Helm, 1978).
5. K. Marx, *Capital*, Vol. 1 (London: Lawrence & Wishart, 1977) p. 19.
6. Trotsky's well-known theory of combined and uneven development is a significant acknowledgement of the difficulties experienced by doctrinaire and eurocentric theories of evolution in Russia and, at the same time, an ingenious but ultimately futile attempt to overcome those difficulties without discarding the overall universal and developmental logic of Marxist thought. For a sympathetic discussion of this theory see M. Löwy, *The Politics of Combined and Uneven Development* (London: Verso, 1981).
7. '... it is always necessary to distinguish between the material transformations of the economic conditions of production which can be determined with the precision of the natural sciences, and the legal, political, religious, artistic or philosophic, in short ideological forms'. K. Marx, *Preface to the Contribution to the Critique of Political Economy*, Various editions.
8. L. Krader, 'The Theory of Evolution' in E. Hobsbawm (ed) *History of Marxism*, (Brighton: Harvester Press, 1982) p. 192. English translation of Vol. 1 of *Storia del Marxismo*
9. *Capital*, p. 20.
10. An important exception to this general trend is the work of Nicos Poulantzas – see *State, Power, Socialism* (London: New Left Books, 1978) pp. 93–120.
11. A. Cutler, B. Hindess, P. Hirst, A. Hussain, *Marx's 'Capital' and Capitalism Today*, Vol. 1 (London: Routledge & Kegan Paul, 1977) Chapters 7, 8, pp. 174–221.
12. C. Mouffe, 'Hegemony and Ideology in Gramsci' in C. Mouffe (ed), *Gramsci and the Marxist Theory* (London: Routledge & Kegan Paul, 1979) p. 168.

13. See for example M. Löwy, 'Marxists and the National Question', *New Left Review*, Vol. 96 (1976) pp. 81–100, and T. Nairn, 'The Modern Janus' in *The Break Up of Britain* 2nd edn (London: Verso, 1981) pp. 327–63.

14. At this point one is left to ponder whether the image of European 'post industrial' societies show to anyone, if at all, the image of their own future. For an illuminating discussion of the significance of the experience of modernity in the West see Marshall Berman, *All That is Solid Melts Into Air* (London: Verso, 1987).

15. Hélène Carrére d'Encausse and Stuart Schram, *Marxism in Asia* (London: Penguin, 1969) p. 4.

16. F. Engels to Kautsky, on 12 September 1882 in *Marx and Engels on Colonialism* (Moscow: Progress Publishers, 1974) p. 342.

17. Anouar Abdel-Malek, *Nation and Revolution*, Vol 2 of *Social Dialectics* (London: Macmillan, 1981) p. 15.

18. For a discussion of these ideas, see Cutler *et. al.*, *Marx's Capital*, Vol 1, Part 3, pp. 167–312 and, specially, E. Laclau and C. Mouffe, *Hegemony and Socialist Strategy* (London: Verso, 1985).

19. (The National Question and Social Democracy), 2nd edn (Vienna: Wiener Volksbuchhandlung, 1924). Reprinted in the collected works of Otto Bauer, *Otto Bauer Werkausgabe* (OBW), Vol. 1 (Vienna: Europa-Verlag, 1975). Surprisingly, there is no English translation of this important work. There is a Spanish translation, *La cuestión de las nacionalidades y la social democracia*, (Mexico: Siglo XXI editores, 1979) and a French translation: *La Question des nationalités et la Social Démocratie*, Nicole Prune-Perrin et Johannès Brune (Paris: EDI, 1988).

CHAPTER 1

1. See for example, S. Zubaida, 'Theories of Nationalism' in G. Littlejohn *et. al.*, *Power and the State* (London: Croom Helm, 1978) p. 64; H. B. Davis, *Socialism and Nationalism*, Monthly Review Press, 1967; M. Löwy, 'Marxists and the National Question', *New Left Review*, 96, March-April 1976, pp. 81–100; J. L. Talmon, *The Myth of the Nation and the Vision of Revolution* (Berkley: University of California Press, 1981) p.38; Z. A. Pelczynski, 'Nation, Civil Society, State, Hegelian sources of the non-Marxist theory of nationality', in Z. A. Pelczynski (ed.) *The State and Civil Society* (Cambridge: Cambridge University Press, 1984) p. 262; G. Haupt, 'Les Marxistes face à la question nationale: l'histoire du problème' in G. Haupt, M. Löwy and C. Weill, *Les Marxistes et la question nationale* (Paris: Maspero, 1974) pp. 13ff. For a refreshingly different and more interesting approach, see A. Walicki, *Philosophic and Romantic Nationalism: The Case of Poland* (Oxford: Clarendon Press, 1982) pp. 375ff.

2. The term state is used here in the descriptive sense of a centralised unit of political administration and authority and not in the analytical sense of a system of ideological and political organisation that flows from the works of the Austro-Marxists, Gramsci and Poulantzas.

For a discussion of Marxist theories of the state see B. Jessop, *The Capitalist State* (Oxford: Martin Robertson, 1983).

3. F. Engels, 'Über den Verfall des Feudalismus und das Aufkommen der Bourgeoisie' in *Marx Engels Werke* (MEW), (Berlin: Dietz Verlag, 1977) Vol. 21, p. 392ff., English translation in F. Engels, 'Decay of Feudalism and Rise of Nation States' in F. Engels, *The Peasant War in Germany* (Moscow: Progress Publishers, 1977) p. 178ff. See also G. Haupt and C. Weill, 'L'Eredità di Marx ed Engels e la Questione Nazionale', *Studi Storici*, Istituto Gramsci Editore, Vol. 15, no. 2 (1974) p. 281.

4. Haupt and Weill, 'L'Eredità di Marx ed Engels' p. 275

5. S. Bloom, *El Mundo de las Naciones*, Spanish translation of *The World of Nations,* (Buenos Aires: Siglo XXI editores, 1975) p. 44.

6. Pierre Giraud, *Patois et les dialectes français* (Paris: Presses Universitaires de France, 1968) p. 27.

7. C. F. Brunnot, *Histoire de la langue française* (Paris: Nouvelle Edition, 1958) pp. 44–9.

8. Rosdolsky and Salvi quote a revealing passage: 'Federalism and super-stition speak low Breton ... the emigration and hatred to the republic speak German, the counter-revolution speaks Italian and fanaticism speaks Basque (Euzkera) ... It is necessary to popularise the (French) language; it is necessary to stop *this linguistic aristocracy* that seems to have established a civilised nation in the midst of barbaric ones', 'Séance du 8 Pluviôse', *Gazette nationale, ou le moniteur universel* – see R. Rosdolsky, 'Friedrich Engels und das Problem der 'geschichtslosen' Völker (Die Nationälitatenfrage in der Revolution 1848–1849 im Lichte der 'Neuen Rheinischen Zeitung')', *Archiv für Sozialgeschichte*, Vol. 4, 1964, p. 100. For a recent English translation (by J. P. Himka) see J.P. Himka *Engels and the 'Nonhistoric' Peoples* (Glasgow: Critique Books, 1986) p. 31. S. Salvi, *Le Nazione Proibite: Guida a Dieci Colonie 'Interne' Dell'a Europa Occidentale* (Florence: Vallechi Editore, 1973) p. 477.

9. K. Marx to F. Engels, 20 June 1866 in *Marx and Engels' Collected Works* (MECW) (London: Lawrence & Wishart, 1977) Vol. 21, p. 288–9.

10. S. Avineri, *Hegel's Theory of the Modern State* (Cambridge: CUP) p. 142.

11. ibid., and G. W. Hegel, *Philosophy of Right*, para 182.

12. K. Marx, *German Ideology*, students edn (London: Lawrence & Wishart, 1974) p .57.

13. In his influential study on Catalonia, Pierre Vilar argues that: 'Une étude critique de l'emploi du vocabulaire montre en effet combien il est facile de mettre sur fiches un nombre imposant d'emplois discuta-bles ou manifestement abusifs des mots "nation", "national", "nationalisme", "patriotisme" ou "patrie"', *La Catalogne dans L'espagne moderne*, Vol 1 (Paris: Bibliothèque Générale de L'ecole pratique des hautes études, 1962) p. 29.

14. As G. Haupt argues: 'La difficulté première se traduit par la grande 'misere' terminologique qui a entravé les tentatives de clarification'. See *Les Marxistes face à la question nationale*, p. 21.

15. In other Western European languages, the term has a more restricted meaning because 'people' (*peuple, pueblo, Volk* in French, Spanish and German respectively) has a wider ethno-political denotation. In German the term 'Nationalität' acquires almost exclusively the denotation (b), since the denotation (a) is covered by the word 'Staatsangehörigkeit'. Also the term 'deutsche Volkszugehörigkeit' defines people of German ancestral ethnic origin, and it is enshrined in the Transitional Provisions of the Basic Law of the Federal Republic of Germany, article 116 (1) definition of German Citizenship. The other well-known case of an ethnic criterion enshrined in the basic laws of a state is in the state of Israel; see sections (1) and (4) of the Law of Return. In Slavic languages, the term 'Narod' and related forms has also an ethno-political denotation. For a recent discussion of the lack of an English equivalent for the Russian 'narod'nost' see T. Shanin, 'Soviet theories of ethnicity, the case of the missing term', *New Left Review*, Vol. 158 (1986) pp. 113ff.

16. R. Rosdolsky, 'Workers and Fatherland', *Science and Society*, Vol. 29 (1965) p. 337.

17. 'God!, is there anybody in this earth that will do justice to the Slavs?': the desperate plight of the Czechs disdainfully quoted by Engels in a letter to Kautsky on 2 February 1882 (MEW, Vol. 35, p. 272), quoted by Rosdolsky, 'Friedrich Engels', p. 197; *Federico Engels*, p. 136; *Engels and the Non Historic Peoples'*, p. 137. (These volumes are hereafter cited as Rosdolsky 1964, 1980 and 1986, respectively.)

18. see K. Kaustky, 'Die moderne Nationalität' in *Die Neue Zeit*, Vol. 5 (1887). Spanish translation in Marmora (ed.), *La Segunda Internacional y el problema nacional y colonial*, part 1, series Cuderno de pasado y presente (Mexico: Siglo Editores, 1978); Davis, *Socialism and Nationalism*, p. 73; G. Haupt, *Les Marxistes et la question nationale*, p. 22; M. Löwy, 'Marxists and the National Question', p. 83. However the most detailed and illuminating discussion of this unfortunate use of Hegelian terminology can be found in R. Rosdolsky, 1986.

19. I. Cummings, *Marx, Engels and National Movements* (London: Croom Helm, 1980) p. 31.

20. A. D. Smith, '"Ideas" and "Structure" in the Formation of Independence Ideas', *Philosophy of Social Sciences*, Vol. 3 (1973) p. 21.

21. R. Gallisot, 'Nazione e Nazionalitá nei Dibattiti del Movimento Operaio' in Hobsbawm *et. al.* (eds), *Storia del Marxismo*, Vol. 2, p. 809.

22. Davis, *Socialism and Nationalism*, p. 2.

23. Hegel, *Philosophy of History*, quoted by H. Marcuse, *Reason and Revolution* (Boston: Beacon, 1969) p. 237.

24. Hegel, *'Encyklopädie der philosophischen Wissenschaften im Grundrisse'*, quoted and translated by C. Herod, *The Nation in the History of Marxian Thought* (The Hague: Martinus Nijhoff, 1976) p. 30.

25. Hegel, *Philosophy of Right*, para 347, translated with notes by T.M. Knox (Oxford: Clarendon Press, 1953) p. 217–18.

26. ibid., para 351, p. 219.

27. Marx and Engels correspondence, 2 December 1847, quoted by L. Aguilar, *Marxism in Latin America* (New York: W. Knopf, 1969) p. 67.
28. MECW, Vol. 7, p. 422.
29. K. Marx, 'Revolution in China and in Europe' New York Daily Tribune, 14 June 1853, quoted in S. Avineri, *Karl Marx on Colonialism and Modernisation* (London: Anchor, 1969) p. 68.
30. Quoted by I. Cummings, *Marx, Engels and National Movements*, p. 54
31. 'It is now perfectly clear to me that, as testified by his cranial formation and hair growth, he is descended from the negroes who joined Moses' exodus from Egypt (unless his paternal mother or grandmother was crossed with a nigger). Well this combination of Jewish and Germanic stock with the negroid basic substance is bound to yield a strange product', K. Marx to F. Engels on 30 July 1862, *MEW*, Vol. 30, p. 259; English translation in F. J. Raddatz (ed.) *Marx and Engels Personal Letters* (London: Weidenfeld & Nicholson, 1981).
32. F. Engels, 'The Democratic Panslavism' pp. 362–8, and 'The Magyar Struggle', p. 227, in *MECW*, Vol. 8.
33. K. Marx, 'Panslavism – The Schleswig Holstein War' in *Revolution and Counter Revolution*, Eleanor Marx Aveling (ed.) (London: Unwin, 1971) p. 48.
34. F. Engels, 'The Magyar Struggle' in *MECW*, Vol. 8 pp 234–5.
35. Rosdolsky, 1964, p. 100; 1980, p. 24; 1986, p. 34.
36. *MECW*, Vol 7, pp. 350–1.
37. K. Marx, *Capital*, Vol. 1 (London: Lawrence & Wishart, 1977) pp. 652–66. The term underdevelopment is of course a modern term, associated with the dependency school. However, the intellectual meaning of the term, namely the prevention of economic development in a peripheral country by the intervention of a more powerful dominant economy, is at the heart of Marx's conceptualisation of the Irish problem.
38. K. Marx, 'Confidential Communication' (written in 1870), in K. Marx and F. Engels, *On Colonialism* (Moscow: Progress Publishers, 1974) p. 259.
39. See Davis, *Socialism and Nationalism*, pp. 79–82. M. Löwy, argues that 'Marx offered neither a systematic theory of the national question, a precise definition of the concept of "nation", nor a general political strategy for the proletariat in this domain.' ('Marxists and the National Question', p. 81)
40. Bloom, *El Mundo*, p. 49.
41. Rosdolsky, 1964, p. 87; 1980 p. 10; 1986, foreword.
42. F. Mehring, *Aus dem literarischen Nachlass von K. Marx, F. Engels und F. Lasalle*, quoted in Herod *The Nation*, p. 19.
43. Haupt and Weill, *L'Eredità di Marx ed Engels*, p. 284ff. Similar ideas are expressed in the introductory essay by Haupt in Haupt *et al.*, *Les Marxistes et la question nationale*.
44. This situation was, half a century later, well understood by the Austrian socialists, who in the Brno (Brünn) Programme, incorporated

a number of important safeguards to protect the rights of these small national communities. See 'Protokoll über die Verhandlugen des Gesamt-Parteitages der sozialdemokratischen Arbeiterpartei in Österreich, Brünn', Spanish translation, in Marmora (ed.), *La Segunda Internacional*, Vol. 1, pp. 181–217. For a summary and evaluation in English of the Brno (Brünn) programme, see Kogan (1949, pp. 204–17).

45. *MEW*, Vol. 18, p. 586; Herod, *The Nation*, p. 33.
46. Letter from F. Engels to August Bebel in Berlin, on 17 November 1885, *MEW*, Vol. 36, p. 390 (my own translation). Also quoted by Herod, *The Nation*, p. 33.
47. *OBW*, Vol. 1, pp. 270–92.
48. The excellent English translation of Rosdolsky's work by John-Paul Himka (1986) is from the second edition published in Berlin and Vienna by Olle & Walter in 1979, while most contemporary references, as well as the Spanish translation (1980), refer to the first German edition in *Archiv für Sozialgeschichte* (1964). While, according to Himka, the second edition is 'a photographic reprint of the first' (Introduction, p. 10) it includes some revised notes by Rosdolsky's widow. Also, the English translator performed the painstaking task of checking and correcting all citations against original sources as well as referring to standard English translations of the works of Marx and Engels. Consequently, wherever possible, I refer to the first German edition (1964), to the Spanish translation (1980) and to the revised second edition translated into English (1986).
49. The word *Hintersassen* has no precise English equivalent; in the English translation it has been translated as 'subject'. According to Garcia Pelayo, it is a juridical term of medieval origin that designates all those who did not have property rights and were in a servile relation to feudal landlords. At a later period, this term was used to designate the lower and poorer classes who had only restricted rights to citizenship and property. The term was used up to the nineteenth century. See M. Garcia Pelayo, *El tema de las nacionalidades en la teoria de la Nación en Otto Bauer*, (Madrid: Pablo Iglesias, 1979) p. 34. See also E. Haberkern and J. F. Wallach, *Hilfswörterbuch für Historiker* (Bern: 1964) entries on 'Hintersassen' and 'Schutzverwandter'.
50. Rosdolsky, 1964, p. 91–2; 1980, p. 15; 1986, pp. 25–6.
51. *MEW*, Vol. 14, p. 507.
52. 'A thorn in the flesh of the future Great German Reich' (!?), Rosdolsky, , p. 93, 1980, p. 16, 1986, p. 26.
53. Rosdolsky, 1964, p. 194; 1980, p. 133; 1986, p.131.
54. Rosdolsky, 1964, p. 194; 1980, p. 133; 1986, p. 131.
55. ibid, 1964, pp. 240ff; 1980, pp. 184ff; 1986, pp. 180ff.

CHAPTER 2

1. L. Kolakowski, *Main Currents of Marxism* (Oxford: Clarendon, 1978) Vol. II: *The Golden Age*, p. 1.

2. On a number of occasions Kautsky acknowledged Darwin's influence on his own thought, defining, for instance, morality as an ethical impulse derived from the natural social condition of humans. However, as Steenson argues, Kautsky subsumed under the name of Darwin a number of diverse influences in his interpretation of Marxism. For a further discussion on the subject see G. P. Steenson, *K. Kautsky, Marxism in the Classical Years* (Pittsburgh: University of Pittsburgh Press, 1978) pp. 24–5.

3. K. Kautsky, *The Class Struggle* (New York: W.W. Norton, 1971).

4. Kautsky, *The Class Struggle*, p. 104.

5. R. Luxemburg, *The Accumulation of Capital*, (London: Routledge & Kegan Paul, 1951) p. 446. This deterministic understanding of the development of capitalism contradicts Luxemburg's emphasis on political activism and radical action by the working class. This contradiction in Luxemburg's work has been discussed at some length by her biographers, for instance J. P. Nettl, *Rosa Luxemburg*, abridged edn (Oxford: Oxford University Press, 1969 and P. Froilich, *Rosa Luxemburg* (London: Pluto Press, 1972).

6. K. Kautsky, *Die Moderne Nationalität*, in Haupt *et al.*, *Les Marxistes et la question nationale*, p. 114. This argument is also found in the work of Poulantzas; see *State, Power Socialism* (London: New Left Books, 1978) p. 95.

7. K. Kautsky, *Die Moderne Nationalität, Neue Zeit*, Vol. 5 (1887), quoted and translated by H. Mommsen and A. Martiny in 'Nationalism and the Nationalities Question' in Renning (ed.) *Encyclopaedia of Marxism*, p. 42.

8. Kautsky, *Moderne Nationalität*, in Haupt *et al.*, p. 119.

9. This probably reflects Kautsky's tribulations about his own nation, the Czechs, to whom he recommended a prompt assimilation to the more 'civilised' Germans.

10. Kautsky, *Moderne Nationalität*, in Haupt *et al.*, p. 121.

11. ibid., p. 122.

12. ibid., p. 116.

13. Kautsky was not familiar with the existence of Gaelic-speaking areas (An Gaeltach) and of the influence they exercised in the modern development of Irish national consciousness.

14. ibid., p. 122.

15. ibid., p. 122.

16. ibid., p. 121.

17. K. Kautsky, *Nationalität und Internationälitat*, p. 17, quoted by H. Mommsen and A. Martiny in 'Nationalism, Nationalities Question' *Encyclopaedia of Marxism, Communism and Western Society* (New York: Herder & Herder, 1972–3) p. 43.

18. Nettl, *Rosa Luxemburg*, p. 505.

19. 'Der Sozialpatriotismus in Polen' in *Die Neue Zeit*, Vol. 2, no. 14 (1895–96) pp. 459–70. Spanish translation El desarrollo industrial de Polonia y otros escritos sobre el problema nacional, (Mexico: Cuadernos de pasado y Presente, 71 Siglo XXI editores, 1979) pp. 195–209.

20. S. Hacker, 'Der Sozialismus in Polen' in *Die Neue Zeit*, Vol. 14, no. 2 (1895–1896) pp. 324–32.

21. R. Luxemburg, *Die Sozialpatriotismus in Polen*, in *El desarrollo Industrial de Polonia*, pp. 206–7 (my own translation from Spanish). A similar quote could be found in Davis, *Socialism and Nationalism*, p. 136.

22. Luxemburg, *Die Sozialpatriotismus*, p. 207.

23. ibid., p. 208; my own translation from Spanish.

24. 'Industrielle Entwicklung Polens', (The industrial development of Poland). The thesis was submitted on 12 March 1897 and examined on 1 May of the same year by Professor Julius Wolf.

25. Luxemburg, *El desarrollo Industrial de Polonia*, p. 155.

26. Lenin's arguments will be discussed in detail in the next chapter. For an appreciation of Lenin's arguments see 'Critical Remarks on the National Question' and 'The Right of Nations to Self Determination', in which Lenin develops a strong polemic against Luxemburg's discussion of the national question, in V. I. Lenin, *Collected Works*, Vol. 20 (Moscow: Foreign Language Publishing house, 1963).

27. H. B. Davis, 'The Right of Nations to Self Determination, Luxemburg vs Lenin', introductory article in H. B. Davis (ed.) *The National Question, Selected Writings by Rosa Luxemburg*, (New York: Monthly Review Press, 1976) p. 13. Davis underestimates the socialist commitment of the PPS and overestimates the popularity of Luxemburg's arguments among Polish socialists.

28. See for example Nettl, *Rosa Luxemburg*, Vol. II, p. 859.

29. R. Luxemburg, 'The Problem of the Hundred Nationalities' in *Die Neue Zeit*, Vol. 1, no. 20 (1904/1905), quoted by Herod, *The Nation*, p. 88.

30. In Herod, *The Nation*, p. 88.

31. ibid., p. 88.

32. Nettl, *Rosa Luxemburg*, p. 860.

33. This series of articles was originally published in the Polish journal *Przeglad Socjaldemokratyczny, Organ Socjaldemokrajci Krolestwa Polskiego i Litwy (Social Democratic Review, the organ of the social democracy of the Kingdom of Poland and Lithuania)* nos. 6–10, (August–December 1908). There is an English translation of this series of articles in H. B. Davis (ed.) *The National Question*, op. cit. p. 101 to 288

34. R. Luxemburg, *The National Question and Autonomy*, in Davis (ed.) *The National Question*, p. 111.

35. ibid., p. 112.

36. 'even if present day governments were forced to declare a universal right to work it would remain only a fine sounding phrase, and not one member of the reserve army of labor waiting on the sidewalk would be able to make a bowl of soup for his hungry children from that right' (ibid., p. 123).

37. Luxemburg, *The Question of Nationality and Autonomy*, quoted by Nettl, *Rosa Luxemburg*, p. 507, and Davis (ed.) *The National Question*, pp. 135–6.

38. Kolakowski, *Main Currents of Marxism*, p. 98.

39. L. Labedz (ed.), *Revisionism* (London: Allen & Unwin, 1962). For a more recent use of the term in way described by Labedz see R. Miliband, The New Revisionist Spectrum in *New Left Review*, Vol. 150, pp. 5–45.

40. See R. Miliband, 'New Revisionist'.

41. J. Joll, *The Second International* (London: Routledge & Kegan Paul, 1974) p. 77.

42. This debate is far from over. For a contemporary discussion of this subject see among others G. Therborn, 'What Does the Ruling Class do When It Rules?', in A. Giddens and D. Held (eds) *Classes, Power, and Conflict* (Basingstoke: Macmillan, 1982) pp. 224–48; E. O. Wright, *Class, Crisis and the State* (London: New Left Books, 1978), N. Poulantzas, *Classes in Contemporary Capitalism* (London: New Left Books, 1975).

43. Laclau and Mouffe, *Hegemony*, p. 29

44. Translated as *Evolutionary Socialism*, with an introduction by Sidney Hook, (New York: Schocken paperbacks, 1961).

45. ibid., p. 48.

46. Kolakowski, *Main Currents of Marxism*, Vol. 2, p. 109.

47. E. Bernstein, 'Ignaz Auer, der Fuhrer, Freund und Berater', in *Sozialstische Monaschefte*, organ of the revisionist section of the SPD, quoted by Joll, *The Second International*, p. 95.

48. Laclau and Mouffe, *Hegemony*, p. 30.

49. ibid., p. 31.

50. Bernstein, *Evolutionary Socialism*, p. 14.

51. P. Gay, *The Dilemma of Democratic Socialism*, (New York: Octagon Books, 1979) p. 143.

52. E. Bernstein, 'Der Revisionismus in der Sozialdemokratie' in *Handbuch de Politik*, Vol. 2, p. 55, quoted and translated into Italian by Vernon L. Lidtke, 'Le premesse teoriche del socialismo in Bernstein' in *Annali*, Istituto Giacomo Feltrinelli, Vol. 15 (1973) p. 156.

53. Bernstein, *Evolutionary Socialism*, pp.169–70.

54. H. Mommsen, *Arbeiterbewegung und Nationale Frage* (Göttingen: Vanderhoeck & Ruprecht, 1979), p. 123.

55. E. Bernstein, 'Der Staat und die Staatsnotwendigkeiten' in *Die Neue Zeit*, Vol. 35, 2 Band, no. 12 (June 1917) p. 272. Also quoted in Mommsen, *Arbeiterbewegung*, p. 123.

56. Mommsen, *Arbeiterbewegung*, p. 121.

57. ibid., p. 120.

58. Bernstein, *Evolutionary Socialism*, p. 170.

59. ibid., p. 175.

60. ibid., p. 178.

61. ibid.

62. ibid., pp. 178–9

63. Organs of the German Socialist Party and the revisionist wing of the party respectively.

64. E. Bernstein, *Einigen Uber Des Indische Problem, Die Neue Zeit*, Vol. 15, (1896–7) quoted by L. Marmora (ed.) in his introduction to *La Segunda Internacional* (Mexico: Siglo XXI Editores, 1978) p. 11.

65. E. Bernstein, *Die Deutsche Sozialdemokratie und Die Turkische Wirren* (*The German social democracy and the Turkish disturbances*) translated into Spanish by C. Cerreti and published in Marmora (ed.) *La Segunda Internacional*, p. 48; my own translation from Spanish.

66. ibid., p. 49; my own translation.

67. ibid., pp. 47ff. Unfortunately Bernstein does not provide a more precise reference to this article. Luxemburg's contemptuous perception of small national minorities in Czarist Russia was outlined above.

68. Kautsky's ambivalences on the colonial question are discussed in Marmora's introduction to *La Segunda Internacional*. Kautsky's position on the question of colonialism is spelled out in *Sozialismus und Kolonial Politik* (Socialism and Colonial Policy) (Berlin, October 1907, translated into Spanish by Juan Behrens in Marmora (ed.), *La Segunda Internacional*, pp. 39–120.

69. Kautsky, *Sozialismus und Kolonialpolitik*, my own translation from Spanish (Behrens in Marmora (ed.), *La Segunda Internacional*, p. 64).

70. E. Bernstein, *Deutsche Sozialdemokratie*, p. 49.

71. ibid., p. 53.

72. The term 'racialism' used in this context follows the definition provided by John Rex in his book on race relations: 'In our belief the common element in these [racialist] theories is that they see the connection between membership of a particular group and the genetically related sub-groups (i.e. families and lineages) of which that group is compounded and the possession of evaluated equalities as completely deterministic. It doesn't really matter whether this is because of men's genes, because of the history to which their ancestors have been exposed, because of the nature of their culture or because of divine decree.' *Race Relations in Sociological Theory* (London: Routledge & Kegan Paul, 1983) p. 159.

73. Bernstein, *Deutsche Socialdemokratie*, pp. 49–53.

74. Edward Said, *Orientalism* (London: Routledge & Kegan Paul, 1978).

75. E. Said, 'Orientalism Reconsidered' in *Race and Class*, Vol. 27, no. 2 (1985) p. 10.

76. Kolakowski, *Main Currents of Marxism*, Vol. 2, p. 5.

CHAPTER 3

1. See for example, 'Who are the Friends of the People?' and 'The Development of Capitalism in Russia', Lenin, *Collected Works*, Vol. 1. In his study of the *Politics of Combined and Uneven Development*, (London: Verso, 1981), Michael Löwy argues that 'A close reading of Lenin's most important political text of the period, *Two Tactics of Social Democracy in the Democratic Revolution*, reveals with extraordinary clarity the *tension* in Lenin's thought between his profound revolutionary realism and the limitations imposed by the straitjacket of so-called Orthodox Marxism' (p. 34).

2. Marcel Liebman, *Leninism under Lenin*, (London: Merlin, 1980) p. 19.

3. Lenin, *Collected Works*, Vol. 5, p. 430.

4. This is the essence of class reductionism: all superstructural occurrences are determined by classes even if they are mediated by a complex chain of causality. To conceptualise a bourgeois democratic revolution blending with a socialist revolution is unthinkable in terms of the class reductionist paradigm. Trotsky stretched this paradigm to its conceptual limits by arguing that this blending was possible under certain historical circumstances, but at the same time he did not provide us with the analytical tools to conceptualise this situation.

5. Laclau and Mouffe, *Hegemony*, pp. 55–60.

6. 'The country that is more developed industrially only shows to the less developed, the image of its own', Marx, *Capital*, Vol. 1, p. 19.

7. This last argument was fully conceptualised by Trotsky in his *History of the Russian Revolution*, (London: Victor Gollancz, 1965), summarising arguments developed in previous works.

8. Sergei Baruzdin, 'Glasnost ili poluglasnost? Pravda ili polupravda?' (Openness or half-openness? truth or half truth?) in a discussion: 'Natsional'nyi vopros segodnia' (The national question today), *Druzba Narodov*, Moscow, no. 12 (December 1988), p. 227.

9. Quoted by Lenin from the official German report of the resolutions of the congress. See V. I. Lenin, 'The Right of Nations to Self Determination', in *Questions of National Policy and Proletarian Internationalism*, (Moscow: Progress Publishers, 1970); also in *Collected Works*, Vol. 20.

10. See Chapter 2 on the controversy on self determination between Rosa Luxemburg's SKDPiL and the PPS.

11. H. B Davis, 'The Right of Self Determination in Marxist Theory – Luxemburg vs. Lenin', in Davis (ed.) *The National Question*, p. 20.

12. Lenin, *Collected Works*, Vol. 20, p. 397.

13. Lenin, 'Self determination', in *Collected Works*, Vol. 20, footnote p. 441.

14. V. Lenin, Letter to Shahumyan in Haupt *et al.*, *Les Marxistes et la question nationale*, p.352. Also Lenin, *Collected Works*, Vol. 19, p. 500.

15. Lenin, 'Self Determination', in *Questions of National Policy*, p. 46.

16. ibid. pp. 46–7.

17. An epiphenomenalist position is always class reductionist, while the reverse is not the case. Epiphenomenalism refers to transparent and deterministic relations of causality, while class reductionism only refers to the paradigmatic location of a superstructural phenomenon in the area of influence of a class position.

18. Lenin, *Self Determination*, p. 47 and 'Theses for a Lecture on the National Question' in *Collected Works*, Vol. 41, p. 313.

19. Lenin, 'State and Revolution' in *Selected Works*, vol. 2, p. 247. For an interesting discussion of the contemporary implications of this idea, see B. Jessop, 'Capitalism and Democracy, the best possible political shell?', in G. Littlejohn *et al.* (eds.) *Power and the State*, (London: Croom Helm, 1978).

20. Lenin, 'Self Determination', p. 51.
21. ibid.
22. ibid. p. 55.
23. Indeed, the general rule is the exact opposite: multinational states. Consider the UK, France, Spain, Belgium, and so on.
24. Lenin, 'Self Determination', p. 56.
25. Lenin, *Collected Works*, Vol. 20, footnote p. 452.
26. ibid. p. 57.
27. Given that there is no direct English equivalent to the Russian 'natsional'nost' and 'narod'nost', the term ethnicity is used here as the closest substitution. For a very interesting and thought provoking discussion of this situation see Shanin's 'Soviet Theories of Ethnicity', pp. 113–22.
28. Lenin 'Determination', p. 55.
29. See Chapter 3. Lenin devotes a substantial part of 'Self Determination', to polemise against R. Luxemburg.
30. Davis, 'Luxemburg vs. Lenin', p. 17.
31. ibid. p. 19.
32. Otto Bauer, *Die Nationalitätenfrage*, Chapter 30, quoted by Lenin in 'Self Determination', p. 129.
33. Lenin, 'Self Determination', p. 129–130.
34. Lenin, 'Self Determination', p. 159.
35. J. Stalin, *Works* (Moscow: Progress Publishers, 1952) Vol. 6, p. 443.
36. M. Löwy, 'Marxists and the National Question', p.97.
37. Lenin, *Collected Works*, Vol. 19, pp. 17–51.
38. ibid., p. 33.
39. *Protokoll uber die Verhandlungen des Gesamtparteitages der sozialdemok-ratischen Arbeiterpartei in Österreich, Brünn*, Vienna, 1899, translated into Spanish by Conrado Ceretti in Mormora (ed.) *La segunda Internacional* pp.181–3. The protocol of the debate that took place in the Austrian socialist party congress shows an amazing similarity with the recent (1990) constitutional debate over the status of the autonomous republics in the Soviet Union.
40. Which was only the position of the minority at the Brno congress; the majority supported territorial federal autonomy, see Chapter 5.
41. V. I. Lenin, 'How does Bishop Nikon defend the Ukrainians?' in *Collected Works*, Vol. 19, p. 380.
42. Lenin, 'Critical Remarks on the National Question' in *Collected Works*, Vol. 20, p. 19.
43. ibid., p.24.
44. ibid., p. 32.
45. ibid., p. 27.
46. ibid., p. 34.
47. ibid., p. 35.
48. ibid., p. 45.
49. Lenin, 'Letter to Shahumyan', in *Collected Works*, Vol. 19, p. 499.
50. ibid.

51. Lenin, *Selected Works* (Moscow, Progress Publishers, 1961) Vol I, part 2, p. 349, quoted by S. Shaheen *The Communist Theory of National Self Determination* (The Hague: W. Van Hoeve, 1956) p. 103.
52. This was expressed in a round table discussion organized by the journal *Voprosy filosofi*, on the topic 'Philosophical problems of the theory and practice national relations under socialism', *Voprosy filosofi*, Moscow, No. 9 (September 1988) p. 43.
53. ibid., p. 46 (Roderic Pitty translated from Russian).
54. See for example M. Löwy, *Marxists and the National Question*.
55. ibid., p. 95.
56. Lenin, 'Letter to Gorki' in *Collected Works*, Vol. 5, p. 84. The article in question is 'Marxism and the National Question', Stalin's 'magna opera'.
57. Quoted by Davis, *Socialism and Nationalism*, p. 81.
58. Stalin, *Works*, Vol. 2 (Moscow: Foreign Languages Publishing House, 1952 and 1953.) pp. 300–81.
59. Stalin, 'Marxism and the National Question', in *Works*, Vol. 2, pp. 300–1.
60. ibid., 307.
61. See Chapters 6 and 7 for a discussion of Bauer's work.
62. M. Löwy, *Marxists and the National Question*, p. 95. It seems that for Löwy the only possible Marxist interpretation of the national question is the Leninist interpretation; if cultural elements are integrated into the definition of a nation this is 'pre-scientific folklorism'. One wonders if this is also the case of Mao, Fanon, Cabral, etc.
63. Stalin, 'Marxism and the National Question' pp. 310–11.
64. O. Bauer, *The Nationalities Question and Social Democracy* Russian translation quoted by Stalin in 'Marxism and the National Question' p. 309.
65. Stalin, 'Marxism and the National Question', p. 321.
66. Lenin, *Collected Works*. Vol. 19, p. 501.
67. Stalin, 'Marxism and the National Question', p. 364.
68. ibid., p. 350.
69. Lenin, 'The Question of Nationalities or "Autonomisation"', in *Questions of Nationality* p. 165.

CHAPTER 4

1. A. Gramsci, 'L'Unita Nazionale', in *L'Ordine Nuovo*, 4 October 1919, quoted by R. Absalom in 'Gramsci's Contribution', in, E. Cahm and V. Fisera (eds) *Socialism and Nationalism* Vol. 1 (London: Spokesman, 1978) p. 29.
2. Perry Anderson, 'The Antinomies of Antonio Gramsci', *New Left Review* Vol. 100, (November 1976) pp. 5–78.
3. ibid., p. 20.
4. Laclau and Mouffe, *Hegemony*.
5. ibid., p. 66.
6. Besides the seminal works of Laclau & Mouffe, similar interpretations could also be found in C. Buci-Glucksmann, *Gramsci and the State*,

(London: Lawrence and Wishart, 1980); S. Hall, 'The Problem of Ideology, Marxism without Guarantees', in B. Matthews (ed.) *Marx 100 Years On*, (London: Lawrence & Wishart, 1983); B. Jessop, *The Capitalist State* (Oxford: Martin Robertson, 1982); Anne Showstack Sasson (ed.) *Approaches to Gramsci* (London: Writers and Readers, 1982).

7. A. Gramsci, 'Notes on the Southern Question', in *Selections from Political Writings 1921-26* selected and edited by Q.Hoare (London: Lawrence and Wishart, 1978), p. 443. See also Laclau & Mouffe, *Hegemony* p.66. As Tom Nairn argues in a fascinating article, the conditions of the south of Italy were not that different from those peripheral societies experiencing uneven development and which are normally called Third World. See T. Nairn, *Antonu Su Gobbu*, in Showstack Sassoon (ed.), *Approaches to Gramsci*, pp. 159–79.

8. See Lenin, *'Two Tactics of Social Democracy'*, in Selected Works, Vol. 1. However, H. Portelli disagrees with this interpretation. He argues that Gramsci was only taking into account 'the real class relations existent in Italy at that time', and that the working class was proposing a broad compromise taking into account the interests of the peasants on the face of the nature of bourgeois power. In Portelli's words 'this equalitarian alliance ... must not hide the hegemonic character of proletarian direction', see *Gramsci y el Bloque Historico*, (Buenos Aires: Siglo XXI Editores, 1974) p. 88. However, the identity of the working class remains unchanged through the hegemonic relation and therefore the description of the event is not incompatible with the Leninist concept of class alliances.

9. Laclau and Mouffe, *Hegemony*, pp. 66–8.

10. For a penetrating critique of the concept of dominant ideology see N. Abercrombie, S. Hill and B. Turner, *The Dominant Ideology Thesis* (London: Allen & Unwin, 1980).

11. This reading of Gramsci is common in British interpretations of his work. Besides the previously mentioned article by Anderson see J. Hoffman, *The Gramscian Challenge* (London: Blackwell, 1984).

12. The problem here is not only a class reductionist logic. There is a manifest difficulty in translating concepts. The Italian verb *'dirigere'* is translated into English as 'to rule' or 'to lead', and the adjective *'dirigente'* as 'ruling' (*'Classe dirigente'* = ruling class). This form of translation over-emphasises the aspects of domination and coercion of the concept (which are clearly there), and under-emphasises the educational aspects of the Italian term used by Gramsci (which in English is conveyed by different words, such as intellectual persuasion or supervision). G. Nowell Smith and Q. Hoare point out the difficulties in translating the term in the preface to their translation of Gramsci's *Selection from Prison Notebooks* (London: Lawrence & Wishart, 1971) p. XIV. However, the over-emphasis on the coercive aspects of the terms used in translation is not fully discussed. This may explain why British commentators (who on the whole rely on translations) tend

to understand the Gramscian concept of hegemony as a a form of domination.

13. D. Grisoni and R. Maggiori, *Guida a Gramsci* (Milan: Biblioteca Universali Rizzoli, 1977) p. 263.
14. Gramsci, *Prison Notebooks*, p. 359.
15. ibid., p. 240.
16. See for example the article by N. Bobbio and subsequent criticism by J. Texier in C. Mouffe (ed.), *Gramsci and the Marxist Theory* (London: Routledge & Kegan Paul, 1979) pp. 19–79.
17. Portelli, in his very illuminating study of the concept, was able to find only six theoretical references to it in the whole *Prison Notebooks*, and all of them appear to sketch an organic relation between base and superstructure. See his *Gramsci y el Bloque Historico*, p. 8.
18. A. Gramsci *Il Materialismo Storico* (MS in the notation of the *Quaderni*) (Turin: Edizioni Einaudi, 1966), p. 96.
19. Gramsci, *Prison Notebooks*, p. 5.
20. See Marx, *German Ideology*, part I, pp. 51–2.
21. Gramsci, *Prison Notebooks*, pp. 8–9.
22. ibid., pp. 60–1.
23. ibid., p. 7.
24. ibid., pp. 58–9. Note in particular the historical example of the Risorgimento.
25. Gramsci, *Prison Notebooks*, p. 132.
26. Laclau and Mouffe, *Hegemony*, p. 69.
27. Tom Nairn, 'Antonu su Gobbu', in Showstack Sassoon, *Approaches to Gramsci*, p. 161. The title of the article is in Sardinian (which is spoken by the majority of the Sardinian population) meaning Antonio the Hump-backed, a reference to a handicap that made him both the object of fear and mockery in the superstitious and fatalistic peasant culture of his country of origin. This bitter experience was undoubtedly important for his subsequent discussions of folklore and popular culture.
28. A Gramsci, 'The Southern Question', in *The Modern Prince & Other Writings*, (New York: International Publishers, 1968) p. 28.
29. ibid., pp. 45–6.
30. ibid., p. 36.
31. For a penetrating discussion of the concept of orientalism see Said, *Orientalism* and B. S. Turner, *Marx and the End of Orientalism* (London: Allen & Unwin, 1978).
32. Gramsci, 'Southern Question', p. 31.
33. ibid., p. 41. The translator rightly argues in a footnote that it is impossible to convey in English the bitter witticism of the contextual use of the referents 'sudici' (southeners) and 'nordici' (northerners) in the quoted phrase. This idiomatic peculiarity is highly indicative of the complex and persistent nature of the social problem it represents.
34. Gramsci, *Prison Notebooks*, p. 349.
35. ibid., p. 418.

36. Laclau and Mouffe, *Hegemony*, p. 69.
37. Gramsci, *Prison Notebooks*, pp. 394–5.
38. A. Gramsci, 'Letteratura e Vita Nazionale', (LVN in the standard abbreviation of the *Prison Notebooks*) in *Quaderni del Carcere* Vol. 5 (Turin: Einaudi Editore, 1966) p. 105.
39. Gramsci, *Prison Notebooks*, p. 421. In an enigmatic footnote on the same page, the editors and translators argue that the Gramscian concept of national popular is 'one of the most interesting and also most widely criticised ideas in Gramsci's thought ... it is perhaps best taken as describing a sort of "historic bloc" between national and popular aspirations in the formation of which the intellectuals, in the wide, Gramscian use of the term play an essential mediating role'. To this fairly accurate description, the editors add: 'It is important to stress however, that it is a cultural concept, relating to the position of the masses within the culture of the nation, and radically alien to any form of populism or "national socialism".' It is difficult to ascertain the meaning of this comment. National-popular is a populist concept par excellence and it would be absurd to suggest any connection between Gramsci and national socialism.
40. ibid., p. 78.
41. ibid., p. 79.
42. ibid., p. 77.
43. ibid., p. 79.
44. ibid., pp. 52–4.
45. ibid., pp. 56, footnote.
46. ibid., p. 82.
47. A large part of the volume on the 'Risorgimento', in the *Quaderni* is devoted to this issue.
48. E. Hobsbawm, 'Gramsci and Marxist Political Theory', in Showstack Sassoon, *Approaches to Gramsci*, p. 29. It is extraordinary that Hobsbawm, the most prominent contemporary Marxist historian, argues here that Gramsci was 'the only Marxist thinker who provides us with a basis of integrating the nation as an historical and social reality to the Marxist theory.' Why does he ignore the 600 plus pages of the original and pioneering work of his fellow Viennese, Otto Bauer? Moreover Bauer is only briefly mentioned in Hobsbawm's later work *Nations and Nationalism since 1780: Programme, Myth, Reality* (Cambridge: Cambridge University Press, 1990).
49. A. Gramsci, *Quaderni del Carcere*, edizione critica dell'Istituto Gramsci a cura di V. Gerratana, (Turin: Einaudi Editore, 1975) 21, 1934–5: 19, quoted by F. Lo Piparo, *Lingua, Intellectuali, Egemonia in Gramsci*, (Rome: Laterza, 1979) p. 155–6; my own translation from Italian.
50. This pattern of tight state centralisation initiated by the Jacobins is not unconnected with subsequent French colonial policies, of which the political euphemism 'Territoires d'Ultramer' is an adequate summary. In this sense the problematic process of independence of

Algeria and today's problems in New Caledonia are not unconnected with the slogan of a 'one and indivisible republic'.

51. Gramsci, *Prison Notebooks*, p. 79.
52. The Peasants Communist International.
53. Quoted by S. Salvi, *Le Nazione Proibite*, (Florence: Vallecchi Editore, 1973) p. 576.
54. Gramsci, *Prison Notebooks*, p. 240.
55. 'Is it not true that in becoming national, a literature takes a more universal signification, a more human general interest?'
56. A. Gramsci, *Gli Intelletuali e l'Organizzazione della Cultura* (Rome: Editore Riuniti, 1977) p. 87; my own translation from Italian.
57. Gramsci, 'Letteratura e Vita Nazionale', in *Quaderni*, Editore Riuniti, p. 127; my own translation from Italian.
58. Laclau and Mouffe, *Hegemony*, p. 69.
59. Which are not only national, but ethnic as distinct from national, cultural, sexual, and so on.
60. Gramsci, *Prison Notebooks*, p. 416.

CHAPTER 5
1. See Otto Bauer, *Die Nationalitätenfrage und die Sozialdemokratie*, 1924 edn, in *Otto Bauer Werkhausgabe(OBW)* (Vienna: Europa-Verlag, 1975) Vol. 1, pp. 49–50.
2. B. F. Pauley, *The Habsburg Legacy* (New York: Holt, Rinehart and Winston, 1972) p. 23.
3. 'Die im Reichsrate vertretenen Königreiche und Länder'. For a very good discussion of the nationalities problem in the dual system, see Oskar Jaszi, *The Dissolution of the Habsburg Monarchy*, Chapter 16 (Chicago: University of Chicago Press, 1929) pp. 106–18 and Robert Kann, *The Multinational Empire*, 2 volumes (New York: Octagon Books, 1950).
4. K. Stadler, *Austria* (London: Ernest Benn, 1971) p. 41.
5. O. Bauer, *Geschichte Österreichs* (Vienna: Weiner Volksbuchhandlung, 1911) quoted and translated by Stadler, in *Austria*, p. 41.
6. I. Oxaal, 'The Jews of Pre-1914 Vienna', Working Paper (Dept of Sociology & Social Anthropology, University of Hull, 1981) p. 62.
7. O. Jászi, *Dissolution of the Habsburg Monarchy*, p. 109, Pauley, *Habsburg Legacy*, p. 8.
8. Oxaal, *Jews of Pre-1914 Vienna*, p. 74. For a detailed analysis of the demographic structure of the Galician population see Oxaal pp. 72–6.
9. Pauley, *Habsburg Legacy*, p. 17.
10. Garcia Pelayo, *La teoria de la nación en Otto Bauer*, p. 3.
11. Z. A. B. Zeeman, *The Twilight of the Habsburgs* (London: Purnell & Sons, 1971) p. 33.
12. ibid., p. 35.
13. I. Oxaal and W. Weitzmann, 'The Jews of Pre-1914 Vienna: An Exploration of Basic Sociological Dimensions', *Leo Baeck Yearbook* XXX (1985), p. 398.

14. Bauer was a personal friend of Freud, and his sister Ana was one of his famous case studies of hysteria. She was referred to in Freud's writings with the pseudonym of Dora.

15. For a discussion of this extraordinary intellectual and cultural environment see Carl. E. Schorske, *Fin de Siècle Vienna* (London: Weidenfeld and Nicholson, 1980); on Wittgenstein see A. Janik and S. Toulmin *Wittgenstein's Vienna* (London: Weidenfeld & Nicholson, 1973). For a critique of the Schorske thesis see S. Beller, *Vienna and the Jews 1867–1938* (Cambridge: Cambridge University Press, 1989), which emphasizes the Jewish character of Viennese cultural and intellectual life.

16. Quoted in Joll, *Second International*, p. 122.

17. Stadler, *Austria*, p. 67. For the high levels of residential integration of Viennese Jews see I. Oxaal, *Aspects of Jewish Social Life in Vienna*, in I. Oxaal, 'The Jews of Young Hitler's Vienna: Historical and sociological Aspects' in I. Oxaal, M. Pollak and G. Botz (eds) *Jews, Antisemitism & Culture in Vienna* (London: Routledge, 1987) pp. 25–33 and Peter Schmidtbauer, 'Zur sozialen Situation der Wiener Juden in Jahre 1857' in *Studia Judaica Austriaca*, Vol. VI, pp. 57–91.

18. 'German Austria must return to the great German motherland ... People of the same blood belong in the same Reich', Hitler, *Mein Kampf*, p. 1, quoted in the original German by Stadler, *Austria*, p. 70.

19. Stadler, *Austria*, p. 67.

20. For a detailed discussion of the Christian Social Movement and its charismatic leader Karl Lueger see John Boyer, *Political Radicalism in Late Imperial Vienna* (Chicago: University of Chicago Press, 1981).

21. ibid., p. X–XI.

22. I. Oxaal and W. Weitzmann, 'The Jews of Pre-1914 Vienna', p. 423.

23. Theodor Herzl, the founder of the Zionist Movement, was a Budapest-born, German-speaking journalist working during this period on the Viennese newspaper *Neue Freie Presse*. The First Zionist congress took place in Basle in 1897, the same year that Karl Lueger, the anti-semitic leader of the Christian Social Movement, became the mayor of Vienna. For the ideological connection between Zionism and anti-semitism see Moshe Machover and Mario Offenberg, 'Zionism and its Scarecrows' in *Khamsin* Vol. 6 (1978) pp. 33–59 and N. Weinstock, *Zionism, False Messiah* (London: Inklinks, 1978).

24. For a detailed analysis of the contradictory nature of the anti-semitic narrative see Jean Pierre Faye, *Los Lenguajes Totalitarios* Spanish translation of *Théorie du récit, Introduction aux Langages Totalitaires*, (Madrid: Taurus Ediciones, 1974), and Jean Pierre Faye, 'Migrations du récit sur le peuple juif', *Collection Éléments* (Paris, 1974).

25. For a controversial discussion of the anti-semitic echos of K. Waldheim's electoral campaign, see R. A. Berman, 'Fascinating Vienna' in *Telos* Vol. 68 (summer 1986) pp. 7–38. On p. 30, Berman argues: 'The centrality of anti-semitism in Nazi ideology hardly needs

to be pointed out; its virulence in the same turn of the century Vienna which gave birth to the cultural wealth now making way through the museums of the world is more significant. Waldheim is a direct heir to Lueger, both exponents of an Austrian political anti-semitism framing the Vienna fascination.' While it is important to recognize the anti-semitic dimension of Waldheim's electoral campaign, the pseudo-psychoanalitic explanation offered in Berman's article appears to be more of an outdated cliché than an original, let alone convincing, argument. For a more interesting discussion of turn-of-the-century Austrian cultural life, see A. Ajtony, 'Vienna and Budapest, Complementary Figures at the turn of the century' in the same issue of *Telos*, pp. 137–50.

26. Stadler, *Austria*, p. 67.
27. For a discussion of the concept of historyless peoples and the way in which Marx and Engels used it in relation to what they called South Slavs see Chapter 2, p. 66ff. and R. Rosdolsky 'Friedrich Engels'; Kann, *Multinational Empire*, Vol 1 Chapter 16, pp 40–51; Herod, *The Nation*, and E. Nimni, 'Marx Engels and the National Question', *Science & Society*, vol. 53, no. 3 (Fall 1989) pp. 308ff.
28. A. Rabinbach, *The Crisis of Austrian Socialism* (Chicago: University of Chicago Press, 1983) p. 7.
29. Kurt L. Shell, *The Transformation of Austrian Socialism* (New York: State University of New York, 1962) pp. 8–9; Rabinbach, *Crisis of Austrian Socialism*, p. 10; W.M. Johnson, *The Austrian Mind* (Berkeley: University of California Press, 1972) p. 99; Garcia Pelayo, *La teoria de la nación en Otto Bauer*, p. 15; Kann, *Multinational Empire*, Vol. 1, p. 104.
30. Kann, *Multinational Empire*, Vol. 1, p. 104.
31. Shell, *Transformation of Austrian Socialism*, p. 11.
32. M. Sully, *Continuity and Change in Austrian Socialism, The Eternal Quest for the Third Way* (New York: Columbia University Press, 1982) p. 13.
33. H. Mommsen, *Die Sozialdemokratie und die Nationalitätenfrage im habs-burgischen Vielvölkerstaat* (Vienna: Europa Verlag, 1963) p. 175–6.
34. J. R. Recalde, *La Construcción de las Naciones* (Madrid: Siglo XXI de España Editores, 1982) p. 279.
35. 'Protokoll über die Verhandlungen des Gesamtparteitages der sozialde-mokratischen Arbeteiterpartei in Österreich Brünn', Vienna 1899. All references in this work are from the Spanish translation by Conrado Ceretti in Marmora (ed.), *La Segunda Internacional*, pp. 181–217. There is a good English summary of the discussion in Kogan, 'The Social Democrats and the Conflict of Nationalities'.
36. Ceretti in Marmora (ed.), *La Segunda Internacional*, p. 184.
37. Kogan, 'The Social Democrats and the Conflict of Nationalities', p. 207; Ceretti in Marmora (ed.), *La Segunda Internacional*, p. 184–5.
38. ibid., pp. 192, 200.
39. ibid., p. 198; A. Agnelli, *Questione Nazionale e Socialismo, Contributo allo studio del pensiero de K. Renner e O. Bauer* (Bologna: il Mulino, 1969) p. 67.

40. Synopticus, *Staat und Nation* (Vienna, 1899). Spanish translation in *La Segunda Internacional y el Problema Nacional y Colonial* Cuadernos de Pasado y Presente, No. 73, pp. 145–80.

41. In the Russian debates it was called national-cultural autonomy.

42. Ceretti in Marmora (ed.), *La Segunda Internacional*, p. 193; A. Agnelli, *Questione Nazionale e Socialismo*, pp. 67–9, Kogan, 'The Social Democrats and the Conflict of Nationalities', p. 209.

43. Ceretti in Marmora (ed.), *La Segunda Internacional*, p. 211; A.G. Kogan, 'The Social Democrats and the Conflict of Nationalities', p. 210; H. Konrand, *Nationalismus und Internationalismus* (Vienna: Europaverlag, 1976) p. 70.

44. For a discussion of the similarities and differences between Otto Bauer and Karl Renner on the national question see Mommsen, *Arbeiterbewegung*, pp. 75–8. The discussion of Renner's constitutional work on the nationalities question is beyond the scope of the present work; for an evaluation of Renner see Kann, *Multinational Empire*, Vol. 2, pp. 157–67 and R. Kann, 'Karl Renner' in *Journal of Modern History*, Vol. 23 (1951) pp. 243–9. In contrast to Bauer, Renner's most significant work has been translated into English see K. Renner, *The Institutions of Private Law and their Social Functions* (London: Routledge & Kegan Paul, 1949, reprinted 1976).

45. K. Renner, *Das Selbstbestimmungsrecht der Nationen in besonderer Anwendung auf Österreich*, Vienna, 1916, p. 36, quoted by Kann, *Multinational Empire*, Vol. 2, p. 157. No connection with Lenin's work of the same title.

46. Agnelli, *Questione Nazionale e Socialismo*, p. 74. While this is undoubtedly a most interesting problem, it unfortunately falls beyond the scope of the present work. The author hopes to return to this discussion in the near future on a work on ethnocentrism and the national state. For the moment it will be sufficient to say that Renner's conceptualisation of the constitutional arragement in a multinational state curiously resembles the Ottoman Millet system. In a period in which new forms of struggle against state centralisation in East and West are constantly emerging, Renner's project on ethno-national decentralisation deserves a fresh consideration.

47. Norbert Leser, 'Austro-Marxism, a reappraisal', *Journal of Contemporary History*, Vol. 11 (1976) p. 134.

48. *OBW*, Vol. 1, p. 49.

49. According to Bauer the term Austro-Marxism was first coined by an American socialist, L. Boudin, who in 1907 published *The Theoretical System of K. Marx*, a book defending classical Marxism from revisionism and the Austrian Marginal utility school of economics. See Bottomore (ed.) *Austro-Marxism* (Oxford: Clarendon, 1976), pp. 1, 45.

50. Sully, *Continuity and Change*, p. 1.

51. O. Bauer, 'Was ist Austromarxismus?', in the organ of the Austrian Socialist Party, *Arbeiter-Zeitung*, on 3 November 1927, translated and reproduced by Bottomore (ed.), *Austro-Marxism*, p. 45. See also G.

Marramao, *Austromarxismo e Socialismo di Siniestra fra le due Guerre*, (Milan: La Pietra, 1977) p. 11.

52. Marramao, *Austromarxismo e Socialismo*, p. 13.
53. Bottomore (ed.), *Austro-Marxism*, editor's introduction, p. 3; Marramao, *Austromarxismo e Socialismo*, introductory essay, p. 10.
54. Bauer, 'Was ist Austro-Marxismus?' in Bottomore *Austro-Marxism*, p. 45–6 and in Marramao, *Austromarxismo e Socialismo*, p. 12. Words in parenthesis appear only in the Italian translation.
55. A number of contemporary discussions of Austro-Marxism understand its intellectual heritage as crucial for building a third way strategy between Revisionism and Marxist-Leninism. This interpretation is supported by the emergence of eurocommunism which inevitably draws a number of parallels with the political project of Austro-Marxism between the two world wars. It explains in part the popularity of Austro-Marxism in Italy. See D. Albers (ed.), *Otto Bauer und die 'Dritte Weg'* (Frankfurt: Campus Verlag, 1979) and D. Albers, *Versuch über Otto Bauer und Antonio Gramsci* (Berlin: Argument-Verlag, 1983). For an excellent discussion in English of the issues involved in Austro-Marxism and the third way strategy see G. Ananiadis, *Austro-Marxism and the 'Third Way' to Socialism*, unpublished thesis (Dept. of Government, University of Essex, 1981).
56. Ananiadis, *Austro-Marxism and the Third Way*, p. 1.
57. *Kausalität und Teleologie im Streite um die Wissenschaft*, Marx Studien Vol. 1 (Vienna: Wiener Volksbuchandlung, 1904). All references in this work are from the Italian translation, *Causalitá e Teleologia nella Disputa sulla Scienza*, with an introduction by R. Racinaro (Bari: De Donato Editori, 1976).
58. For a discussion of revisionism see Chapter 3 and P. Gay, *Dilemma of Democratic Socialism*.
59. As Gay correctly argues, there is a substantial difference between Bernstein's revisionism and neo-Kantian socialism, despite Bernstein's alleged adherence to the principles of Kantian philosophy (see the last chapter of Bernstein's *Evolutionary Socialism*). For Bernstein 'science is free from bias', and 'ethics is not a Wissenschaft', that is, a subject of disciplined and rational understanding. Both claims could be hardly accepted by neo-Kantians. See Gay, *Dilemma of Democratic Socialism*, p. 159. However, it is probably the case that Bernstein confused neo-Kantianism with empiricism, since epistemological issues had never been his strength, and this perhaps explains his eclectic approach to politics.
60. T. E. Willey, *Back to Kant* (Detroit: Wayne State University Press, 1978) p. 103.
61. ibid., p. 108.
62. ibid.
63. E. Cassirer, 'Hermann Cohen' in *Social Research*, Vol. 10 (1943) p. 220.
64. ibid., p. 125.
65. Willey, *Back to Kant*, p. 113.

66. ibid., p. 122.
67. Cassirer, *Cohen*, p. 232.
68. Lenin's main philosophical work, *Materialism and Empirocriticism*, only makes passing references to the neo-Kantians, since the bulk of the work is directed to polemicise with Russian followers of Avenarious and Mach, who were not, strictly speaking, neo-Kantians.
69. These terms are normally translated as 'natural sciences' and 'cultural sciences', however the English translation is only an approximation since the words 'Wissenschaft' and 'science' are not exactly equivalent. 'Wissenschaft' is far more comprehensive than the English equivalent normally used. Gay argues 'the German term refers to any discipline which attempts to establish a system, generality, or some definite method. "Science" on the other hand is largely limited to the natural sciences of physics, chemistry, etc. with their special methodology which stresses induction and empirical content' (*Dilemma of Democratic Socialism*, p. 157). See also H. Stuart Hughes, *Consciousness & Society* (Brighton: Harvester Press, 1979) p. 195. Consequently ethics and logic are 'Wissenschaften' but not sciences. This is symptomatic of the intellectual paradigms that dominated the German and English intellectual life at the time of the consolidation of their respective languages.
70. Quoted in Willey, *Back to Kant*, p. 134.
71. P. Heintel, 'Neo Kantianism' in C. D. Renning (ed.)*Encyclopaedia of Marxism*, p. 101; Stuart Hughes, *Consciousness and Society*, pp. 183–200; Willey, *Back to Kant*, p. 137.
72. Kolakowski, *Main Currents of Marxism*, Vol. 2, p. 259.
73. H. Rickert, *Science and History: a Critique of Positivist Epistemology*, translated by G. Reisman (Princeton: Princeton University Press, 1962) p. 19; quoted by Willey, *Back to Kant*, p. 147.
74. A good summary of Adler's work can be find in Kolakowski, *Main Currents of Marxism*, Vol 2, pp. 258–68 and in Bottomore, *Austro-Marxism*, pp. 15–22 and excerpts from 'Causality and Teleology' and other works in pp. 57–78.
75. Peretz Merhav, 'Marxismo e Neokantianismo in Max Adler' in *Storia del Marxismo Contemporaneo* (Turin: Istituto Feltinelli, 1974) p. 394.
76. Kolakowski, *Main Currents of Marxism*, p. 260.
77. Adler, *Kausalität und Teleologie*, quoted by Heintel, 'Neo Kantianism', in Renning (ed.), *Encyclopaedia of Marxism*, p. 104.
78. Adler, *Causalitá e Teleologia*, pp. 176–7
79. Adler, 'The Relation of Marxism to Classical German Philosophy', in Bottomore, *Austro-Marxism*, p. 65.
80. See V.I. Lenin, *Materialism and Empirocriticism, Collected works*, Vol. 3.
81. M. Adler, *Lehrbuch der materialistischen Geschichtsauffassung*, quoted by Heintel, 'Neo-Kantianism' in Renning (ed.), *Encyclopaedia of Marxism*, p. 104.

CHAPTER 6

1. *Die Nationalitätenfrage,* 1924 edn, in *OBW*, Vol. 1, pp. 168–9.
2. For a recent refreshing discussion on the work of Bauer see R. Munck, 'Otto Bauer, towards a Marxist Theory of Nationalism', in *Capital and Class*, Vol. 25, (1985) pp. 84–97; R. Munck, *The Difficult Dialogue, Marxism and Nationalism* (London: Zed, 1986). Prior to the publication of these works, Kolakowski, *Main Currents of Marxism*, Vol. 2, pp. 285–97 and Mommsen and Martiny, 'Nationalism and the Nationalities question' in Renning (ed.) *Encyclopaedia of Marxism*, pp. 39–45, were some of the very few publications in English with correct interpretations of the work of Bauer.
3. In Bottomore (ed.), *Austro-Marxism*, pp. 102–17.
4. The French translation is *La Question des nationalités et la Social-Démocratie* (traduit de l'allemand par Nicole Prune-Perrin et Johannès Brune), (Paris: Etudes et Documentation Internationales (EDI), 1988, 2 vols).
5. *La Cuestión de las nacionalidades y la social democracia.*
6. *Hashela Haleumit* (Tel Aviv: Sifriat Hapoalim, 1943).
7. Kolakowski, *Main Currents of Marxism*, p. 285. For example, in his book *Theories of Nationalism* (London: Duckworth, 1971, 2nd edition 1984), A. D. Smith only makes a passing reference to Bauer, and in a recent article he wrongly equates Bauer's work with the voluntaristic theory of E. Renan. See his 'Nationalism and Classical Social Theory' in *British Journal of Sociology*, Vol. 34, no. 1 (March 1983) p. 23. On the same misinterpretation see Davis, *Socialism and Nationalism*, p. 151 and A. Touraine, 'Sociological Intervention on the Internal Dynamics of the Occitanist Movement' in E. Tiryakian and R. Rogowski, *New Nationalisms of the Developed West* (London: Allen & Unwin, 1985) p. 167. In fact, Bauer *explicitly rejects* Renan's theory arguing that it is 'unsatisfactory [because it ignores the all important question of why] we wish to link our fate with one group of humans and not with others', and that it is equally incorrect to say that 'all human beings who wish to belong to a nation are ipso facto a national community'. Besides, for Bauer, awareness of nationhood is not an essential aspect of belonging to a national community. See *OBW*, Vol. 1, p. 229. For an English translation of E. Renan's essay 'Qu'est-ce qu'une Nation?', see J. Figgs & R. Lawrence (eds), *The History of Freedom and other essays* (London: Macmillan, 1919).
8. K. Kautsky wrote an article in *Die Neue Zeit* to polemicise against Bauer's work. See 'Nationalität und Internationalität', to which Bauer wrote a rejoinder 'Bemerkungen zur Nationalitätenfrage', *Die Neue Zeit*, March 1908. Both articles have been translated into Spanish and included in Marmora (ed.), *La Segunda Internacional*. Stalin's monograph *Marxism and the National Question* was mainly written to counteract Bauer's influence in Russia. Lenin also repeatedly took issue with Bauer; see 'Critical Remarks on the National Question', in *Collected works*, Vol. 20.

9. Kolakowski, *Main Currents of Marxism*, p. 255; Davis, *Socialism and Nationalism*, p. 149.

10. M. Croan, 'Prospects for the Soviet Dictatorship: Otto Bauer', in Labedz (ed.) *Revisionism*, pp. 282-3. Labedz also argues that Bauer made a significant contribution to the analysis of social change in the interwar period and to the development of democratic socialism.

11. See for example, V. J. Shveitser, *Sotsial-Demokratiia Avstrii: kritika politicheskikh kontseptsii i programm* (Austrian Social Democracy: a critique of political conceptions and programmes) (Moscow: Nauka, 1987) and the article by the same author 'Avstromarksisty o revoliutsii i stroitel'stva sotsializma v SSSR' (Austro-Marxists on revolution and the construction of socialism in the USSR) in *Rabochii Klass i Sovremennyi Mir*, no. 2, March–April 1988, pp. 147–55. The publication of both works represented a lifting of the Soviet intellectual embargo on Bauer and Austro-Marxism. This generated a lively discussion in the Soviet specialised literature; see the orthodox Leninist review by V. Ierusalimsky 'Puti, tupuki i obreteniia avstromarksizma' (The paths, dead-ends and abodes of Austro-Marxism), *Mirovaia Ekonomika i Mezhdunarodnye Otnosheniia*, No. 7, July 1988, pp. 139–42, and L. Georgiev, 'Nasledie Avstromarksizma' (The Heritage of Austro-Marxism), *Rabochii Klass i Sovremennyi Mir*, no. 4, July–August 1988, pp. 185–7. A more sympathetic review was published in *Voprosy Istorii* no. 12, December 1988, see B.S. Orlov, 'Austromarksizm s pozitsii segodniashnego dnia' (Austro-Marxism from present day positions) pp. 138-40. Another recent work on the topic is D. Mironov & A. Petersev, *Avstromarksizim, Pozitivizm i Rabocheie Dvizhenie* (Sverdlovsk: Urals University Press, 1990). The unusual number of reviews indicates the importance given to the topic. I am grateful to R. Pitty for translating the material and to S. Fortescue for directing me to the discussion.

12. See Lenin 'Self Determination' and 'Critical Remarks on the National Question' in *Collected Works*, Vol. 20. On the Bund, see H.Tobias, *The Jewish Bund in Russia from its Origins to 1905* (Stanford: Stanford University Press, 1965).

13. For the essential arguments of this mistaken criticism, see *Great Soviet Encyclopaedia*, A. M. Prokhorov, editor-in-chief (New York: Macmillan, 1983), sections on Bauer and 'Cultural National Autonomy'.

14. Mommsen, *Arbeiterbewegung*, p. 75.

15. See *OBW*, Vol 1, pp. 571–82.

16. ibid., Vol 1, p. 66.

17. Haupt, 'Les Marxistes face à la question nationale' in Haupt *et al.*, *Les Marxistes et la Question Nationale*, p.47.

18. Mommsen, *Arbeiterbewegung*, pp. 75–6.

19. *OBW*, Vol 1, p. 70.

20. ibid., Vol. 1, p. 71–2ff.

21. W. P. Metzger, 'Generalizations about National Character: An Analytical Essay' in L. Gottschalk (ed.), *Generalization in the Writing of History* (Chicago: University of Chicago Press, 1963) p. 77.

22. W. McDougall, *Character and Personality*, quoted by W. Metzger, 'Generalizations about National Character' in Gottschalk (ed.), *Generalization in the Writing of History*, p. 79.

23. *OBW*, Vol 1, p. 71.

24. ibid., Vol. 1, p. 72.

25. ibid., Vol 1, p. 74.

26. Adler argues that an 'absolute prerequisite' in conceptualising 'Man's existence, preservation and development' is the existence of a human community. (*Causalitá e Teleologia*, Italian translation of *Kausalität und Teleologie*, p. 167. See also chapter 15.) Bottomore too argues that Adler's concepts of 'socialised humanity' or 'social association' are to be understood in the neo-Kantian fashion as being 'transcendentally given as a category of knowledge'. Bottomore (ed.), *Austro-Marxism*, p. 16. See also G. Mozetic, *Die Gesellschaftstheorie des Austromarxismus* (Darmstadt: Wissenschaftliche Buchgesellschaft, 1987) pp. 48–50.

27. Adler, *Causalitá e Teleologia*, pp. 20–2.

28. Bauer, as will be seen below, refers to a form of 'subjective selectivity', but this is not an identity in the sense of a subjective positional definition.

29. *OBW*, Vol. 1, p. 77.

30. Garcia-Pelayo *La teoria de la nación en Otto Bauer*, p. 23.

31. *OBW*, Vol. 1, p. 170.

32. Meaning the constitution of human subjectivity out of social forms of existence (interaction). In this sense individuality is strictly unthinkable outside the social arena. The concept of socialisation used in mainstream sociology refers to the same process but from the opposite point of view, namely that of an individual who pre-exists society but learns social attitudes.

33. *OBW*, Vol. 1, p. 171.

34. Duhem's biographer, Stanley L. Jaki, argues that Duhem's antisemitism was above all a by-product of his anti-republicanism and that his devout catholicism did not impede him from opposing Pope Leo XIII's Encyclical 'Inter innumeras sollicitudines'. See S. L. Jaki, *Uneasy Genius: The Life and Work of Pierre Duhem* (The Hague: Martinus Nijhoff, 1984) pp. 91–2.

35. The edition quoted by Bauer is the German translation *Ziel und Struktur der physikalischen Theorien*, published in Leipzig in 1908; *OBW*, Vol. 1, pp. 53–4. There is an English translation of Duhem's *The Aim and Structure of Physical Theory* (New York: Atheneum, 1981). The chapter referred to by Bauer is Chapter 4, pp. 55–104.

36. *OBW*, Vol. 1, p. 54.

37. *OBW*, Vol. 1, p. 55. Duhem, English translation, p. 64.

38. *OBW*, Vol. 1, p. 55. Duhem, English translation, p. 64–8.

39. *OBW*, Vol. 1, p. 56–7.

40. ibid., p. 57.

41. ibid.

42. For reasons that will be discussed below, the concept of 'Schicksalsgemeinschaft' is difficult to translate. Tom Bottomore translates it as 'common destiny' (see Bottomore, *Austro-Marxism*, p. 107). Perhaps 'Community bound by a common destiny' or 'Community of fate' or 'commonalty of fate' might be a better ways of translating this ambiguous notion, given that the term 'Gemeinschaft' (community) is used by Bauer not in its current sociological meaning, but to denote the collective experience which finds its concrete expression in a societalised individual subjectivity.

43. Garcia Pelayo, *La teoria de la nación en Otto Bauer*, p. 24.

44. *OBW*, Vol. 1, p. 173.

45. *OBW*, Vol. 1, p. 172. This is derived, as Bauer acknowledges, from Kant's third analogy of experience: the principle of community: 'All substances so far as they coexist, stand in thoroughgoing community, that is, in mutual interaction' I. Kant, *Critique of Pure Reason* (New York: Random House, 1958) p. 131. In the introduction to the second edition of the *Nationalitätenfrage* Bauer argues that in his student years (this work was his doctoral thesis written at the age of 24!), he was 'fascinated' by the critical philosophy of Kant, but subsequently overcame his 'kantian childish illness' ('kantianischen Kinderkrankheiten', p. 53). However, over this crucial aspect of his work – the definition of community – the Kantian influence as well as the impact of Max Adler's work is clear, and Bauer still sustained the validity of this conceptualisation in the new 1924 introduction and in later works.

46. Agnelli, *Questione Nazionale e Socialismo*, p. 135; Garcia Pelayo, *La teoria de la nación en Otto Bauer*, p. 26.

47. *OBW*, Vol. 1, p. 174.

48. *OBW*, Vol. 1, p. 185; Adler *Kausalität und Teleologie*, quoted by Bauer from Marx-Studien Vol. 1, pp. 369ff., in the Italian translation, *Causalità e Teleologia*, pp. 166ff. While the term 'Satzung' etymologically translates as 'statute' or 'standing rule', in this case it is derived from the work of the neo-Kantian legal philosopher R. Stammler, *Wirtschaft und Recht nach der materialistischen Geschichtsauffassung*, here it means the formal convention that makes possible the rule of law. Stammler's work was a critique of historical materialism against which Adler took issue in *Causality and Teleology*. (see Chapter 5). Stammler uses the concept of 'Gemeinschaft' to indicate 'the final expression of unity under the law' (Willey, *Back to Kant*, p. 125). Bauer strongly disagrees with Stammler's interpretation of 'Gemeinschaft': see *OBW*, Vol. 1, p. 186.

49. *OBW*, Vol. 1, p. 186.

50. K. Kautsky, 'Nationalität und Internationalität', in *Ergänzungshefte zur Neuen Zeit*, Vol. 1 (January 1908), translated into Spanish by U. Köchmann in Marmora (ed.), *La Segunda Internacional*, Vol. 2, p. 127.

51. O. Bauer, 'Bemerkungen zur Nationalitätenfrage' in *Die Neue Zeit*, no. 26, Vol. 1 (March 1908), translated into Spanish by Ceretti in

Marmora (ed.), *La Segunda Internacional*, Vol. 2, pp. 175–6. For a review of the debate between Kautsky and Bauer over the pages of *Die Neue Zeit*, see Mommsen, *Arbeiterbewegung*, p. 76–8.

52. 'Der Begriff der Nation' (the concept of the nation), in *OBW*, Vol. 1, pp. 170–97.
53. ibid., p. 173.
54. ibid., p. 175.
55. *OBW*, Vol. 1, p. 62.
56. Garcia Pelayo, *La teoria de la nación en Otto Bauer*, p. 25.
57. K. Marx, 'On the Jewish Question' in *Early Writings*, introduced by L. Colletti (London: Penguin Books, 1975) pp. 211–41.
58. *OBW*, Vol. 1, p. 416.
59. ibid., p. 417. While this is a valid description of the process that affected Bauer's paternal ancestors, the middle-class Jewish population of Vienna, it is not valid as a general description of the Jewish population of Eastern and Central Europe. Besides the obvious class reductionist analysis of Jewish life, it is clear that an important group of Yiddish speaking Jews of Eastern Europe remained a national community long after the emergence of capitalism, fulfilling all of Bauer's theoretical criteria for national existence, with a strong working-class base and a combative socialist party (the Bund). This characterisation of Jewish national life in Eastern Europe should, of course, be carefully confined to the geographical area and the period under consideration. To include the predominately urban and culturally assimilated Jewish communities of Central and Western Europe – let alone Jews from other parts of the world with vastly different ethnic cultures – under this single national criterion, is a transcendentalist mystification of the process of national development. This is, in essence, the Zionist position. For a critical analysis see Machover and Offenberg, *Zionism and its Scarecrows*.
60. In a nutshell, Bauer attributes the persistence of the Yiddish-Jewish national community in Eastern Europe to the relative underdevelopment of that part of the world, particularly when compared with Western Europe where Jews were no longer a national community, because they lost a common language and became therefore more and more assimilated through a greater interactive relationship with the national communities with which they lived. While Bauer's description of the differences between Eastern and Western European Jews is undoubtedly correct, it does not follow, particularly in view of his own insightful conceptualisation of the national phenomenon, that the Yiddish speaking Eastern European Jews will experience the same developmental path as the Western Jews and cease to be a national community. See 'Nationale Autonomie der Juden?' (National Autonomy for Jews?) in *OBW*, Vol. 1, pp. 414–35.
61. 'Die Nation ist die Gesamtheit der durch Schicksalsgemeinschaft zu einer Charaktergemeinschaft verknüpften Menschen', *OBW*, Vol. 1, p. 194.

62. ibid., p. 170. English version in T. Bottomore (ed.), *Austro-Marxism*, p. 102.
63. See footnote 7 in this chapter.
64. ibid., and Garcia Pelayo, *La teoria de la nación en Otto Bauer*, pp. 26–7.
65. *OBW*, Vol. 1, p. 192. English translation Bottomore (ed.), *Austro-Marxism*, p. 105.
66. *OBW*, Vol. 1, p. 190. English version Bottomore (ed.), *Austro-Marxism*, p. 103.
67. *OBW*, Vol 1, p. 187.
68. ibid., p. 202; also Garcia Pelayo, *La teoria de la nación en Otto Bauer*, p. 35.
69. 'If I think of my nation, I remember my beloved motherland, my parental home, my first childish play, my old schoolteacher, that young woman that gave me happiness with her kisses, and from all those representations a feeling of pleasure overlaps the representation closely linked to it, that of the nation that I belong to', *OBW*, Vol. 1, p. 202.
70. For a discussion of this idea in a different context see E. Laclau, 'Towards a Theory of Populism' in Laclau, *Politics and Ideology in the Marxist Theory* (London: New Left Books, 1977) p. 143ff.

CHAPTER 7

1. Mommsen, *Arbeiterbewung*, p. 75–6.
2. *OBW*, Vol. 1, pp. 92ff.
3. This term is also difficult to translate. Garcia Pelayo argues that it is a juridical term of medieval origin that designates all those who did not have property rights and were in a servile relation to feudal landlords. At a later period, it denoted the lower and poorer classes that had only restricted rights to citizenship and property. The term was used up to the nineteenth century. (Garcia Pelayo, *La teoria de la nación en Otto Bauer*, p. 34.) In translation, 'tributary classes' is hesitantly used in the absence of a better term. This is also the way in which the term is translated in the Spanish edition.
4. *OBW*, Vol. 1, p. 115.
5. Garcia Pelayo, *La teoria de la nación en Otto Bauer*, p. 34–5.
6. *OBW*, Vol. 1, p. 151.
7. For a discussion of the notions of historical versus non-historical nations in Marx and Engels, see Chapter 1 of this work and R. Rosdolsky, *Friedrich Engels;* Herod, *The Nation* and Nimni, 'Marx, Engels and the National Question'.
8. For a discussion of these issues see Mommsen, *Arbeiterbewung*, pp. 127–220; Kogan, 'The Social Democrats and the Conflict of Nationalities'; Kann, *The Multinational Empire*, pp. 154–68, and Jaszi, *The Dissolution of the Habsburg Monarchy*, pp. 177ff.
9. Bauer refers to 'The Magyar Struggle' and 'Democratic Panslavism'; see Marx and Engels, *Collected Works*, Vol. 8. For a critical discussion of those articles see Chapter 1.

10. *OBW*, Vol. 1, pp. 323–4.
11. ibid, p. 324.
12. ibid., pp. 245ff., summarised by Herod, *The Nation*, pp. 50–1.
13. *OBW*, Vol. 1, p. 247.
14. ibid., pp. 270–1; also quoted and translated by Herod, *The Nation*, p. 49.
15. *OBW*, Vol. 1, p. 284; Garcia Pelayo, *La teoria de la nación en Otto Bauer*, pp. 42–3.
16. 'Nationaler Hass ist transformierter Klassenhass': *OBW*, Vol. 1, p. 315.
17. This argument was also influential in the development of the ideology of the Poale Tzion so-called left-wing Zionism. The work of Ber Borochov, *Nationalism and Class Struggle*, reflects a similar interpretation of the situation of Jews in Europe. While Bauer himself, like most Austro-Marxists, was a decided anti-Zionist and recommended Jewish assimilation, Max Adler expressed a distant sympathy for Poale Tzion; see J. Jacobs, 'Austrian Social Democracy and the Jewish Question in the First Republic' in A. Rabinbach (ed.), *The Austrian Socialist Experiment* (Boulder, Colorado: Westview Press, 1985) pp. 161–2.
18. Herod, *The Nation*, p. 47.
19. R. Rosdolsky, *Friedrich Engels Völker*, p. 191 (Spanish translation, p. 130; English translation, p. 135, footnote 25).
20. This idea was developed above all in Bauer's later work, *Die österreichische Revolution* (Vienna: Wiener Volksbuchhandlung, 1923), English abridged translation *The Austrian Revolution*, translated by H. J. Stenning (London: L. Parsons Ltd., 1925) pp. 183ff.
21. *OBW*, Vol. 1, p. 223.
22. ibid., p. 224.
23. ibid., p. 228.
24. ibid., p. 231. Almost ninety years after it was first formulated, this question has neither lost its urgency – as the current crisis of the Soviet State and the restructuring of the EC appear to indicate – nor has it been satisfactorily answered (including in Bauer's work). For recent attempts to provide answers to this question see E. Gellner, *Nations and Nationalism* (Oxford: Basil Blackwell, 1983) and B. Anderson, *Imagined Communities* (London: Verso, 1983), the latter thought provoking, but with an overdose of third worldism, the compensatory but no less distortive mirror image to orientalism. Also, Anderson joins the long list of scholars who dismiss the work of Bauer without properly understanding his theory, see pp. 101–2. Gellner ignores Bauer completely.
25. *OBW*, Vol. 1, p. 233.
26. ibid., pp. 234–5.
27. ibid., p. 234.
28. ibid., pp. 242–3.
29. ibid., p. 243.
30. ibid.

31. W. Connor, 'Nation Building or Nation Destroying?' *World Politics*, Vol. 24 (1972) p. 319. In this interesting article Connor argues that of the 132 states represented in the UN in 1971, 9.1 per cent were ethnically homogeneous, 18.9 per cent have a single ethnic community representing more than 90 per cent of the population. In 30 per cent of all states represented the largest ethnic community is less than 50 per cent of the population, while in a total of 40 per cent of all states represented there are more than five significant ethnic communities. On Connor's figures, Bauer is not that mistaken in arguing that the national state is a historical exception. In sharp contrast with the quality of his articles on nationalism, W. Connor wrote a theoretically ill-informed work on Marxism and nationalism; see W. Connor, *The National Question in Marxist Leninist Theory and Strategy* (Princeton: Princeton University Press, 1984).

32. Unfortunatelly, limitations of space do not permit a discussion of this interesting programmatic proposal. It was initially raised by K. Renner under the pseudonym of Synopticus in *Staat und Nation*; Spanish translation in Marmora (ed.), *La Segunda Internacional*, Vol. 1, pp. 145–80.

33. *OBW*, Vol. 1, pp. 192–4; Bottomore (ed.), *Austro-Marxism*, p. 106.

34. Bauer wrote a number of important works on the Soviet Union and the Bolshevik Revolution; see 'Die russische Revolution und das europäische Proletariat' (1917), 'Bolshewismus oder Sozial-demokratie?' (1919), 'Der "neue Kurs" in Sowjetrussland' (1921) as well as his major work 'Zwischen Zwei Weltkriegen?' all in *OBW*. For a discussion of Bauer's analysis of the Soviet Union and the revolution in the West see the excellent introductory article in Marramao (ed.) *Austromarxismo e Socialismo*, particularly pp. 105–15. Another important work is Y. Bourdet (ed.), *Otto Bauer et la Revolution*, with an introduction by the editor and a French translation of some of Bauer's works on the Soviet Union (EDI: Paris, 1968). See also M. Croan, 'Prospects for the Soviet Dictatorship: Otto Bauer', in Labedz, *Revisionism*, pp. 281–96 and Bauer's political biography, O. Leichter, *Otto Bauer, Tragödie oder Triumph?* (Vienna: Europa-Verlag, 1970).

35. Otto Bauer, 'Zwischen Zwei Weltkriegen? (Bratislava, 1936) p. 166, quoted and translated by Croan, 'Prospects for the Soviet Dictatorship', in Labedz, *Revisionism*, p. 291.

36. See footnote 11, Chapter 6. An unprecedented 'post-perestroika' sympathetic criticism of Bauer can be found in V. Y. Shveizer, 'Avstromarksisty o revoliutsii' (Austro-Marxists on revolution) in *Rabochii Klass i Sovremennyi Mir*.

37. See Stalin, *Marxism and the National Question* and Lenin, 'Cultural National Autonomy', 'Critical Remaks on the National Question' and 'The Right of Nations to Self Determination', in *Collected Works*, Vols. 19, 20.

38. A contemporary Soviet historian at the Institute of Social Sciences attached to Central Committee of the CPSU, V. P. Ierusalimsky,

laments that the work of the Austro-Marxists was once considered by the Comintern as 'Still more dangerous [... than] social fascism. He then argues that 'about Austro-Marxism what we have written is petty, fragmentary and largely one sided prejudice'. V. Ierusalimsky, op. cit. 'Puti, tupiki i obreteniia avstromarksizma', *Mirovaia Ekonomika*, p. 140.

39. V. Kozlov, 'The classification of ethnic communities, the present position in the Soviet debate', *Ethnic and Racial Studies* vol. 3, no. 2 (1980), pp. 123–39.

40. *Leninism and the National Question* (Moscow: Progress publishers, 1977) p. 26.

41. Shveiser, 'Austromarksisty o revoluliutsii', p. 154; translation from Russian by R. Pitty.

42. Ierusalimsky, 'Puti, tupiki i obreteniia avstromarksizma', in *Mirovaia Ekonomika*, p. 142

43. 'Filosofskie problemy teorii i praktiki natsional'nykh otnoshenii pri sotsializme' (Philosophical problems of the theory and practice of national relations under socialism) round table discussion, *Voprosy filosofii*, September 1988, no. 9, pp. 43–6; translation from Russian by R. Pitty.

44. In *The Break Up of Britain*, p. 329.

CONCLUSION

1. Nairn, *The Break Up of Britain*, p. 329.
2. Both in the sense of a tradition that sees social classes as privileged actors in the process of social transformation, and in the sense of the traditional and original theoretical stance of historical materialism.
3. This of course did not prevent Engels from arguing a few years later in a letter to Marx that 'the more I think over the business the more clear it becomes to me that the Poles as a nation are done for and can only be made use of as an instrument until Russia herself is swept into the agrarian revolution.' F. Engels, 'Engels an Marx' 23 May 1851, Enclosure 94, Vol. 1, Dritte Abteilung, *Marx Engels Gesamtausgabe* (MEGA) (Berlin: Dietz Verlag, 1930) pp. 204ff., quoted by Herod, *The Nation*, p. 34.
4. Kolakowski, *Main Currents of Marxism*, Vol. 2, p. 1.
5. Lidtke, 'Socialismo in Bernstein', in *Annali*, p. 147.
6. L. Kolakowski, *Main Currents of Marxism* (Oxford: Clarendon, 1978) Vol. II: *The Golden Age*, p. 1.
7. Prazauskas, 'Filosofkie problemy teorii' in *Voprosy filosofii*, p. 46.
8. *Kausalität und Teleologie.*

References

Primary Sources

COLLECTIONS

Bauer, O. *Otto Bauer Werkeausgabe* (OBW) (Vienna: Europa-Verlag, 1975).
Gramsci, A. *Quaderni del carcere* (Turin: Einaudi Editore, 1966) 10 volumes.
La Segunda Internacional y el problema nacional y colonial, Part I and II, series Cuadernos de Pasado y Presente, 73 and 74 (Mexico: Siglo XXI editores, 1978–79).
Lenin, V.I. *Selected Works*, (Moscow: Progress Publishers, 1961).
——. *Collected Works*, (Moscow: Foreign Language Publishing House, 1963).
Marx Engels Werke (MEW) (Berlin, GDR: Dietz Verlag, 1964).
Marx and Engels Collected Works (MECW) (London: Lawrence & Wishart, various editions).
Stalin, J. *Works*, (Moscow: Progress Publishers, 1952 and 1953).

BOOKS

Adler, M. *Kausalität und Teleologie im Streite um die Wissenschaft*, Marx Studien Vol. 1 (Vienna: Wiener Volksbuchhandlung, 1904); Italian translation *Causalita e teleologia nella disputa sulla scienza*, introduction by R. Racinaro (Bari: De Donato Editori, 1976).
——. *El socialismo y los intelectuales*, Spanish translation of 'Der Sozialismus und die Intellektuellen', (Mexico: Biblioteca Pensamiento Socialista, Siglo XXI editores, 1980).
——. *La concezione dello stato nel Marxismo*, Italian translation of 'Die Staatsauffassung des Marxismus' (Bari: De Donato Editore, 1979).
Aguilar, L. (ed.) *Marxism in Latin America* (New York: W. Knopf, 1969).
Avineri, S. (ed.) *Karl Marx on Colonialism and Modernisation* (London: Anchor Books, 1969).
Bauer, O. *Die Nationalitätenfrage und die Sozialdemokratie* (Vienna: Wiener Volksbuchhandlung, 1924).
——. *The Austrian Revolution*, English translation by H.J. Stenning of 'Die Österreichische Revolution' (London: L. Parsons, 1925).
——. *La cuestión de las nacionalidades y la socialdemocracia*, Spanish translation of 'Die Nationalitätenfrage' (Mexico: Biblioteca Pensamiento Sociaista, Siglo XXI editores, 1979).
——. *La Question des Nationalités* (traduit de l'allemand par Nicole Prune-Perrin et Johannès Brune) (Paris: Etudes et Documentation Internationales (EDI), 1988; 2 vols).
Bernstein, E. *Evolutionary Socialism* (New York: Schoken paperbacks, 1961).

Borochov, B. *Nationalism and the Class Struggle* (Connecticut: Greenwood, 1973).

de Sausurre, F. *Course in General Linguistics* (London: Fontana, 1974).

Engels, F. 'Über den Verfall des Feudalismus und das Aufkommen der Bourgeosie', in *MEW* Vol. 21; English translation, 'Decay of Feudalism and Rise of Nation States', in F. Engels, *The Peasant War in Germany* (Moscow: Progress Publishers, 1977).

Gramsci, A. 'The Southern Question', in *The Modern Prince & Other Writings* (New York: International Publishers, 1968).

——. *Selection from Prison Notebooks*, preface by G. Nowell Smith and Q. Hoare (London: Lawrence & Wishart, 1971).

——. *Gli intelletuali e l'organizzazione della cultura* (Rome: Editore Riuniti, 1977).

Haupt, G., Löwy, M., Weill, C. (eds), *Les Marxistes et la question nationale, 1848–1914* (Paris: François Maspero, 1974).

Hilferding, R. *Das Finanzkapital* Marx Studien Vol. 3 (Vienna: Wiener Volksbuchhandlung, 1910); English translation with an introduction by T. Bottomore, *Finance Capital* (London: Routledge & Kegan Paul, 1981).

Kant, I. *Critique of Pure Reason* (New York: Random House, 1958).

Lenin, V.I. *Questions of National Policy and Proletarian Internationalism* (Moscow: Progress Publishers, 1970).

Lukacs, G. in *History and Class Consciousness* (London: Merlin, 1976).

Luxemburg, R. *The National Question, Selected Writings*, ed. H.B. Davis, (New York: Monthly Review Press, 1976).

——. *El desarrollo industrial de Polonia*, Spanish translation of 'Industrielle Entwicklung Polens' (Mexico: Cudernos de Pasado y Presente, Siglo XXI Editores, 1979).

——. *La question nacional y la autonomia*, Spanish translation from a series of articles in *Przeglad Socjaldemokratyczny* (Mexico: Cauternos de Pasado y Presente, Siglo XXI, 1979).

Marx, K. *The Communist Manifesto*, various editors and editions.

——. *Preface and Introduction to a Contribution to the Critique of Political Economy*, (Pekin: Foreign Languages Press, 1976).

——. *Capital*, 3 volumes (London: Lawrence & Wishart, 1977).

——. *German Ideology*, students ed. (London: Lawrence & Wishart, 1974).

——. *Early Writings*, with an introduction by L. Colleti (London: Penguin, 1985).

Marx and Engels on Colonialism (Moscow: Progress Publishers, 1974).

Marx Aveling, E. (ed.) *Revolution and Counter Revolution* (London: Unwin Books, 1971).

Renner, K. *The Institutions of Private Law and their Social Functions* (London: Routledge & Kegan Paul, 1949, reprinted 1976).

Rickert, H. *Science and History: a Critique of Positivist Epistemology*, translated by G. Reisman (Princeton: Princeton University Press, 1962).

Stalin, J. *Marxism and the National Question* (Moscow: 1953).

Tönnies, F. *Community and Society* (Chicago: Michigan State University Press, 1957).

Trotsky, L. *The History of the Russian Revolution* (London: Victor Gollancz, 1965).

Secondary Sources

BOOKS

Abdel-Malek, A. *Nation and Revolution*, Vol. 2 of *Social Dialectics* (London: Macmillan, 1981).

Abercrombie, N., Hill, S., and Turner, B. *The Dominant Ideology Thesis* (London: Allen & Unwin, 1980).

Agnelli, A. *Questione nazionale e socialismo, contributo allo studio del pensiero de K. Renner e O. Bauer* (Bologna: il Mulino, 1969).

Albers, D. (ed.) *Otto Bauer und der 'dritte' Weg* (Frankfurt: Campus Verlag, 1979).

Ananiadis, G. *Austro Marxism and the 'Third Way' to Socialism*, unpublished thesis (Dept. of Government, University of Essex, 1981).

Anderson, B. *Imagined Communities* (London: Verso, 1983).

Avineri, S. *Hegel's Theory of the Modern State* (Cambridge: CUP, 1972).

Basso, L. *Rosa Luxemburg* (London: Andre Deutsch, 1975).

Blaut, J. *The National Question* (London: Zed, 1987).

Bloom, S. *El mundo de las naciones*, Spanish translation of 'The World of Nations' (Buenos Aires: Siglo XXI Editores, 1975).

Boersner, D. *The Bolsheviks and the National and Colonial Question*, (Connecticut: Hyperion Press, 1956).

Bottomore, T. (ed.), *Austro-Marxism* (Oxford: Clarendon, 1976).

Bourque, G. *L'État capitaliste et la question nationale* (Quebec: Les Presses de l'Université de Montreal).

Bourdet, Y. *Otto Bauer et la revolution* (Paris: EDI, 1968).

Boyer, J. *Political Radicalism in Late Imperial Vienna* (Chicago: University of Chicago Press, 1981).

Brunnot, C. F. *Histoire de la langue française* (Paris: Nouvelle Edition, 1958).

Buci-Glucksmann, C. *Gramsci and the State* (London: Lawrence & Wishart, 1980).

Cahm, E. and Fisera, V. (eds) *Socialism and Nationalism* Vol. 2, (London: Spokesman, 1978).

Carrère d'Encausse, H. and Schram, S. *Marxism in Asia* (London: Penguin, 1969).

Carr, E.H. *The Bolshevik Revolution* (London: Macmillan, 1963).

Castoriadis, C. *The Imaginary Institutions of Society* (London: Polity Press, 1987).

Colleti, L. *From Rousseau to Lenin* (London: New Left Books, 1972).

Connor, W. *The National Question in Marxist Leninist Theory and Strategy* (Princeton: Princeton University Press, 1984).

Cummings, I. *Marx, Engels and National Movements* (London: Croom Helm, 1980).

Cutler, A., Hindess, B., Hirst, P., Hussain, A. *Marx' 'Capital' and Capitalism Today*, Vol. II (London: Routledge & Kegan Paul, 1978).

Davis, H.B. *Socialism and Nationalism* (New York: Monthly Review Press, 1967).

——. *Towards a Marxist Theory of Nationalism* (New York: Monthly Review Press, 1978).

Doujot, A. *Le Patois* (Paris: Librairie Delagrave, 1946).

Duhem, P. *The Aim and Structure of Physical Theory* (New York: Atheneum, 1981).

Faye, J.P. *Los lenguajes totalitarios*, Spanish translation of *Théorie du récit, introduction aux langages totalitaires* (Madrid: Taurus Ediciones, 1974).

——. *Migrations du recit sur le peuple juif* (Paris: Collection 'Élèments', 1974).

Figgs, J. and Lawrence, J. *The History of Freedom and Other Essays* (London: Macmillan, 1919).

Froilich, P. *Rosa Luxemburg, Ideas in Action* (London: Pluto, 1972).

Garcia Pelayo, M. *El tema de las nacionalidades en la teoria de la nación en Otto Bauer* (Madrid: Editorial Pablo Iglesias, 1979).

Gay, P. *The Dilemma of Democratic Socialism* (New York: Octagon Books, 1979).

Gellner, E. *Nations and Nationalism* (Oxford: Basil Blackwell, 1983).

Geras, N. *The Legacy of Rosa Luxemburg* (London: New Left Books, 1976).

Giraud, P. *Patois et les dialectes français* (Paris: Presses Universitaires de France, 1968).

Grisoni, D. and Maggiori, R. *Guida a Gramsci* (Milan: Biblioteca Universali Rizzoli, 1977).

Haupt, G. *Socialism and The Great War* (Oxford: Clarendon, 1972).

Haupt, G. and Jean-Jacques, M. *Makers of the Russian Revolution* (London: Allen & Unwin, 1974).

Herod, C. *The Nation in the History of Marxian Thought* (The Hague: Martinus Nijhoff, 1976).

Hindess, B. and Hirst, P. *Mode of Production and Social Formations* (London: Macmillan, 1977).

Hobsbawn, E., Haupt, G., Marek, F., Ragionieri, E. (eds) *History of Marxism* (Brighton: Harvester Press, 1982), English translation of Vol. 1 of *Storia del Marxismo*, 5 volumes (Turin: Einaudi Editore, 1979).

Hoffman, J. *The Gramscian Challenge* (Oxford: Basil Blackwell, 1984).

Howell, D. *A Lost Left*. Three Studies in Socialism and Nationalism (Chicago: University of Chicago Press, 1986).

Jaki, S. L. *Uneasy Genius: The Life and Work of Pierre Duhem* (The Hague: Martinus Nijhoff, 1984).

Janik, A. and Toulmin, S. *Wittgenstein's Vienna* (London: Weidenfeld & Nicholson, 1973).

Jaszi, O. *The Dissolution of the Habsburg Monarchy* (Chicago: University of Chicago Press, 1929).

Jessop, B. *The Capitalist State* (Oxford: Martin Robertson, 1983).

——. *Nicos Poulantzas, Marxist Theory and Political Strategy* (London: Macmillan, 1985).

Johnson, W. *The Austrian Mind* (Berkeley: University of California Press, 1972).

Joll, J. *The Second International* (London: Routledge & Kegan Paul, 1974).

Kann, R. *The Multinational Empire*, 2 volumes (New York: Octagon Books, 1950, reprinted 1964).

Knapp, V.J. *Austrian Social Democracy* (Washington, DC: University Press of America, 1980).

Knei Paz, B. *The Social and Political Thought of Leon Trotsky* (Oxford: Clarendon, 1978).

Kolakowski, L. *Main Currents of Marxism*, 3 volumes (Oxford: Clarendon, 1978).

Konrad, H. *Nationalismus und Internationalismus* (Vienna: Europa-Verlag, 1976).

Korsch, K. *Marxism and Philosophy* (London: New Left Books, 1970).

Labedz, L. (ed.) *Revisionism* (London: Allen & Unwin, 1962).

Laclau, E. *Politics and Ideology in the Marxist Theory* (London: New Left Books, 1977).

Laclau, E. and Mouffe, C. *Hegemony and Socialist Strategy* (London: Verso, 1985).

Leclerq, J.M. *La nation et son idéologie* (Paris: Éditions Anthropos, 1979).

Lefort, C. *The Political Forms of Modern Society* (London: Polity Press, 1986).

——. *Democracy and Political Theory* (Minneapolis: University of Minnesota Press, 1988).

Leichter, O. *Otto Bauer, Tragödie oder Triumph?* (Vienna: Europa-Verlag, 1970).

Leninism and the National Question (Moscow: Progress Publishers, 1977).

Liebman, M. *Leninism under Lenin* (London: Merlin, 1980).

Lo Piparo, F. *Lingua, Intellectuali, Egemonia in Gramsci* (Rome: Laterza, 1979).

Marcuse, H. *Reason and Revolution* (Boston: Beacon, 1969).

Marramao, G. *Austromarxismo e socialismo di siniestra fra le due guerre* (Milan: La Pietra, 1977).

Mironov, D. and Petersev, A. *Austromarksizm, Positivizm i Rabocheie Dvizhenie* (Sverdlovsk: Urals University Press, 1990).

Mommsen, H. *Die Sozialdemokratie und die Nationalitätenfrage im habsburgischen Vielvölkerstaat, Das Ringen um die supranationale Integration der zisleithanischen Arbeiterbewegung (1867–1907)*, (Vienna: Europa Verlag, 1963).

——. *Arbeiterbewegung und Nationale Frage* (Göttingen: Vandenhoeck & Ruprecht, 1979).

Mouffe, C. (ed.) *Gramsci and the Marxist Theory* (London: Routledge & Kegan Paul, 1979).

Mozetic, G. *Gesellschaftstheorie des Austromarxismus* (Darmstadt: Wisselschaftliche Buchgesellschaft, 1987).

Munck, R. *The Difficult Dialogue, Marxism and Nationalism* (London: Zed, 1986).

Nairn, T. 'The Modern Janus' in *The Break Up of Britain*, 2nd edn (London: Verso, 1981).

Nettl, J.P. *Rosa Luxemburg* Vols. 1 and 2 (London: Oxford University Press, 1966).

Oxaal, I. *The Jews of Pre–1914 Vienna*, Working Paper (Dept of Sociology & Social Anthropology, University of Hull, 1981).

Pauley, B. F. *The Habsburg Legacy* (New York: Holt, Rinehart and Winston, 1972).

Pelczynski, Z.A. (ed.) *The State & Civil Society* (Cambridge: CUP, 1984).

Portelli, H. *Gramsci y el bloque historico* (Buenos Aires: Siglo XXI, 1974).

Poulantzas, N. *Classes in Contemporary Capitalism* (London: New Left Books, 1975).

Rabinbach, A. *The Crisis of Austrian Socialism* (Chicago: University of Chicago Press, 1983).

——. (ed.) *The Austrian Socialist Experiment* Social Democracy and Austro-Marxism, 1918–1934 (Boulder, Colorado: Westview, 1985).

Raybourn, A. *The Ethical Theory of Hegel* (Oxford: Clarendon, 1967).

Recalde, J. R. *La construcción de las naciones* (Madrid: Siglo XXI de España Editores, 1982).

Rex, J. *Race Relations in Sociological Theory* (London: Routledge & Kegan Paul, 1983).

Reyburn, H. A. *The Ethical Theory of Hegel* (Oxford: Clarendon, 1977).

Said, E. *Orientalism* (London: Routledge & Kegan Paul, 1978).

Salvatori, M. *Karl Kautsky* (London: New Left Books, 1979).

Salvi, S. *Le Nazione Proibite* (Florence: Vallechi Editore, 1973).

Schorske, C. *German Social Democracy* (New York: Russell & Russell, 1970).

——. *Fin de Siècle Vienna* (London: Weidenfeld & Nicholson, 1980).

Service, R. *The Bolshevik Party in Revolution 1917–1923* (London: Macmillan, 1979).

Shaheen, S. *The Communist Theory of National Self Determination* (The Hague: W. Van Hoeve, 1956).

Shapiro, L. and Reddaway, P. *Lenin: The Man, the Theorist and the Leader* (London: Pall Mall, 1967).

Shaw, M. (ed.) *Marxist Sociology Revisited* (London: Macmillan, 1985).

Shell, K.L. *The Transformation of Austrian Socialism* (New York: State University of New York, 1962).

Shveitser, V.J. *Sotsial-Demokratiia Avstrii: kritika politicheskikh kontseptsii i programm* (Moscow: Nauka, 1987).

Smith, A. D. *Theories of Nationalism* (London: Duckworth, 1971, 2nd impression 1984).

——. *The Ethnic Revival* (Cambridge: Cambridge University Press, 1981).

——. *The Ethnic Origin of Nations* (London: Basil Blackwell, 1986).

Stadler, K. *Austria* (London: Ernest Benn, 1971).

Steenson, G. P. *K. Kautsky, Marxism in the Classical Years* (Pittsburgh: University of Pittsburgh Press, 1978).

Stuart Hughes, H. *Consciousness and Society* (Brighton: Harvester, 1979).

Sully, M. *Continuity and Change in Austrian Socialism, The Eternal Quest for the Third Way* (New York: Columbia University Press, 1982).

Szporluck, R. *Communism and Nationalism* (Oxford: Oxford University Press, 1988).

Talmon, J.L. *The Myth of the Nation and the Vision of Revolution* (Berkeley: University of California Press, 1981).

Tibi, B. *Arab Nationalism* (London: Macmillan, 1981).

Tiryakian, E. and Rogowski, R. *New Nationalisms of the Developed West* (London: Allen & Unwin, 1985).

Tobias, H. *The Jewish Bund in Russia from its Origins to 1905* (Stanford: Stanford University Press, 1965).

Turner, B.S. *Marx and the End of Orientalism* (London: Allen & Unwin, 1978).

Ulam, A. *Lenin and the Bolsheviks* (London: Fontana, 1974).

Vilar, P. *La Catalogne dans L'espagne moderne* (Paris: Bibliotheque Géneralé de L'Ecole Pratique des Hautes Etudes, 1962).

Walicki, A. *Philosophic and Romantic Nationalism: The Case of Poland* (Oxford: Clarendon, 1982).

Weinstock, N. *Zionism, False Messiah* (London: Inklinks, 1978).

Willey, T. *Back to Kant* (Detroit: Wayne State University Press, 1978).

Worsley, P. *Marx and Marxism* (London: Tavistock, 1982).

Wright, E.O. *Class, Crisis and the State* (London: New Left Books, 1978).

Zeeman, Z.A.B. *Twilight of the Habsburgs* (London: Purnell & Sons, 1971).

Zwick, P. *National Communism* (Boulder, Colorado: Westview, 1983).

ARTICLES

Anderson, P. 'The Antinomies of Antonio Gramsci' in *New Left Review* no. 100 (November 1976) pp. 5–78.

Berman, R.A. 'Fascinating Vienna' in *Telos* no. 68 (summer 1986) pp. 7–38.

Bernstein, E. 'Die Deutsche Sozialdemokratie und Die Turkische Wirren' (The German Social Democracy and the Turkish disturbances), Spanish translation in *La Segunda Internacional y el problema colonial*, pp. 47–58.

Carrere d'Encausse, H. 'Unité proletarianne et diversité nationale: Lenin et la theorie de l'autodetermination' in *Revue Française de Science Politique*, Vol. 1, no. 2 (1971).

Cassirer, E. 'Hermann Cohen' in *Social Research*, Vol. 10 (1943), pp. 219–32.

Connor, W. 'Nation Building or Nation Destroying? in *World Politics*, Vol. 24 (1972) pp. 319–55.

Debray, R. 'Marxism and the National Question' in *New Left Review* no. 105 (1977), pp. 25–41.

Gallisot, R. 'Nazione e Nazionalità nei Dibatti dei Movimento Operaio' in *Storia del Marxismo*, Vol. 2.

Georgiev, L. 'Nasledie Avstromarksizma' in *Rabochii Klass i Sovremennyi Mir*, no. 4 July-August (1988), pp. 185–7.

Haupt, G. 'Les Marxistes face à la question nationale: l'histoire du problème' in G. Haupt, M. Löwy and C. Weill, *Les Marxistes et la question nationale* (Paris: François Maspero, 1974), pp. 10–61.

Haupt, G. and Weill, C. 'L'Eredità di Marx ed Engels e la questione nazionale' in *Studi Storici*, Instituto Gramsci Editore, 15, 1977, no. 2, pp. 270–324.

Heintel, P. 'Neo Kantianism' in C.D. Renning (ed.), *Encyclopaedia of Marxism, Communism and Western Society* (New York: Herder & Herder, 1977), pp. 98–105.

Hilary, C. et Mascotto, J. 'Dialectique Materialiste et Nationalisme Historique' in *Les Cahiers du socialisme* (Montreal, Quebec: May 1978), pp. 87–197.

Hobsbawm, E. 'Gramsci and Marxist Political Theory' in Anne Showstack Sassoon (ed.), *Approaches to Gramsci* (London: Writers and Readers Publishing Cooperative, 1982) pp. 20–36.

Ierusalimsky, V. 'Puti, tupiki i obreteniia avstromarksizma' in *Mirovaia Ekonomika i Mezhdunarodnye Otnosheniia* no. 7 (July 1988) pp. 139–42.

Jessop, B. 'Capitalism and Democracy, the best possible political shell?' in G. Littlejohn *et al.* (eds), *Power and the State*, (London: Croom Helm, 1978) pp. 10–51.

Kann, R. 'Karl Renner' in *Journal of Modern History*, Vol. 23 (1951) pp. 243–9.

Kogan, A.G. 'The Social Democrats and the Conflict of Nationalities in the Habsburg Monarchy' in *Journal of Modern History* Vol. 21 (1949) pp. 204–217.

Kozlov, V. 'The classification of ethnic communities, the present position in the Soviet Debate' in *Ethnic and Racial Studies*, Vol. 3, no. 2, (1980), pp. 123–39.

Krader, L. 'The theory of evolution' in E. Hobsbawm *et al.* (ed), *History of Marxism*, Vol. 1 (London: 1982) pp. 192–226.

Leser, N. 'Austro-Marxism, a reappraisal' in *Journal of Contemporary History* Vol. 11 (1976) pp. 133–48.

Lidtke, V.L. 'Le premesse teoriche del socialismo in Bernstein' in *Annali*, Istituto Feltrinelli, Vol. 15 (1973) pp. 155–68.

Löwy, M. 'Marxists and the National Question' in *New Left Review*, no. 96 (1976) pp. 81–100.

Machover, M. and Offenberg, M. 'Zionism and its Scarecrows' in *Khamsin*, no. 6 (1978) pp. 33–59.

Metzger, W.P. 'Generalizations about National Character: An Analytical Essay' in L. Gottschalk (ed.), *Generalization in the Writing of History* (Chicago: University of Chicago Press, 1963).

Mouffe, C. 'Hegemony and Ideology in Gramsci' in C. Mouffe (ed.), *Gramsci and the Marxist Theory* (London: Routledge & Kegan Paul, 1979).

Munck, R. 'Otto Bauer, towards a Marxist Theory of Nationalism' in *Capital and Class*, Vol. 25 (1985) pp. 84–97.

Orlov, B.S. 'Austromarksizm s pozitsii segodniashnego dnia' in *Voprosy Istorii* Vol. 12 (December 1988) pp. 138–40.

Pelczynski, Z.P. 'Nation, Civil Society and State, Hegelian Sources of the Marxian non-theory of Nationality' in Z. A. Pelczynski (ed.), *The State and Civil Society* (Cambridge: Cambridge University Press, 1984), pp. 262–78.

Protokoll uber die Verhandlungen der Gesamtparteitages der sozialdemokratischen Arbeiterpartei in Österreich, Brün, translated into Spanish by C. Ceretti in *La Segunda Internacional y el problema nacional y colonial*, Vol. 1.

Rosdolsky, R. 'Friedrich Engels und das problem der "Geschichtslosen" Völker' in *Archiv für Sozialgeschichte*, Vol. IV, Hannover 1964.

——. *Federico Engels y el problema de los pueblos 'sin historia'* (Mexico: series Cuadernos de Pasado y Presente, numero 88, Siglo XXI editores, 1980).

——. *Engels and the 'Nonhistoric' Peoples: The National Question in the Revolution of 1848*, translated and edited with an introduction by J.P. Himka, special issues of *Critique* (Glasgow: 1987).

——. 'Workers and Fatherland' in *Science and Society*, Vol. 29, 1965.

Said, E. 'Orientalism Reconsidered' in *Race and Class*, Vol. 27, no. 2 (1985), pp. 1–15.

Schmidtbauer, P. 'Zur sozialen Situation der Wiener Juden in Jahre 1857' in *Studia Judaica Austriaca*, Vol. VI, pp. 57–91.

Shanin, T. 'Soviet Theories of Ethnicity, the Case of the Missing Term' in *New Left Review*, no. 158 (1986) pp. 113–22.

Shveitser, V.J. 'Avstromarksisty o revoliutsii i stroitel'stva sotsializma v SSSR' in *Rabochii Klass i Sovremennyi Mir*, no. 2 (March-April 1988) pp. 147–55.

Smith, A.D. '"Ideas" and "Structure" in the Formation of Independence Ideas' in *Philosophy of Social Sciences*, Vol. 3 (1973).

——. 'Nationalism and Classical Social Theory' in *British Journal of Sociology*, Vol. 34, no. 1 (March 1983) pp. 19–39.

Synopticus, *Staat und Nation*, Vienna 1899. Pseudonym of K. Renner. Spanish translation in *La Segunda Internacional y el problena nacional y colonial*, Vol. 73, pp. 145–80.

Wright, A.W. 'Socialism and Nationalism' in L. Tivey (ed.), *The Nation State* (Oxford: Martin Robertson, 1981) pp. 148–70.

Name Index

Subject Index